December 8, 1997

Sylvania

READ to WRITE

An Integrated Course for Nonnative Speakers of English

Jeri Wyn Gillie

Susan Ingle

Heidi Mumford

The McGraw-Hill Companies, Inc.

New York   St. Louis   San Francisco   Auckland   Bogotá   Caracas
Lisbon   London   Madrid   Mexico City   Milan   Montreal   New Delhi
San Juan   Singapore   Sydney   Tokyo   Toronto

This is an EDI book.

McGraw-Hill

A Division of The **McGraw-Hill** Companies

Read to Write
An Integrated Course for Nonnative Speakers of English

This book is printed on acid-free paper.

1 2 3 4 5 6 7 8 9 0   DOC DOC   9 0 3 2 1 0 9 8 7 6

ISBN 0-07-023721-2

This book was set by York Graphic Services.
The editors were Tim Stookesberry, Bill Preston, Don Linder, and Terri Wicks.
The production supervisor was Rich Devitto.
The cover was designed by Suzanne Montazer.
Project supervision was done by York Production Services.
This book was printed and bound by RR Donnelley & Sons Company.

Gillie, Jeri Wyn.
   Read to write: an integrated course for nonnative speakers of English / Jeri Wyn Gillie, Susan Ingle, Heidi Mumford.
       p. cm.
   Includes index.
   ISBN 0-07-023721-2
   1. English language—Textbooks for foreign speakers. 2. English language—Rhetoric—Problems, exercises, etc. 3. College readers.
I. Ingle, Susan. II. Mumford, Heidi. III. Title.
PE1128.G526 1996
808'.0427—dc21   96–46646
                                                                                                                                      CIP

LITERARY ACKNOWLEDGMENTS 1. For "Thinking - A Neglected Art": From *Newsweek*, Dec. 14, 1981, p19. Reprinted by permission of the author. 2. For "American Momma": From *US Express*, Dec. 1990 issue. Copyright© 1990 by Scholastic Inc. Reprinted by permission of the author. 3. For "Tale of Two Schools": Reprinted with permission from the Nov. 1991 *Reader's Digest*. Copyright© 1991 by The Reader's Digest Assn., Inc. 4. For "Go Ahead, Take A Nap": Copyright© 1993 by The New York Times Company. Reprinted by permission. 5. For "You Just Don't Understand": Copyright© 1990 by Deborah Tannen. 6. For "Music Soothes the Savage Brain": From *Newsweek* 10-25-93, Newsweek, Inc. All rights reserved. Reprinted by permission. 7. For "On Friendship": Copyright© 1961...1970 by Margaret Mead and Rhonda Metraux. 8. For "You're Full of Goodness, Spread It Around": Reprinted by permission of the author. 9. For "Take Time to Take on Some Travel Manners": Reprinted by permission: Tribune Media Services. 10. For "Why Do We Cry?": Reprinted with permission from the Feb.© 1987 *Reader's Digest*. Copyright© 1987 by The Reader's Digest Assn., Inc. 11. For "Do You Have a Green Thumb for Marriage?": Reprinted by permission of Norman M. Lobsenz. 12. For "Obituaries: Grave Injustice": Reprinted with permission from *Psychology Today Magazine*, copyright© 1993 (Sussex Publishers, Inc.) 13. For "Envy vs. Jealousy": Reprinted with permission from *Psychology Today Magazine*, copyright© 1994 (Sussex Publishers, Inc.) 14. For "I, Too, Am a Good Parent": From *Newsweek* 7-4-94, Newsweek, Inc. All rights reserved. Reprinted by permission. 15. For "Needing and Wanting Are Different": Reprinted by permission of the author.

PHOTO CREDITS Cover: Daniel Grogan and Bob Llewellyn / Uniphoto; Page 11: Hank Morgan / Science Source / Photo Researchers; 17: Ed Castle / Folio, Inc.; 35: UPI / Corbis-Bettman; 54: Alain Evrard / Photo Researchers; 84: Harald Sund / The Image Bank; 140: Duane Hanson, *Tourists II*, 1988 (by permission of the Estate of Duane Hanson); 178: Gregg A. Rummel 1994 / Folio, Inc.; 183 top: David Young-Wolff / PhotoEdit; 183 bottom: © Jim Ward; 226: Gerard Vandystadt / Agence Vandystsdt / Photo Researchers; 235: Stephen Frisch / Stock Boston; 265: Michel Tcherevkoff / The Image Bank; 281: Joel Gordon.

http://www.mhcollege.com

*To Our Students, from Whom
We Have Learned the Most.*

CONTENTS

Preface

Read to Write: An Integrated Course for Nonnative Speakers of English is for intermediate-level ESOL students. It is composed of eight chapters focusing on traditional rhetorical forms. An important goal of this text is to make students aware of how reading and writing are connected, interrelated processes. Moreover, the dual focus on reading and writing is aimed to show students that developing skills in one area will improve their skills in the other. Our hope is that this text, by leading students through a systematic process of generating and developing ideas, applying the appropriate rhetorical forms, and writing, evaluating, and revising their essays, will provide them with the tools necessary to function successfully in an academic setting.

A key feature of *Read to Write* is the generous number of readings in each chapter, exposing students to several different essays for each rhetorical form and, thus, better preparing them to write in each form. In addition, there is a wide variety of subject matter and writing styles presented in each chapter, including "authentic" material by professional writers and essays written by teachers and international students.

This textbook teaches both reading and writing skills. However, the reading material in this book is not intended to be the students' sole source of reading. Rather, it is intended to give them practice reading *intensively,* using various reading skills and strategies. In order to become fluent readers, students must also read *extensively*, preferably in literature—both fiction and nonfiction.

Chapter Organization

Chapter 1 of *Read to Write* is an introduction to reading and writing. It reviews basic paragraph writing, introduces essay writing, and presents some basic reading skills. Chapters 2 through 8 present the different rhetorical forms, beginning with the more personal styles of biography, description, and narration, and progressing to more formal styles of cause and effect and persuasion. The purpose of this organization is to have students begin with rhetorical forms that relate to subject matter for which they already possess considerable personal schemata—that is, material that allows them to draw on their personal experience and background knowledge. Later, students move to other forms which may require them to learn about subject matter that is somewhat unfamiliar. We suggest that students progress through the book sequentially. You may, of course, vary the order of chapters depending on your particular students' needs.

The objective of each chapter is to allow students to become familiar with the organization of the rhetorical form and the corresponding model readings. Once familiar with a particular form, students then write, evaluate, and rewrite an essay in that form. Each chapter is divided into three parts; in Chapters 2 through 8, which deal with specific rhetorical forms, these parts have the same organization and function.

- In **Part One**, students are introduced to a particular rhetorical form and practice some prewriting strategies and skills. At the end of Part One, they write the first draft of an essay in the rhetorical form.
- In **Part Two**, students identify organizational styles in different readings, focusing on essential rhetorical and stylistic conventions such as topic sentences, supporting details, introductions, conclusions, and paragraph coherence. Students then apply what they have learned by developing and revising their first drafts.
- In **Part Three**, students review skills previously presented and concentrate on fine-tuning their final drafts, focusing particularly on cohesive devices.

Within each of these three chapter parts, the reading skills of skimming, scanning, inferring, guessing meaning from context, and understanding the main idea are presented in conjunction with the writing skills related to the rhetorical forms.

Special Features

Following are highlights of special features included in each chapter.

Chapter Opening Pages. The first page of each chapter contains an illustration relating to the chapter focus, along with a box giving a brief description of the kind of writing that will be presented in the chapter, explaining the uses of the particular rhetorical form, and previewing some of the skills that will be introduced in the chapter.

Activities. After the chapter opener, there is a schema-building activity designed to introduce students to the rhetorical form that is the focus of that chapter. This activity gives students the opportunity to interact with each other. It may also activate ideas for writing that students can use later in the chapter.

Prereading Activities. Prereading material, in the form of a brief introduction to the reading and prereading discussion questions, is meant to activate students' schemata. Sharing what they already know about the subject allows students to pool their knowledge and get the most from the readings.

Vocabulary. Chapter 1 provides students with strategies for learning vocabulary on their own. Other chapters include some vocabulary exercises which give students the opportunity to practice the essential skill of determining the meaning of unfamiliar words from context. In addition, many readings are preceded by special **Vocabulary Watch** boxes, containing lists of vocabulary with which students may not be familiar. Words and expressions listed in these boxes appear in boldface type in the readings.

About the Reading. Questions following many of the readings are meant to give students the chance to think and write about aspects of the readings. Some questions ask for specific information from the readings in order to check comprehension, while others are discussion questions aimed at getting students to share personal information and go beyond the text. You may choose to have students write answers to these questions or discuss them as a class or in groups, depending on your course goals. The last question in these sections is called **What Do You Think?** These open-ended questions are meant to be used as topics for journal entries or informal writing assignments.

Exercises. Explanations of each reading and writing skill are followed by exercises that allow students to practice the skills that have been presented. The exercises also encourage students to apply these skills to their own essays. Answers to excercises are available in a separate Answer Key.

Getting Started. Near the end of Part One in each chapter is a section of brainstorming exercises to help students generate ideas from which they can select or develop their essay topics and write their first drafts.

Checklists. A checklist appears at the end of each chapter part. Students are encouraged to use these checklists to evaluate each draft they have written. Each checklist requires students to review their writing to see if they have incorporated the skills presented in the corresponding part of the chapter. In addition, students are instructed to use the **Second Draft Checklist** as part of a peer-evaluation activity. Because the checklists are cumulative throughout the chapter, they may also be used as criteria for grading the students' essays.

Idea Generator. At the end of each chapter are two "idea generators" designed to creatively reinforce and extend principles taught in the chapter. These activities are intended to stimulate further student reading, writing, group work, and presentation projects.

Acknowledgments

We would like to thank our families, colleagues, and people at McGraw-Hill for their interest in and support of this textbook. In particular, our thanks to the following people at McGraw-Hill: to Tim Stookesberry for having the initial vision of what the book could be, to Bill Preston for directing the project and for tips on the initial organization, and to both Bill Preston and Don Linder for editing the final manuscript. Also, we thank Gina Martinez, Pam Tiberia, and Cheryl Besenjak for their assistance in acquiring permissions.

Many thanks to our colleague Laurie Shin, who was involved in the initial stages of *Read to Write* and who further contributed by writing essays for the book and giving both creative and stylistic feedback.

We give special thanks to Lynn Henrichsen at Brigham Young University for his guidance and encouragement in the early stages of the book, and for his invaluable vision which helped shape its later development.

We thank our fellow ESL teachers at Brigham Young University's English Language Center, who offered their encouragement and expertise.

And, of course, we thank our students, from whom we have learned the most. Their enthusiasm and essays have added so much to our teaching and to this book.

Finally, we wish to thank the following reviewers whose comments, both favorable and critical, were of great value in the development of this text: Laurie Blass; J. Marcia Le Roy, Englobus Communications and Development Group; Joanne Marino, Cape Fear Community College; Gerri McFadden, Babson College; Lisa Rost, State University of New York, New Paltz; and Elizabeth Templin, University of Arizona, Tucson.

About the Authors

Jeri Wyn Gillie has an M.A. in TESL. She teaches ESL at Brigham Young University's English Language Center, where she has coordinated both the reading and writing programs. Currently, she is conducting classroom research on skills integration.

Susan Ingle has an M.A. in TESL. She has developed and taught ESL reading and writing courses in both academic and workplace settings. She is co-founder of Education Works, Inc., a workplace training company located in Salt Lake City, Utah.

Heidi Mumford has an M.A. in TESL. She has taught reading and writing in intensive English programs at Brigham Young University and Utah Valley State College. She has also designed and taught ESL and U.S. culture courses for visiting students and scholars at Arizona State University.

Summary of Reading/Writing Skills and Activities

Following is a chart of the reading and writing skills and the activities in each chapter. Many skills that are embedded into main sections of each chapter have not been included here. For example, the "Prereading" sections will give students practice with predicting and formulating schema. In the "About the Reading" sections, students will practice finding the main idea, topic sentences, and thesis statements, as well as inference, and reading comprehension. In the "Essay Writing" sections, students will practice organizing and writing in a specific genre, revising, peer-reviewing and editing.

Chapter	Reading Skills	Writing Skills	Activities
One	• identifying topics and topic sentences • identifying main ideas • making predictions • skimming for main ideas • scanning for specific information • guessing meaning from context	• identifying audience • understanding purpose • narrowing topics • identifying supporting details • making paragraphs unified • reviewing punctuation and paragraph form • writing introductions to essays • writing conclusions to essays	• writing two letters about weekend plans, each for a different audience • writing synonyms
Two	• guessing meaning from context • identifying main ideas • scanning for specific information • inferring information • identifying chronological connectors	• brainstorming with a timeline • using details to describe events or time periods • using chronological connectors	• sharing stories • making a timeline • talking about important ages and life events • talking about events in the lives of famous people
Three	• identifying descriptive detail • identifying similar meanings • guessing meaning from context • analyzing descriptive detail • identifying spatial organization • identifying topic sentences • identifying supporting detail • identifying similes • making predictions	• adding descriptive detail • brainstorming sensory details • writing supporting details in a paragraph • creating similes • organizing description	• describing objects, people, places • writing descriptions to share and compare • writing a description of a special place, using senses to add detail
Four	• scanning for information • identifying audience and purpose • guessing meaning from context • understanding meaning from context • identifying narrative elements • identifying detail • identifying quoted and reported speech • sequencing • identifying chronological connectors	• brainstorming—writing without stopping • using narrative elements to write a story • adding detail • punctuating quoted speech • changing quoted speech to direct speech • changing reported speech to quoted speech • using chronological connectors	• telling stories • watching short segments on television or video; retelling segments in groups, then writing them down • writing stories of important events in life; exchanging them with peers, and adding details

Chapter	Reading Skills	Writing Skills	Activities
Five	• identifying detail • identifying purpose • guessing meaning from context • identifying expository organization • analyzing introductions to essays • analyzing conclusions to essays • predicting a conclusion • identifying cohesive devices • recognizing textual highlighting techniques • reviewing reading skills • reading carefully for details	• brainstorming by mapping • organizing expository essays • writing sentences using new vocabulary • writing introductory paragraphs • writing concluding paragraphs • adding cohesive devices	• sharing information, ideas, and opinions • creating and conducting a survey • writing and sharing paragraphs
Six	• identifying and expanding descriptive language • comparing major points • identifying similarities and differences • guessing meaning from context • identifying comparison and contrast organization • determining methods of organization in comparison and contrast • understanding how examples are used to support a thesis statement • finding support from the text • scanning for idiomatic expressions • identifying comparison and contrast constructions	• brainstorming topics with partners • brainstorming similarities and differences • outlining • using comparison and contrast constructions • unifying paragraphs	• identifying similarities and differences between pictures • designing an advertising campaign • comparing and contrasting a given product with others on the market • comparing and contrasting what is considered beautiful in different countries
Seven	• inferring meaning • identifying causes and effects • identifying cause-and-effect organization • diagramming causes and effects • completing an outline • understanding idiomatic expressions • identifying connections between paragraphs • identifying thesis statements and their controlling ideas • identifying logical connectors	• brainstorming causes and effects • outlining • writing surprise introductions • writing dramatic introductions • writing transitions between paragraphs • using logical connectors • writing good thesis statements	• identifying causes and effects • discussing causes and effects of global and personal experiences • telling chain reaction stories
Eight	• identifying persuasive support • identifying persuasive organization • identifying strong opinions as thesis statements • guessing meaning from context • identifying coherent paragraphs • skimming	• brainstorming for persuasive support • writing rebuttals • reviewing rhetorical forms • writing thesis statements • reviewing cohesive devices • using cohesive devices • reviewing transitions between paragraphs • writing transitions between paragraphs	• debating an issue • analyzing persuasive advertising • reading and writing editorials

Chapter 1

Introduction to Reading and Writing

I n this book, you will learn how to write paragraphs and essays using various rhetorical forms, such as description, narration, comparison and contrast, and persuasion. Knowing how to use these different forms when you write will enable you to choose a form that will most effectively communicate your ideas to your reader.

To be a good writer, you must also be a good reader. The readings and activities in this book will help you improve both your reading and your writing skills, as well as your understanding of vocabulary.

This chapter provides an overview of several important skills and elements of reading and writing. Each element or skill is discussed again in subsequent chapters of the book, so you will be given ample opportunity to practice them. In later chapters, when you are asked to use these skills, you may want to refer back to this chapter for review.

The Paragraph

A *paragraph* is a group of sentences that are all related to the same idea. Paragraphs contain certain elements, such as topic sentences, controlling ideas, and supporting details. As a reader, you are often not consciously aware of these elements, but learning to identify them can assist you in recognizing and understanding the main idea. As a writer, you should learn to use these elements effectively. Later in this chapter, you will explore these elements of a paragraph in the context of reading and writing. Before you begin to write, however, it is important to consider two things:

1. Your *audience*—to whom you are writing
2. Your *purpose*—why you are writing

Audience

When people write, they usually have in mind a certain *audience,* or group of readers to whom they are writing. That audience influences the writer's style and choice of details and vocabulary. As a writer, you will need to write in a way that will interest your readers and that will enable them to understand what you want to communicate. Before you begin writing, you should ask yourself the following questions:

1. What does my audience already know about this topic?
2. What does my audience need to know about this topic?
3. What form of writing will best communicate this topic to my audience?

Exercise 1 **Audience.** Following are two paragraphs on the same topic: Note, however, that the paragraphs are aimed at two different audiences. As you read each paragraph, think about the intended audience.

Christmas (1)

Christmas is the most widely celebrated holiday in the United States. It is celebrated on December 25th each year. Many people celebrate the whole season surrounding Christmas. This time, referred to as "the holidays," begins after Thanksgiving (the end of November) and continues through New Years Day (the first day of January). Although Christmas is a Christian religious holiday, many people who are not Christians take part in some Christmas customs. On this holiday, people exchange gifts with friends and families. Most people have time off from work, and they spend this vacation time with their families. Students come home from college, and people often travel long distances to return home. Many children receive gifts from "Santa Claus," a legendary character who does good things for children. People also prepare special foods and often bring small gifts of food to their neighbors. Sometimes when people visit their neighbors, they sing special songs of the season, called carols. During this season, it seems as though everything and everyone is filled with happiness and goodwill. Christmas is really a delightful time of year in the United States.

- Who is the audience for this paragraph? How do you know?

Christmas (2)

Christmas is a holiday that brings back many wonderful memories. My favorite part of Christmas was waking up early Christmas morning after not sleeping most of the night to rush to the living room and find the gifts from Santa. Every year without fail there was a huge red, white, and green stocking hanging from the fireplace, filled with treats: crunchy apples, fragrant oranges, rich chocolate, and peppermint candy canes. After we discovered the contents of our stockings, we would open up the brightly colored packages from our family and friends with great anticipation. After the gifts were opened we would have a special breakfast made by our father—crepes filled with fruit and cream. Later that day we would put on our warm winter clothing and go out to sing Christmas carols to our neighbors, who would often invite us in and serve us hot chocolate or cider. When we came home, our father would read us the Christmas story while we stared at the twinkling Christmas lights and tinsel on the huge fir tree. I always fell asleep satisfied and exhausted on Christmas night.

- Who is the audience for this paragraph? How do you know?

Purpose

In addition to knowing the audience for your writing, you must know your *purpose*—the reason why you are writing something. Audience and purpose are very closely tied, in that the purpose usually depends on the audience. For example, the intended audience for the first paragraph on Christmas is someone who is unfamiliar with how Christmas is celebrated in the United States. Hence, the author's purpose is to explain how Christmas is celebrated in the United States. In contrast, the audience for the second paragraph on Christmas is someone who already knows about Christmas. Hence, the author doesn't need to explain *about* Christmas and can simply share a personal experience with the reader.

If your topic were illegal drugs, and your audience were a group of adolescents, your purpose might be to inform them of the consequences of using these drugs and to persuade them to avoid the drugs. On the other hand, if your audience were a group of medical professionals, your purpose might be to explain how to treat drug addiction.

As a reader, determining the author's purpose may help you to focus on the author's message. As you read, ask yourself the following questions about the author's purpose: Is it to inform you about something or to explain a process? Is it to persuade you to believe a particular opinion? Is it to share an experience or a story? Or, is it merely to entertain?

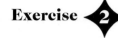 **Exercise** **Identifying a Purpose.** The following two paragraphs are written about the same topic. However, each is written for a different purpose. Read each paragraph, and identify the author's purpose, as well as the intended audience.

Diabetes

Diabetes is a disease that prevents your body from properly using the food you eat. When people eat, food is changed into fuel for the body. This fuel is called "glucose." The glucose is carried to the cells in the body by the blood. The body makes a special hormone called "insulin," which allows the glucose to be used by the cells. When a person has diabetes, his or her body does not make enough insulin. Without enough insulin, the body cannot effectively use the food that it takes in. When glucose can't be used for energy, the body burns fat for energy. When the body burns fat for energy, acid wastes, called "ketones," are formed. If a person's body has too much of this waste, physical problems can occur. Diabetes is a serious disease, and, if left untreated, it may result in death.

- What is the purpose of this paragraph? How do you know?
- Who is the audience for this paragraph? How do you know?

Managing Your Diabetes

There are several things you can do to manage your diabetes. The first way to control diabetes is with good nutrition. Good nutrition helps to keep the amount of glucose in your blood as close to normal as possible. Here are some points to remember for good nutrition: Eat less fat, eat more carbohydrates, eat less sugar, use less salt, and use alcohol only in moderation. Another way to help manage your diabetes is to exercise daily. Daily exercise also aids in keeping the amount of glucose in your blood regulated. Further, exercise keeps you at a reasonable body weight, which is another important factor in fighting the effects of diabetes. Finally, when exercise and good nutrition are not enough to control the disease, you may need to take insulin. By taking daily doses of the hormone insulin, people who cannot produce their own insulin are able to use the food that they consume as energy. Following these three suggestions will help you better manage your diabetes.

- What is the purpose of this paragraph? How do you know?
- Who is the audience for this paragraph? How do you know?

Exercise 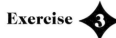 **Writing for Audience and Purpose.** You have practiced identifying the audience and purpose for a few paragraphs. Now you will have a chance to practice writing paragraphs with your own audiences and purposes in mind. First, choose one topic from the following list, or select your own topic.

Sample Topics

1. A social problem
2. Caring for a pet
3. Learning a foreign language

Next, think about two paragraphs you can write on your topic, each with a different audience and purpose. Write each topic, as well as your audience and purpose for each topic, on the lines below. Use these following two examples from the paragraphs on diabetes to help you.

Paragraph 1

Topic: <u>Diabetes</u>

Audience: <u>People unfamiliar with diabetes</u>

Purpose: <u>To inform about the effects of diabetes</u>

Paragraph 2

Topic: <u>Managing your diabetes</u>

Audience: <u>People who have diabetes</u>

Purpose: <u>To explain ways to cope with diabetes</u>

Your paragraphs:

Paragraph 1

Your topic: _____

Your audience: _____

Your purpose: _____

Paragraph 2

Your topic: _____

Your audience: _____

Your purpose: _____

When you have finished writing, exchange papers with a classmate, and talk about how your paragraphs differ from each other, depending on your audience and purpose.

Topic

In addition to considering the audience and purpose for a piece, the writer must choose a topic. A *topic* is the subject about which the paragraph is written. As a reader, it is important to identify the topic in order to see what the author is writing about. The topic is usually located at the beginning of the paragraph, although it is not always found in the first sentence.

Exercise ◆**4**◆ **Identifying Topics.**   Read the following two paragraphs written by students. Identify the topic for each one.

1. Independence Day is my favorite holiday in my country, the Dominican Republic. The day we remember our independence is on the 27th of February. In La Vega, where I live, we celebrate that day beginning very early in the morning. Many people get up at 5:00 A.M. to go to meet the municipal band at Juan Pablo Duarte Park. Later, at 6:00 A.M., the band plays on the main streets, and the people sing, dance, and clap as they follow it through the streets. In the afternoon, we go to the main street to see a parade of people dressed in masquerade costumes. Typical costumes are made of pants, a shirt, and a big cape with many colors and jingling bells. These kinds of costumes are called "Diablos Cojeulos." Later, in two different parks, there are parties with bands playing Merengue, our typical music. This day is always fun and happy. It is the holiday that I enjoy the most in my country.

Topic: _____

2. My first experience with fast food taught me a lot about the necessity of correct pronunciation in a foreign language. In my first month in the United States, I was taking night classes to learn English. One day after class, I was hungry, so I drove to McDonald's to get some dinner. The weather was cold, and I didn't want to get out of my car, so I stopped at the drive through. I ordered a Big Mac and a small Coke. I took my bag and drove home. When I arrived at home and opened it, I was very surprised to find that inside was a Big Mac and cookies. I was frustrated with my English, and I decided to practice my pronunciation of the word "Coke" for a week. My roommates helped me, and I felt confident. Then, after one week, I returned to McDonald's, and I ordered the same thing: one Big Mac and a small Coke. This time, I felt proud of my pronunciation. I was sure I could get what I wanted. When I got home and opened my bag, I was surprised again. I got a Big Mac and a small coffee. This experience helped me learn that in order

to be understood, it is very important to have correct pronunciation in a foreign language.

Topic: _____

Narrowing the Topic

In choosing a topic, writers sometimes make the mistake of choosing a topic that is too general. If a topic is too general, the information is too great to cover in one paragraph. Consequently, the paragraph may merely list several generalizations, which are usually not interesting for a reader. If you begin with a topic that is too general, you should narrow it down. Depending on your audience and your purpose, you might have to narrow your topic several times before you have a topic specific enough for a good, clear paragraph.

The following examples show topics that have each been narrowed down two times.

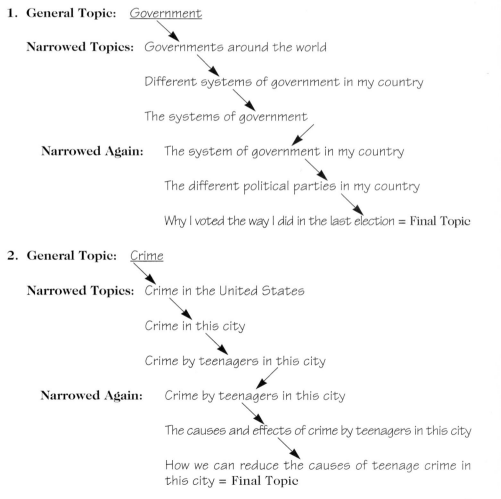

1. **General Topic:** _Government_

    Narrowed Topics: Governments around the world

    Different systems of government in my country

    The systems of government

    Narrowed Again: The system of government in my country

    The different political parties in my country

    Why I voted the way I did in the last election = Final Topic

2. **General Topic:** _Crime_

    Narrowed Topics: Crime in the United States

    Crime in this city

    Crime by teenagers in this city

    Narrowed Again: Crime by teenagers in this city

    The causes and effects of crime by teenagers in this city

    How we can reduce the causes of teenage crime in this city = Final Topic

Exercise ◆**5**▶ **Choosing General and Narrowed Topics.** Now practice narrowing the following general topics at least two times: "Food," "Education," and "Marriage." Refer to the previous examples for help. List each topic on a separate page. For each topic, suggest three or more narrowed topics, then choose one of the narrowed topics, and narrow your topic again. For each general topic, choose a final specific topic. You will be referring to these topics again later (in Exercise 7). Use this outline to help you narrow the first topic.

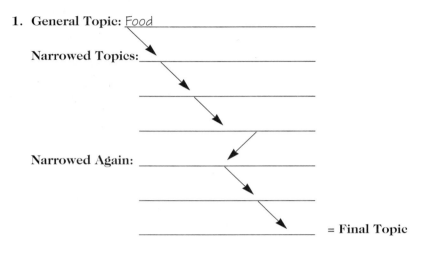

1. **General Topic:** _Food_ _____

   Narrowed Topics: _____

   _____

   _____

   Narrowed Again: _____

   _____

   _____ = **Final Topic**

Topic Sentence

Within a paragraph, the topic is introduced or explained by a *topic sentence,* which tells what the paragraph will be about. The topic sentence is the most general sentence in the paragraph and is often, but not always, the first sentence in the paragraph.

Look back at the first paragraph called "Christmas" on page 2. The topic sentence is, "Christmas is the most widely celebrated holiday in the United States." Now look at the second paragraph on Christmas on page 3. The topic sentence is, "Christmas is a holiday that brings back many wonderful memories." Do you notice how each topic sentence targets a different audience, preparing the reader differently for what he or she will read?

Controlling Idea

Each topic sentence has a *controlling idea,* which controls the topic and content of the paragraph. Its purpose is to focus the topic and to introduce the specific aspect of the topic that will be discussed. Following are three topic sentences from previous paragraphs. In each sentence, the topic is underlined, and the controlling idea is circled. A note following each sentence explains how the topic and controlling idea help you know what to look for when you read.

1. <u>Christmas</u> is the ⟨most widely celebrated holiday in the United States.⟩

     As you read the paragraph, you will look for how Christmas is celebrated and why it is the most widely celebrated holiday in the United States.

2. <u>Christmas</u> is a holiday that brings back ⟨many wonderful memories.⟩

     As you read the paragraph, you will look for the many wonderful Christmas memories the author will share.

3. <u>Diabetes</u> is a disease that ⟨prevents your body from properly using the food⟩ that you eat.

     As you read the paragraph, you will look for ways in which diabetes prevents your body from properly using food.

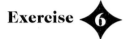

Exercise 6 **Using Topic Sentences.**   Following are five more topic sentences. Underline the topic, and circle the controlling idea in each sentence. Then, on the line below each sentence, write what you would expect to look for as you read the rest of the paragraph.

1. Independence Day is my favorite holiday in my country, the Dominican Republic.

    What you will look for: _____

2. My first experience with fast food taught me a lot about the necessity of correct pronunciation in a foreign language.

    What you will look for: _____

3. U.S. and Japanese hospital childbirth practices differ in several ways.

    What you will look for: _____

4. U.S. attitudes about whether youths should work differ greatly from the attitudes in my country.

    What you will look for: _____

5. In Taiwan, it is becoming more difficult to find good jobs.

    What you will look for: _____

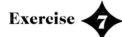

Exercise 7 **Writing Topic Sentences from Narrowed Topics.**   Look back at the work you did in Exercise 5, creating narrowed topics for the general topics of food, education, and marriage. Next, practice writing your own topic sentences from the narrowed topics you chose. Use the following example as a guide for writing your own topic sentences.

Example: General Topic: <u>Crime</u>

                   Narrowed Topic: <u>How we can reduce the causes of teenage</u>
                                     <u>crime in this city</u>

                   Topic Sentence: <u>There are many ways to reduce teenage crime</u>
                                     <u>in this city, but the most important is to make</u>
                                     <u>sure young people have something to do in</u>
                                     <u>their free time.</u>

1. General Topic: <u>Food</u>

    Narrowed Topic: _____

    Topic Sentence: _____

    _____

2. General Topic: <u>Education</u>

    Narrowed Topic: _____

    Topic Sentence: _____

    _____

3. General Topic: <u>Marriage</u>

    Narrowed Topic: _____

    Topic Sentence: _____

    _____

Support

Once you have written a topic sentence, you need to build your paragraph by providing *support,* the ideas that expand, explain, or describe the controlling ideas. All the sentences in a paragraph should work together to support the ideas expressed in the topic sentence. Support can be given in the form of examples (e.g. personal experiences, facts) or descriptions. While the topic sentence gives the reader the controlling idea, the supporting sentences give the reader the specific ideas that will elaborate on the topic and its controlling idea. For example, in an earlier paragraph, the topic was "diabetes," and the controlling idea was how to manage diabetes. Three specific things were explained that could help manage diabetes: nutrition, exercise, and insulin. More specifically, they were as follows:

Topic sentence: There are several things a person with diabetes can do to manage the disease.

First supporting idea: Monitoring nutrition

- Helps to maintain the amount of glucose at levels close to normal
- Includes several specific nutritional points to remember—
  - eat less fat
  - eat more carbohydrates
  - eat less sugar
  - use less salt
  - use alcohol only in moderation

Second supporting idea: Getting exercise

- Helps regulate the amount of glucose
- Keeps you at a reasonable body weight

Third supporting idea: Taking insulin

- Helps people convert the food they eat into a form they can use as energy

Exercise ◆8◆ **Identifying Supporting Details.** Read the following student-written paragraph. The topic sentence has been underlined. Notice that the topic sentence isn't the first sentence, but it still contains the controlling idea of the paragraph—the differences in hospital childbirth practices between the United States and Japan. In the lines following the paragraph, list the specific support that is used to expand, explain, or describe the topic and the controlling idea. Some of the lines have been filled in for you. Fill in the rest.

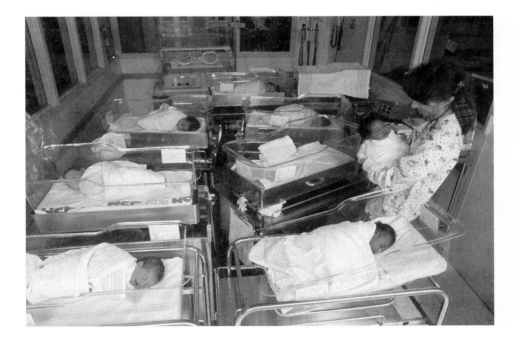

Childbirth

Giving birth is one of the most important yet most difficult things that women do all over the world. However, there are many international differences in the routines that accompany childbirth. <u>For example, U.S. and Japanese hospital childbirth practices differ in several ways.</u> In both countries, the women see the doctor several times during their pregnancy. Japanese women go to the hospital for their prenatal checkups, whereas American women usually go to the doctor's office. Another difference is the use of drugs during labor. Japanese women are not given any drugs because Japanese doctors feel that drugs are not healthful during delivery. Consequently, the mother is expected to feel any pain that accompanies childbirth. In contrast, American women commonly are given epidural anesthetics so they can feel nothing from the waist down. The two countries also differ in terms of the length of the hospital stay. Japanese mothers stay in the hospital for one week after delivery so that the newborn and the mother can be monitored. During this time, the mother learns to nurse, bathe, and care for her baby. In contrast, American women often go home 12–24 hours after they have had their babies. They usually have to learn to take care of their babies by themselves. Because of the differences in hospital childbirth practices between Japan and America, I would rather give birth to my babies in a Japanese hospital.

by Sanae

Topic sentence: U.S. and Japanese hospital childbirth practices differ in several ways.

First supporting idea: Prenatal doctor visits

- Japanese women go to the hospital
- American women go to the doctor's office

Second supporting idea: The use of drugs during labor

- Japanese women _____

- American women _____

Third supporting idea: _____

- _____

- _____

Exercise 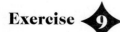 **Writing a Paragraph.** Now that you have practiced identifying support in someone else's writing, you are ready to write your own supporting sentences. Pick one of your topic sentences from Exercise 7, and write the rest of the paragraph. Each sentence in the paragraph should discuss some aspect of your topic, as expressed by the controlling idea. Save your unfinished paragraph; you will be referring to it again later.

Read to Write

Unity

In order for supporting sentences to be effective, they must show *unity*. This means that all of the supporting details in each paragraph must help to expand, explain, or describe the controlling idea. If any of the ideas in the paragraph don't relate to the controlling idea, the reader may become confused.

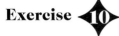 **Exercise 10 Recognizing Paragraph Unity.** Read each paragraph once, then go back and underline the topic sentence and circle the controlling idea. Cross out any sentences that do not support the topic and the controlling idea.

Pressure in School

In Taiwan, if students want jobs with good salaries they need a higher education. Before students can ever think of this, however, they must do well in junior high school and high school. The pressure is tremendous. Americans don't have this pressure to enter a good school. Some of the pressure to enter a good high school comes from parents. Parents always hope that their sons or daughters will have a good future. Pressure also comes from the students themselves. They realize that if they don't pass the exams to get into a good high school and then a good university, their future will not be the best it can be. As a result, they put a lot of stress on themselves. They study hard and go to special schools after regular school in order to be able to succeed in high school. Some of my friends skipped these night schools. For these reasons, junior high school and high school can be a greatly stressful time in a Taiwanese teenager's life.

Two Seasons in My Hometown

The weather in my hometown is very important to everyone there. With the different seasons, our lives change in many ways. In Huancayo, Peru, where I live, there are only two seasons—summer and winter. Summertime is from May to October. During those months, the weather is dry and calm. In Los Angeles it also gets very hot. The sun shines every day, and we have clear, blue skies. The people dress lightly and spend a lot of time outside working on the harvest. In the afternoon, the temperature drops and it gets cool and pleasant, so the people enjoy playing games or doing other activities during this time. Later on in the evening, it gets very cold. The temperature drops to zero degrees Fahrenheit. The people stay inside and wear heavy clothes. Winter, on the other hand, lasts from November to April. The weather is wet and windy during this half of the year. The temperature is cool and humid, but it rarely gets cold. The sun shines sometimes, but the skies are cloudy most of the time. It rains a lot but it doesn't snow. As a result, very few people ski in my hometown. People wear heavy clothes and water boots in order to walk through the mud and water. The two seasons give us variety that we enjoy.

Making Your Paragraph Unified. Now go back to the paragraph you wrote for Exercise 9 and make sure it is unified. Delete any sentences that do not support both the topic and its controlling idea.

Revising Your Paragraph

During the writing process, you will revise your writing several times. Each revised version is called a "draft." It is a good idea to have another classmate read your drafts to give you feedback on what you have written. Exchanging drafts with another student will also give you the experience of being a reader whose job it is to give helpful feedback to the writer.

First Draft

Exchange the first draft of your paragraph (see Exercise 11) with one of your classmates. Read each other's paragraphs. Make sure you both have included all the necessary elements that have been discussed in this section. Use the following checklist as a guide.

First Draft Paragraph Checklist

✓ Identify the audience.
✓ Identify the purpose.
✓ Identify the topic.
✓ Is the topic narrowed appropriately? If not, why not?
✓ Is there a topic sentence with a controlling idea? (Underline the topic sentence, and circle the controlling idea.)
✓ Are there sufficient supporting details? (Is there missing information? Do you have any unanswered questions?)
✓ Is the paragraph unified? (Are there any sentences that don't seem to belong?)

Second Draft

After talking with your partner, write a second draft of your paragraph. Include any elements you may have left out. Make any other changes that you think are necessary.

Punctuation and Paragraph Form

A very important part of writing is *form*—how the writing looks on the page. You can help your readers better understand what you write if you remember the following rules:

Some Rules of Paragraph Form

Indentation. In order to tell where a new paragraph begins in an essay, *indent* the type five spaces from the left margin.

Capital Letters. Use *capital letters* at the beginning of every sentence.

Periods, Question Marks, Exclamation Points. *Periods* come at the end of complete sentences. They indicate the end of one complete thought. *Question marks* also indicate the end of sentences. Look at the following examples:

   (a) *The concert is tonight.* Sentence (a) ends in a period because it is a statement.

   (b) *Is the concert tonight?* Sentence (b) ends in a question mark because it is a question.

Like periods and question marks, *exclamation points* also mark the ends of sentences. However, they are used for dramatic emphasis, to call attention to something surprising, exciting, and so on. For example:

   (c) *I can't believe the concert is tonight!* Sentence (c) ends in an exclamation point because it shows the speaker's surprise or excitement.

Do not use exclamation points too much, or you will lose the emphasis you are trying to create.

Exercise 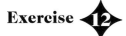 **Using Punctuation and Paragraph Form.** The following descriptive essay has some errors in punctuation and paragraph form. Capitalization, indentations, periods, and question marks are missing. As you read the essay, insert capital letters, periods, or question marks wherever necessary. Indicate where each paragraph should be indented by drawing an arrow. The first sentence has been fixed for you. You must find and fix 8 words that should be capitalized, 2 missing indentations, 4 missing periods, and 4 missing question marks.

Have You Ever Looked at Snow?

H
→ Have you ever looked at snow? have you caught one snowflake on the tip of your finger and studied its shapes, the angles sticking out this way and that way sometimes they look so sharp that you wonder why they don't hurt when they fall on your cheeks or your tongue as you try to catch them in midair
have you watched a snowflake melt into water in your warm hand at first the snowflake is so beautiful, but within a moment or two it has disappeared and left nothing behind but a drop of water like a tear drop
when was the last time that you watched a snow storm and noticed the thousands of white spots falling and whirling like tiny dancers in white skirts, finally piling up on each other at your feet then, after the storm stops and the sun comes out again, have you looked at the freshly fallen snow, glistening in the sunlight all of the individual flakes and all of their individual shapes reflect the sunlight, creating thousands of rainbows you can look at the snow and see spots of blue and red and silver and gold covering the purest white

Final Draft

Now that you have reviewed paragraph form and punctuation, write a final draft of the paragraph you have been working on for this section. Make sure the form, punctuation, and spelling are correct. Use the following checklist as you look over your paragraph one last time.

Final Paragraph Checklist

✓ Can you identify the audience?
✓ Can you identify the purpose?
✓ Can you identify the topic?
✓ Is the topic narrowed appropriately?
✓ Is there a topic sentence with a controlling idea?
✓ Are there sufficient supporting details?
✓ Is the paragraph unified?
✓ Is the paragraph indented?
✓ Are capital letters used at the beginning of each sentence?
✓ Is there a period, question mark, or exclamation point at the end of each sentence?
✓ Is the spelling correct?

If you can answer "yes" to the preceding questions, then you have written a well-focused paragraph with a narrowed topic or main idea, which is supported with relevant details.

Part Two

The Essay

An *essay* is a group of paragraphs. Like a single paragraph, it is developed around a main topic; it is written with a specific audience and purpose in mind, and it has a narrowed topic, supporting details, and unity. On the other hand, the essay also contains certain unique elements, such as an introduction, a thesis statement, and a conclusion. To help you identify and understand the various parts of an essay, you will be asked to refer to the following essay, "Culture Shock."

✦ Prereading Activity

The following essay, written by a student, is about a subject with which you are probably familiar: culture shock. Before you read, discuss the following questions in small groups.

1. What is culture shock?

2. Have you ever experienced culture shock? Are you experiencing it now?

3. What things about life in North America seem strange to you?

Culture Shock

(A)   Studying in a different country is something that sounds very exciting to most people. Many young people who leave their home to go study in another country think that they are going to have a lot of fun. Certainly, it is a new experience, which brings us the opportunity of discovering new things and a feeling of freedom. In spite of these advantages, however, there are also some difficulties we will face. Because of the different beliefs, norms, values, and traditions that exist among different countries, we may have difficulty adjusting to a new culture and to all of the parts of the culture that are not familiar to us. This is culture shock. There are at least four essential stages of culture-shock adjustment.

(B)   The first stage is called "the honeymoon." In this stage, we are excited about living in a different place, and everything seems to be marvelous. We like everything, and everybody seems to be so nice to us. Also, the amusement of life in a new culture seems as though it will never end.

(C)   Eventually, however, the second stage of culture shock appears. This is the "hostility stage." We begin to notice that not everything is as good as we had originally thought it was. We become tired of many things about the new culture. Moreover, people don't treat us like a guest anymore. Everything that seemed to be so wonderful at first is now awful, and everything makes us feel sick and tired.

(D)   Usually at this point in our adjustment to a new culture, we develop some defense mechanisms to help us feel better and to protect us against the effects of culture shock. One type of defense mechanism is called "repression." This is when we pretend that everything is okay and that nothing bothers us. Another type of defense mechanism is called "regression." This is when we start to act as if we are younger than we actually are; we act like children. We forget everything, and sometimes we become careless and irresponsible. The third kind of defense mechanism is called "isolation." We would rather be home alone, and we don't want to talk to anybody. With isolation, we try to avoid the effects of culture shock, or at least that's what we think. Isolation is one of the worst defense mechanisms that we can use because it separates us from those things that could really help us. The last type of defense mechanism is called "rejection." With this defense mechanism, we think that we don't need anybody. We feel we are doing okay alone, so we don't try to ask for help.

(E)   The defense mechanisms that we use in the hostility stage are not helpful. If we only occasionally use one of these defense mechanisms to help ourselves feel better, that is okay. We must be careful, however. These mechanisms can really hurt us because they prevent us from making necessary adjustments to the new culture.

(F)   After we deal with our hostility, we begin to know that the shock of the new culture is only temporary; then we come to the third stage, called "recovery." In this stage, we start to feel better, and we try to find an answer to everything that we don't understand. The whole situation starts to get better; we recover from the symptoms of the first two stages of culture shock, and we adjust ourselves to the new norms, values, and even beliefs and traditions of the new country. We begin to see that even though the culture is different from our own, it has things that we can learn to appreciate.

(G)   The last stage of culture shock is called "adjustment." In this stage, we have reached a point where we actually feel good because we have learned enough to understand the new culture. So the things that at first made us feel uncomfortable or strange are now things that we understand. This understanding alleviates much of the stress. Now we feel good; we have adjusted to the new culture.

(H)   In conclusion, culture shock is something that those of us living in a foreign country cannot avoid. It does not seem like a very good experience when we are going through the four stages of culture shock. However, when we have completely adjusted to a new culture we can more fully enjoy it. We learn how to interact with other people, and we learn a lot about life in a culture that is not our own. Furthermore, learning about other cultures and how to adjust to the shock of living in different cultures helps us learn more about ourselves.

by Flavia

Introduction

A well-written essay always begins with a good *introduction*. The introduction introduces the essay's topic to the reader and provides a general idea of what will be said in the essay. An introduction should also get the reader interested in reading the essay. The introduction is always the first one or two paragraphs of an essay.

Exercise 1 Predicting from Introductions. The following introductions are taken from essays found in this book. Read each introduction, and discuss what you think the essay will be about, based on the introductory paragraph. Discuss with your classmates whether the introduction has interested you enough to read the rest of the essay.

1. I'll never forget my eleventh-grade writing teacher. She was unforgettable not because of her great knowledge of writing, her love for teaching, or because she was a wonderful teacher who taught me all about life. The reason I won't forget her is because she was different. She was different from anyone that I had ever met before. I will always remember her because she

didn't care at all about what others thought about her. She didn't care at all that she was different from absolutely everyone around her.

2. I look into the old box that contains my memories of my time in Uruguay, and I discover the shoes. They are old, ugly, worn out, having served their owner well. I smell the old leather, and the memories begin coming, taking me back in time. I take the shoes out, put them on the table, and study them.

3. I know that most people don't think there are ghosts in the world, especially those people who believe in a religion. However, I had an experience that makes me think that ghosts might exist.

4. Who talks more then, women or men? The seemingly contradictory evidence is reconciled by the difference between what I call "public" and "private speaking". More men feel comfortable doing "public speaking," while more women feel comfortable doing "private" speaking. Another way of describing these differences is by using the terms "report-talk" and "rapport-talk".

Exercise 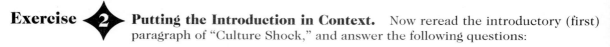 **Putting the Introduction in Context.** Now reread the introductory (first) paragraph of "Culture Shock," and answer the following questions:

1. Has the author prepared you for the rest of the essay?
2. Does the author interest you in reading the essay? Why or why not?

Thesis Statement

In an introductory paragraph, there is a *thesis statement,* one sentence that contains the topic and the controlling idea for the entire essay. The writer usually needs to give the reader some background information before introducing the essay's thesis statement. For this reason, the thesis statement is usually found near the end of the introductory paragraph.

Exercise **3** **Identifying a Thesis Statement.** Reread the introductory paragraph of "Culture Shock," and do the following:

1. Find the thesis statement.
2. Underline the topic.
3. Circle the controlling idea.

Supporting Paragraphs

Once the thesis has been introduced, the essay provides *supporting paragraphs,* which follow the introduction and support the thesis statement. Just as each sentence in a paragraph should support the topic sentence, each paragraph in an essay should support the thesis statement.

Exercise 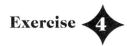 **Identifying Supporting Paragraphs.** Use the following examples as a guide for writing out the topics and controlling ideas of paragraphs D–H in "Culture Shock."

Thesis Statement: *There are at least four essential stages of culture-shock adjustment.*

Paragraph B

Topic: <u>first stage of culture shock</u>

Controlling idea: <u>honeymoon</u>

Paragraph C

Topic: <u>second stage of culture shock</u>

Controlling idea: <u>hostility</u>

Paragraph D

Topic: _____

Controlling idea: _____

Paragraph E

Topic: _____

Controlling idea: _____

Paragraph F

Topic: <u>third stage of culture shock</u>

Controlling idea: _____

Paragraph G

Topic: _____

Controlling idea: _____

Paragraph H

Topic: _____

Controlling idea: <u>we can't avoid culture shock; what we can learn from culture</u>

<u>shock</u>

Unity

The paragraphs in an essay must be unified, just as the sentences in a paragraph need to be unified. To create *unity* in an essay, all of the paragraphs need to relate to the thesis, the controlling idea of the essay. When a paragraph contains information that doesn't relate to the essay topic, the unnecessary material can confuse the reader.

 **Observing Essay Unity.**   Look back at "Culture Shock" again, and determine whether all of the information presented relates to the controlling idea of the essay.

Conclusion

A well-written essay always ends with a clear *conclusion*. A good conclusion restates what was said in the thesis statement or summarizes the main points presented in the essay. The author may also use the conclusion to comment on the whole issue discussed in the essay, or the author may offer solutions, suggestions, or hope for the future. In short, a conclusion ties all of the main ideas in the essay together.

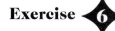 **Observing a Conclusion.**   Reread the conclusion of "Culture Shock." Does it remind the reader of the controlling ideas in the essay and tie them together well? How does it do so?

In summary, the following three elements make an essay clear to read and easy to understand:

1. A good introduction with a strong thesis statement

2. Unified supporting paragraphs

3. A good conclusion that ties all the writer's ideas together

You may want to use the explanations about the parts of an essay found in this chapter for reference when writing your own essays, later on.

Part Three

Basic Reading Skills

This section focuses on three reading skills that can help you become a more efficient reader. Two of the skills—*skimming* and *scanning*—can help you find information quickly. The third skill, knowing how to learn new vocabulary, is an essential skill for becoming a good reader and writer. In this section, you will learn and practice each of these skills.

Skimming

When you *skim* a text—for example, an article, report, or a book—you are making a quick survey to find out the main idea of the information contained in the text. Skimming is also a useful way to activate background information you may already know about a subject. Skimming before you read can increase your efficiency as a reader.

Skimming

Definition. To find out the main idea of a text before you begin reading.

Purpose. To prepare yourself for what you will read. Having an idea of what you will read before you read will make it easier for you to understand the text.

How to Skim.
1. Read the title. Ask yourself what kind of information this text will contain.

2. Read the first and last paragraphs.

3. Read the first sentence of each paragraph in the text.

4. Look at any pictures or highlighted words.

5. Again, ask yourself what kind of information the rest of this text will contain.

Exercise  **Skimming.** Practice your skimming skills with the following article by carrying out the steps listed in the box on skimming. As you skim the article, answer the following questions.

1. Based on the title, what do you think this essay is about?

2. What do the first sentences of each paragraph tell you about the organization of this essay?

3. In general terms, what information does the writer want to convey in this essay? What is the main idea?

Fight Sleepism Now

(A)   American society is not, in general, nap-friendly. It is actually sleepist in the extreme. "There's such a prohibition against admitting that we need sleep!" says David F. Dinges, a nap specialist at the University of Pennsylvania. Nobody wants to get caught napping, to be found asleep at the switch. Even children know that it's bad to be a sleepyhead. To quote an obscure Minnesota proverb worthy of Lake Wobegon, "Some sleep five hours, nature requires seven, laziness nine and wickedness eleven."

(B)   Wrong. The way not to fall asleep at the switch is to take naps when you need them. Listen to William Dement of Stanford University, the godfather of sleep research: "We need to totally change our attitude toward napping." Taking a nap, he says, should be viewed as a "heroic" act. "If we see someone taking a nap, we should stand in awe." Our latest hero leading us all in sleep policy is none other than President Clinton. According to recent reports, he has begun taking a half-hour nap in the afternoon.

(C)   . . . . there is a clear consensus among sleep researchers that, as Dinges writes, napping can be "normal, appropriate and beneficial." Sleeping for 15 minutes to two hours in the early afternoon can reduce stress, improve alertness and perhaps even help prevent heart disease. In healthy people, napping is not a cause of sleep disorders, and it's usually not a symptom of them either. About 60 percent of American adults nap at least once a week. They usually do it roughly midway between waking up in the morning and going to sleep at night, and not because of big lunches or warm weather. Human beings seem to have "a midafternoon quiescent phase," also called "a secondary sleep gate."

(D)   In other words, we were born to nap. . . .

(E)   There is an exquisite pleasure to be had in giving oneself over to drowsiness during the day, particularly if you're supposed to be doing something else. And we should all note, it's one of the few pleasures left that is not life-threatening. . . .

(F)   I myself have napped standing up on the Paris Metro, sitting in New York City buses and subways, in an incredibly noisy helicopter flying over the spectacular Trans-Atlantic Mountains, in lectures, in cars and airplanes, on sailboats and cruise liners, on a United States Coast Guard icebreaker while it was breaking 10-foot thick sea ice (which is like napping inside a food processor), on floors, couches and beds, in libraries and offices and museums, at the Metropolitan Opera House (often), and once, briefly, while I was in the process of interviewing someone for a magazine story. I savor half-hour naps, but given the chance I will sleep for as little or as long as I can.

(G)   The pathologically alert like to think they get more done than nappers. Wrong again. There are scores of stories about successful nappers (successful at something besides napping, that is). Winston

Churchill slept every afternoon when he was the wartime Prime Minister of England. Napoleon is said to have napped on the battlefield (a common practice among generals, who don't get a lot of good sack time when a war is on). Alfred Hitchcock slept at parties. Jack Warner, of Warner Brothers, took a nap in his office every afternoon. Once, Bette Davis interrupted his sleep, charging in with complaints about a script. "Without opening his eyes," recounts "The Little Brown Book of Anecdotes," Warner reached for the phone and called his secretary. "Come in and wake me up," he said. "I'm having a nightmare." . . .

(H) If there is to be a transformation of American sleep behavior, we nappers, the sleep elite, will have to learn to share our expertise with those less fortunate than us. I am prepared to lead the way in this matter, and here, for starters, are a few of my favorite naps. Review them, think about them, try them out. Don't be afraid to try out your own ideas for a good nap. And don't be ashamed if you don't fall asleep on your first try. At least one scientific article I read referred to sleeping "skills." Say to yourself: I can learn. I can change. I will nap.

(I) In the office: Sleeping at work is superbly satisfying, and in some cases necessary. Truck drivers should pull over at the first sign of drowsiness. As should anyone operating heavy machinery, including a word processor. . . .

(J) In class: Students sleep in class all the time. These naps can be very sweet because of the edge of risk associated with them. In high school I once succumbed to uncontrollable drowsiness in French class and was awakened by my teacher singing, "Frere Jacques, Frere Jacques, dormez-vous?" William Dement has designated sleeping sections in his courses at Stanford. . . .

(K) In the opera house: Music is wonderful for napping, and sleeping (discreetly) at a concert, or even better, at an opera, can be one of life's great experiences. One rides the music, being wafted this way and that on themes and leitmotifs. Wagner in particular (I recommend the second act of "Die Walküre") promotes vivid dreams.

(L) In the great outdoors: Napping out of doors is considered by some to be the peak dozing experience. Several years ago *The New Yorker*, in one of its unsigned pieces, stated, "Sleeping in the park in a city is the height of true civilization." (I suspect the author favored cities because they have fewer insects than the countryside.) . . .

(M) The best nap of all: The opera nap would be my favorite, except for the presence of other people. And music does adulterate the pure nap experience, however pleasantly. My No. 1, top-of-the-line, all-time-favorite way to nap is in a hammock on a screened-in porch, on a mild summer day with a breeze wafting gently over me and—this is what makes it perfect—a huge, important book lying on my chest, open and unread. . . .

by James Gorman

**Checking Your Answers.**   Now, read the entire text slowly and carefully to check your answers to the questions in Exercise 1.

Scanning

You *scan* to find specific information from any text you read, from a newspaper, to a bus schedule, to a college textbook. Scanning can help you go back to a text and find important pieces of information without having to read every word.

Scanning

Meaning. To find specific information in a text without having to read every word.

Purpose. To help you quickly find the information you seek.

How to scan. Quickly move your eyes back and forth across the text, looking for just one or a few words that will give you the information you want.

Exercise 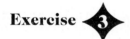 **Scanning.**   Now, practice your scanning skills to find the following information in the essay, "Fight Sleepism Now."

1. How many adults nap at least once a week?

2. Who is called the "godfather of sleep research"?

3. According to the author, where is the best nap of all?

4. What special area has William Dement designated in his courses at Stanford?

5. Where did Napoleon nap?

6. What is the name of the sleep specialist from the University of Pennsylvania School of Medicine mentioned in this article?

Vocabulary

Vocabulary knowledge is integral to both reading and writing. As a reader, your vocabulary knowledge is essential to your understanding of meaning. Learning a few basic vocabulary strategies will help you when you come across unfamiliar words as you read. As a writer, your vocabulary choice will affect the quality of your writing, by adding variety, interest, and detail.

Vocabulary Strategies

1. **Find the Meaning from Context.** When you read an unfamiliar word, you can often determine its meaning by reading the words around it. The words before and after a new word will often give you clues to its meaning.
2. **Get the Big Picture.** Don't panic if you don't understand a word when you first read it. Try to read on and complete the reading. Often, the meaning of an unfamiliar word will become clear after you understand the main idea the writer is trying to convey.
3. **Ask Others.** Asking a native speaker, your teacher, or another student to explain the meaning of a word is a quick way to help you understand the meaning. When asking for help, be sure to explain the context in which the word was found.
4. **Use the Dictionary.** Sometimes, another person is not available, and the meanings of words cannot be found by looking at their context or by trying to grasp the main idea. In these cases, and when you sense that the word is essential to understanding the full meaning of the text, look it up in a dictionary. Avoid doing this too often, however, because it can interrupt the flow of your reading.

Exercise 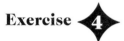 **Building Vocabulary through Context.** In the following sentences, a word has been removed, but by using the words that remain (the context), you should be able to think of a word that can be used in the blank space. Write the word that makes sense to you, based on the surrounding context. Compare answers with your classmates. More than one correct answer is possible.

1. My new little _____ is so funny! He can run after balls for hours, and he loves to chase his own tail.
2. When Tomas _____ the glass, there was a loud crash, and glass went flying everywhere!
3. Avi really doesn't like to travel by _____. He says he doesn't like the thought of being thousands of feet in the air, crowded into an uncomfortable seat, eating bad food.
4. Don't move! There is a great big _____ on your forehead. Hold still while I hit it.
5. Oh, I'm so _____! Every time Sharon borrows my car, she leaves the gas tank on empty, and the seats are covered with fast-food containers.

Exercise 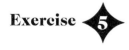 **Using Vocabulary Strategies.** Read the following story, and complete the vocabulary exercise that follows it. Some words in the story may be new to you. Try to either determine each word's meaning from the surrounding context, or skip over the word as you work on getting the big picture (main idea).

The following story is one of the many famous fables by the Greek writer Aesop. A *fable* is a story that usually has animals as the main characters and that teaches a moral or a lesson.

The Fox and the Grapes

One hot, dry summer's day, a fox was passing through a large orchard, lined with vines loaded with ripe, juicy fruits of all kinds. As the fox passed under one tree, he spied a beautiful clump of purple grapes hanging from a vine that had grown into the branches of the tree.
5   The fox was very thirsty, and he thought how good a few sweet grapes would taste just then. Although the grapes were out of the fox's reach, he was determined to get those grapes one way or another. The fox walked a little way from the tree. He turned toward the tree and ran as fast as he could until he was almost directly under the grapes;
10   then he leaped into the air—just missing the clump. The fox landed with a loud thump. He brushed himself off and tried to run and jump for the grapes again—and again—and
15   again—each time with no success. The luscious fruit hung safely out of his reach. Finally, the fox had to give it up, and as he walked away with his nose in the air, he
20   was heard to say, "Those grapes were probably sour anyway."

It's easy to despise what you can't get.

by Aesop

1. What does the word "spied" (line 3) mean? _____

   What strategy did you use to determine the word's meaning?

2. What does the word "clump" (line 3) mean? _____

   What strategy did you use to determine the word's meaning?

3. What does the word "leaped" (line 10) mean? _____

   What strategy did you use to determine the word's meaning?

Read to Write

4. What does the word "luscious" (line 16) mean? _____

   What strategy did you use to determine the word's meaning?

5. What does the word "despise" (line 22) mean? _____

   What strategy did you use to determine the word's meaning?

In this final section, you have reviewed three different types of reading skills—skimming, scanning, and using strategies for understanding the meanings of unfamiliar vocabulary words. You will have additional opportunities to practice these skills as you work through this book. If you practice these reading skills in other situations outside of the classroom, you will quickly become a more effective reader.

 # Going Further: Idea Generator

Activity  **Tell Me What I Want to Hear.**   You often choose details to include in your writing, based on what your intended audience wants to hear or what you know they will understand. Think about what you will be doing this weekend, and make a list of as many activities as possible. Then, write two letters about your plans for the weekend: Address one letter to your best friend and the other letter to your parents.

Activity  **Word Association.**   You probably know more words in English than you think you do. Get together with your classmates in groups of four. Each person should make a list of 10 words in English. Take turns slowly reading your lists to the rest of your group. As each person reads the words on his or her list, the others in your group should quickly write the first *synonym* (word that has the same meaning) that comes to mind. Compare your lists after each student's turn.

Chapter 2

Biography

A *biography* is the story of a person's life. The person may be a scoundrel or a hero, well-known or obscure. Many people even write their own biographies, in which case their stories are called "autobiographies." Usually, both biographies and autobiographies highlight the major events and accomplishments in a person's life. As such, biographies are excellent sources of history, showing us how other people's lives resemble or differ from our own. In addition, by writing our autobiographies, we have an opportunity not only to enhance our writing skills, but also to learn more about ourselves.

Reading and Writing Biography

Like other people, you have experienced important events and accomplishments in your life. In this section, you will be able both to share parts of your life story with your classmates and to hear about parts of theirs. You will read biographies of both famous and ordinary people, and you will have a chance to begin writing your own autobiography.

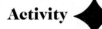

Activity

Sharing Stories. You and your classmates have fascinating stories to share about your lives. In small groups, ask each other the following questions.

1. When were you born?

2. Where were you born?

3. How many children are in your family? Which siblings are older or younger than you are?

4. What were your school days like?

5. What is your most exciting memory?

6. What is your happiest memory?

7. What is your saddest memory?

8. What is your greatest accomplishment in life so far?

9. What places have you visited in the world?

10. If you died today, what things would people remember about your life?

Biography in the Real World

There are two main types of biographies—biographies and autobiographies. A *biography* is an account of one person's life, written by another person. Usually, a biography focuses on the events in the life of a person who influenced society and perhaps even the world. In addition, many ordinary and extraordinary people write their *autobiographies,* describing their own life events and accomplishments. You might write an autobiography for many reasons: to understand yourself better, to leave your family a personal history, or to understand how you are similar to and different from others around you.

Prereading Activity

The following autobiography was written by Merlinda, a student from the Philippines, after she had lived in the United States for a year. On a separate sheet of paper, make a list of questions that you would like to ask Merlinda before you read her story.

My Life

(A)   I was born in Villa Hermosa, Calumbian Leyte, Philippines, on June 11, 1957. The first years of my life were quite ordinary. I went to school, made new friends, and learned many things. As a young girl, my life with my parents was a happy one, but later, when I was in high school, my happy life changed very suddenly.

(B)   One week before I graduated from high school, my mother died. It was very hard for me to accept my mother's death because I had always been Mama's girl. We were close. She watched out for me and gave me everything that I needed. After my mother died, I had to work hard to earn money for my personal expenses. In order to make a little money, I cooked sweet bananas and sold them on the street. After I did that for a while, however, my father told me that it was better that I go to Manila City. Since the city was new to me and very large, he said that I should stay with my uncle.

(C)   So in 1980 I went to live with my uncle. My uncle promised me that I could continue my studies and that he would pay the fees for school. I told my uncle that I was unsure of how I would do this since I couldn't pass the necessary tests in high school. He said that it was okay, and that he would support me so that I could take a secretarial course.

(D)   However, he didn't keep his promise. I stayed at my uncle's house for one year, waiting to continue my studies, but all of his promises meant nothing. They were just words, "bla bla." I could see that nothing was going to happen if I stayed with my uncle in Manila, so I decided to go with my friend to her parent's hometown. I never returned to my uncle's home. I stayed at my friend's boarding house for a few weeks. One day, one of my friends told me that they needed a salesperson in the tourist store where she worked. I applied for and was offered the job, and I took it. The store sold many different Philippine products, such as clothing, lamp shades, necklaces, and other things. I worked at this store for about four years, from 1984 to 1988.

(E)   In 1990, I found another job. I worked at a small beauty shop as a manicurist and a beautician cutting hair. However, after a few months, the beauty shop was closed because the owner moved. Once again, I was left without work.

(F)   I was still living at my friend's boarding house and wondering what I should do with my life. One day I decided to write a letter to my cousin in Switzerland, to ask her if there was a possibility I could work there. She told me that working there was not possible because I wasn't a Swiss citizen. However, she said I could visit her as a tourist, and she would be my sponsor. So, a month later, I moved to Switzerland. At first I was homesick because I didn't have any friends there. Luckily, this homesickness did not last for long. Soon after I arrived, I met a very nice Swiss man, and you can guess the rest. . . .

(G)   I am now living in the United States with my Swiss husband and our little
boy. Both my husband and I are studying English. I have had a lot of experiences in my life that have helped me to be strong and independent. I hope to
have many more wonderful experiences with my family in this country.

by Merlinda

About the Reading

1. Who was Merlinda's audience?

2. Did Merlinda answer the questions you wrote down before you read her story?

What Do You Think?

Merlinda was in some difficult situations, but she did her best to succeed.
What do you think helped her to try so hard?

Prereading Activity

In addition to telling about the major events in a person's life, biographies often
focus on how those events contributed to society. The following biography is
about a well-known person who dedicated her life to serving other people. Before you read, discuss the following questions in small groups, and then review
the vocabulary words highlighted here.

1. Have you ever heard of Mother Teresa? If so, what do you know about her life?

2. What other famous person do you think has done a great deal to help others? Why do you think so?

✦ VOCABULARY WATCH

NOUNS	VERBS	EXPRESSIONS
charity	dedicate	give up
nun	accomplish	take care of
poverty	sacrifice	a great deal
purity		
obedience		
superiors		
recognition		
shelter		
lepers		
clinic		

Read to Write

Mother Teresa

(A)   Mother Teresa is known throughout the world for her life spent in the service of the poorest of the poor in the world. Her life of service to others began on August 27, 1910 in the town of Skopje, Macedonia. When she was born, she was named Agnes Gonxha Bojaxiu, the third child of Nikola and Drana Bojaxiu, who were strong Albanian Catholics. Her parents believed deeply in helping the poor to have a better life. Agnes's mother taught her well that true **charity** meant caring for others. She always invited their poor neighbors into her home, and she often visited the sick, the elderly, and the lonely.

(B)   Agnes learned much about service from her family. She also learned about the importance of service through her religion. One man in particular, named Father Jambrekovich, helped Agnes decide what to do with her future. When Agnes was 12 years old, he told her in exciting detail about the Catholic missionaries that helped the poor in Calcutta, India.

(C)   At the age of 18, Agnes decided that she wanted to become a **nun.** She applied to work with the Order of Loreto, the missionary nuns who worked in eastern India. Making the decision to become a nun was not easy for Agnes because there was much that she would have to **give up:** marriage, children, her family, her music, and her writing. Nevertheless, on September 25, 1928, Agnes left her family and friends in Skopje to begin her life of service in India. She knew that she would never change her mind about becoming a nun.

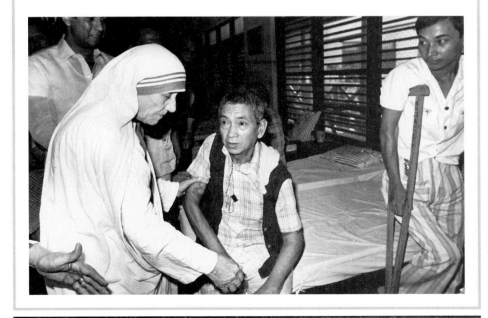

(D)   First, Agnes had to travel to the Loreto Abbey in Dublin, Ireland, where new nuns learned to speak English, the language they would teach the schoolchildren in India. They also learned how to lead the life of a nun. It was at the Abbey in Ireland that Agnes was given a new name, Mary Teresa.

(E)   In January of 1929, Sister Teresa arrived in India. Soon after arriving, Sister Teresa **dedicated** herself to a life of **poverty, purity,** and **obedience.** She continued her study of the English language and began to study Hindi and Bengali, which were the major languages in Calcutta, India. She also began to help nurses at a medical clinic, where she learned how to **take care of** the sick and dying. Her next assignment was at the Loreto convent school in Calcutta, where she taught history and geography to wealthy children. In May 1937, Sister Teresa took her final vows as a nun and then became the head of the school as Mother Teresa.

(F)   Mother Teresa had **accomplished** a lot in her short life as a nun; however, she was not happy. All around her, especially outside of the convent school, were the poor people that she wanted to help, yet she was not helping any of them. She began to pray that she would somehow be able to do what she came to India to do—help the poorest of the poor. Nine years later, Mother Teresa felt as though she had heard the voice of God telling her that she needed to leave the comfort of the convent and go out to help the poor as she lived with them, not separated from them. However, because she had promised to spend her whole life with the nuns of the Loreto order, Mother Teresa had to ask for permission to leave. Her **superiors** did not want to allow her to go because they did not believe that she could help the poor outside the convent walls. Finally her request was approved, and on August 6, 1948, she left the convent.

(G)   After leaving the convent, Mother Teresa went to Patna, India, to study medicine with the Medical Missionary Sisters. Then in December of 1948, Mother Teresa returned to Calcutta to begin serving the poor. She had no idea where to start her mission, so one day, she began to walk among the poor. After a few children began to follow her, she sat down under a tree and began to write the Bengali alphabet in the dirt. Soon, there were 40 children watching her. This is how she began her outdoor school. She continued to teach the children during the day, and she visited the sick and the elderly at night. The work was never ending.

(H)   Soon, there were others who wanted to help her. Mother Teresa's first helper was Subhasini Das, one of her students at the Loreto convent. Later, when 12 sisters had also joined her, Mother Teresa felt they could start their own order. In 1950, Mother Teresa asked the church officials in Rome for official **recognition** of their new order of nuns. Several months later, their order was approved, and they officially became the Order of the Missionaries of Charity.

(I)   In 1952, Mother Teresa wanted to help the poor in another way. Many of the sick people that she was trying to help were too poor to pay for hospital care, so they would return to the streets of Calcutta to die. Mother Teresa was given permission from the city officials to use the back rooms of a former Hindu temple as a **shelter** for the dying. She wanted to give these people, who had nothing, a "beautiful" death. This place became known as Nirmal Hriday, the Place of the Immaculate Heart, and it could provide care for about 120 people at a time.

(J)   Three years later, Mother Teresa found yet another way to further her work among the poor. In 1955, she opened Shishu Bhavan, the Children's Home of the Immaculate Heart. Mother Teresa and her nuns took care of orphans and sick children at this home, caring for these children as if they were her own. She provided education for the boys and gave the girls the things they needed when they were married.

(K)   In 1957, a small group of **lepers** visited Mother Teresa. She was one person they knew would care about them and their disease. After listening to them, Mother Teresa decided that it was time to help another group of people in need. The Missionaries of Charity helped by opening Shanti Nagar, a place where the lepers could learn a trade and support themselves. They also set up **clinics** throughout Calcutta where the lepers could receive treatment. For those who could not come to the clinics, Mother Teresa rode through the streets in a van equipped with medical supplies.

(L)   In a short time, Mother Teresa became famous throughout the world. Volunteers from all over the world came to India to help Mother Teresa with her work. In addition, she opened homes throughout the world to help the poor in Venezuela, Italy, Tanzania, Great Britain, and the United States. By 1990, she had helped to open 430 homes in 95 countries.

(M)   In 1979, the world decided to recognize Mother Teresa for her great work. In that year, she was awarded the Nobel Peace Prize. Along with the award, she received $190,000, which she used to help the poor in India.

(N)   Although Mother Teresa has grown old and become ill herself, she continues to serve those in need. Mother Teresa's goal has been to help the poorest of the poor and she has **sacrificed a great deal** to reach this goal. Through the example of her life, we are reminded that everyone deserves compassion and that we can all help those in need.

About the Reading

1. What is the purpose of this biography? How is it different from the purpose of Merlinda's autobiography?

2. Why did Mother Teresa decide to become a nun?

3. What was Mother Teresa's greatest desire in life?

4. Who did Mother Teresa help besides the people in India?

5. What were some of the challenges that Mother Teresa had to face as she tried to help others?

6. After reading Mother Teresa's biography, what other things would you like to know about her life?

7. How has Mother Teresa changed the world?

What Do You Think?

Mother Teresa served the people of India because it was her greatest desire. However, she had to give up many things to do this. What is one of your greatest desires? What would you be willing to give up to do it?

Exercise 1

Guessing Meaning from Context. Read the following sentences, which use some words that may have been new to you as you read Mother Teresa's biography. By looking at the sentence contexts, try to guess the meaning of the underlined words. Write your own definitions of what these words mean in the blanks below.

1. When the rain started falling, we found a warm, dry place that would protect us from the weather. We decided that it would be a good <u>shelter</u>.

   _____

2. In order to study in America, Mercedes has to <u>give up</u> many things. She can't live with her parents. She can't see her friends. She can't eat the food from her country, and she can't hear her favorite songs on the radio.

   _____

3. Anya began to do poorly at work. Her <u>superiors</u> told her that she needed to improve or she would lose her job.

   _____

4. The people in the countryside lived in <u>poverty</u>; they had no money, very little food or clothing, and often no shelter.

   _____

5. When Omar got the best grade on the national exam, he was given a lot of <u>recognition</u>. His picture was in the newspaper, he was invited to many formal dinners, and he was given a large scholarship from the university.

   _____

Main Idea

In a biography, each paragraph generally focuses on one period or significant event in a person's life. A paragraph may also focus on some special characteristic or quality of that person. As you learned in the previous chapter, the focus of a paragraph is the controlling idea, often called the "main idea."

Exercise 2   **Identifying the Main Idea.**   Reread Mother Teresa's biography. For the following items, circle the letter of the phrase that best expresses the main idea of each paragraph. The letter in parentheses identifies the paragraph in which you can find each item.

1. (A)   a. The birth of Mother Teresa
          b. The service of Mother Teresa
          c. The background of Mother Teresa

2. (C)   a. Deciding to become a nun
          b. Giving up a normal life
          c. Serving in India

3. (F)   a. Her original purpose in India
          b. Her many accomplishments
          c. Her dissatisfaction with what she was doing

4. (G)   a. Starting her mission in Calcutta
          b. Studying medicine in Patna
          c. Writing the Bengali alphabet in the dirt

5. (K)   a. Taking supplies to the lepers
          b. Helping the lepers to support themselves
          c. Trading with the lepers

Few of us have influenced others as greatly as Mother Teresa has. Thus, most autobiographies about ordinary people lack the historical significance found in the biographies of famous persons. Nonetheless, these autobiographies can still be very interesting to read. Like biographies, autobiographies are organized around the significant events in a person's life.

Prereading Activity

The following autobiography was written by Quynh, a student from Vietnam. Quynh had lived in the United States for 11 months when she wrote this autobiography. Before you read it, make a list of ideas you think might appear in Quynh's autobiography. Write your list on a separate sheet of paper, so that you can refer back to it later.

My Journey

(A)   I was born in Saigon, Vietnam, on March 5, 1973. I was my parent's first child. At that time, my father was at war as a pilot in the army, so he was not there when I was born.

(B)   We lived in Saigon until I was one and a half years old. It was dangerous to live in Saigon at that time, though, so my family moved to my grandmother's house in Nhatrang, which is in the western part of Vietnam.

(C)   My father was a political prisoner for four years. When he was finally set free, he and my mother got a divorce. My father married another woman when I was seven years old. He and his new wife lived in a home in Saigon. About the same time, my mother also remarried and her new husband adopted us.

(D)   When I turned 12 years old, my mother and stepfather left Vietnam and moved to Japan. I had to stay in Vietnam with my grandmother. This was the saddest time of my life because I had no parents close by me. My mother and stepfather were far away, and my father and his wife were not close to me either. Without my parents, I felt like an orphan.

(E)   However, after a while, life began to get better. Four months after my parents left, I began junior high school. I was so happy to meet many people my same age, and we became very good friends. We always walked to school and back home together, and we often made food and ate together. Sometimes we went to see movies or to the beach. In contrast to how I had felt right after my parents left, these were some of the most happy years of my life. I no longer felt so sad that I had been left behind by my parents.

(F)   Three years went by. When I was 15 years old, I went to Japan to live with my mother and stepfather. At first, I was very sad because I missed my grandmother and my friends. My homesickness caused me not to eat or sleep well. Soon, however, I began high school. In the beginning, I couldn't speak Japanese at all, but I kept practicing. After about one year, once I could speak Japanese and I had some friends, I really enjoyed going to high school there.

(G)   In March 1992, I graduated from high school. I worked for three months at an electric company, where I met a very nice boy who became my first boyfriend. I was very happy, but as I began to think about my future, I decided that I needed to learn English if I really wanted to succeed in life. So in December 1992, I left Japan, my family, and my boyfriend, and I came to the United States to study English.

by Quynh

Exercise 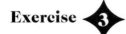 **Identifying the Main Idea.** For Quynh's autobiography, write the main idea of each paragraph in the blanks below.

Paragraph A: _____

Paragraph B: _____

Read to Write

Paragraph C: _____

Paragraph D: _____

Paragraph E: _____

Paragraph F: _____

Paragraph G: _____

Getting Started:
Brainstorming with a Time Line

As you may already know, *brainstorming* is a prewriting strategy that many writers use to develop ideas for writing. Writers don't begin with a blank piece of paper and immediately write a perfect essay. Rather, most writers brainstorm a list of possible ideas they may use in their essay, then they select their best ideas before they start to write. Just as a rainstorm is made of many individual rain drops, a brainstorm is made of many individual ideas. It doesn't matter whether all the ideas in a brainstorm are perfect for the essay. You may not even use many ideas you come up with while you brainstorm, but write them all down anyway. Often, one good idea leads to an even better one, and you can choose the best ideas to use after you have finished brainstorming.

Because most biographies are organized *chronologically* (according to time), one of the best ways to brainstorm for a biography is by using a *time line* that begins with the person's birth and progresses through his or her life. If you look at the main ideas of the previous essays, you will notice that they are in *chronological order*. That is, they are in order according to when they happened in the person's life. If Quynh had brainstormed for ideas before writing her biography, she might have used a time line such as the following one to organize her ideas.

Time Line of Quynh's Life

1973	1974	1979	1980	1985	1988	1989	1992
I was born. Father was at war.	Moved to Nhatrang with grandmother	Parents divorced	Father remarried	Began junior high school Mother and stepfather left Vietnam	Moved to Japan	Began to feel comfortable in Japan	Graduated from high school Came to U.S.

Notice that each main event in Quynh's life is indicated by a specific point on the time line.

Exercise ◆**4** **Brainstorming and Making Your Time Line.** To brainstorm possible ideas and events to use in your autobiography, write some important events and the years when they occurred on a time line on a separate sheet of paper. Begin with your birth and continue up to the present. Add as many events as you like, especially events that were interesting, unusual, funny, or meaningful in other ways.

After you have finished, exchange time lines with a classmate. Ask each other questions about the events listed. Discussing the events on your time lines can help you decide which ones are most important. If you have too many events on your time line, choose some events that you can best describe in a short autobiography like Quynh's.

Essay Writing: First Draft

Now that you have seen a few examples of biographies and have created your own time line, you are ready to write the first draft of your autobiography. Using the events on your time line as a guide, write your own short autobiography. As in the biographies you have read so far, each paragraph should focus on a particular major event, period, or personal trait.

Before you write your first draft, read over the following First Draft Checklist, to guide you in your writing. Then, after you have written your draft, use the checklist to evaluate what you have written. Make any changes that will improve your writing.

First Draft Checklist

✓ Are the main events included?

✓ Are the main events listed in the correct chronological order?

✓ Does each paragraph contain a main idea, such as a significant event, period, or character trait?

Part Two

Developing Biographies

In Part One, you read a few biographies, practiced identifying the main ideas of biographies, and began writing your own autobiography. In Part Two, you will learn how to organize and develop your own autobiography, through use of supporting details.

Organizational Style in Biographical Writing

The main events or time periods of biographies are usually written in *chronological order*, which means that the different events are presented in the order in which they happened.

⬧ Prereading Activity

The following is a short biography of Mahatma Mohandas Gandhi. In this biography, each event is reported in chronological order, beginning with his birth in 1869 and ending in his death in 1948. Before you read, discuss the following questions in small groups, and then review the vocabulary highlighted here.

1. What do you know about Mohandas Gandhi?
2. What do you know about the *caste system* in India?

✦ VOCABULARY WATCH

NOUNS	VERBS	ADJECTIVES	ADVERBS
caste	inspire	Hindu	eagerly
discrimination	imprison	traditional	
race			
fasts			

Gandhi: Man of Truth

(A)   Mohandas Karamchand Gandhi was born October 2, 1869, in Porbandar, India, where his father worked for the Indian government. Gandhi was the youngest child of a large family that belonged to the **Hindu** Vaisya (merchant) **caste**. His mother had strong **traditional** Hindu beliefs of how a person should live. Her beliefs **inspired** Gandhi greatly throughout his life.

(B)   According to Hindu custom, a wife was chosen for Gandhi while he was still quite young; at 13, he was married to a young girl named Kasturba. They remained married for 62 years until her death in 1944. In 1888, at the age of 19, Gandhi went to London to study law.

Following his studies in England, he returned to India to practice law. He was not a successful lawyer, however, and soon after his return to India, he **eagerly** accepted an opportunity to work in South Africa for a business that was owned by Indians living there. In South Africa, however, Gandhi, along with all other Indians, suffered greatly from practices of **discrimination** against their **race.** This unfair treatment of Indians led to Gandhi's efforts to help other Indians living in South Africa. He taught them his belief in *satyagraha,* which means "holding on to truth," and he encouraged them to work as individuals to improve their conditions without using violence.

(C)   In 1906, Gandhi encouraged Indians in South Africa to stand up for their beliefs, even if they were **imprisoned** for those beliefs. He never encouraged violence, however. He himself was imprisoned many times for his work to make life better for other Indians in South Africa. While he was in prison, he was often treated very cruelly. Even during these terrible times, though, he never lost his belief in nonviolence and in individual responsibility.

(D)   After several years, Gandhi left South Africa, and in 1915, he returned to India. As he had done in South Africa, Gandhi began to educate people about *satyagraha.* He publicly expressed his views and often held **fasts,** in which he and his followers went without food for long periods in order to obtain rights for others. His work often benefited people such as the *untouchables,* Indians of a lower caste who didn't enjoy many of the rights of higher caste members. He also worked very hard to overcome the differences between the two main religious groups in India—the Hindus and the Muslims. Improving the conditions for the poor and the minority groups and working for peace between the Hindus and the Muslims was not the end of Gandhi's efforts. He desired to improve the conditions of his entire country. Through two weekly newspapers, he promoted the idea that every village should produce its own food, clothing, fuel, and small industries.

(E)   At this time, Britain controlled India; Gandhi encouraged Indians to unite in an effort to correct the problems of the British-controlled government and to move toward self-rule—independence—for India. Though he served only one term as president of the Indian Congress, he was always looked to for his strong leadership. By the mid-1920s, he had come to be known as *Mahatma,* which means "Great Soul."

(F)   In 1947, the British announced that they would leave India by June 1948. The Indian Congress, the British, and a Muslim group decided to split India into two nations—India and Pakistan—based on the country's religious differences. It was thought that the Hindus could live in India, and the Muslims could live in the new country of Pakistan. Although in principle, Gandhi opposed this idea of splitting India, he supported the agreement and worked to reduce the dangers he believed the separation would cause. After the division of India, he traveled to many areas to promote peace, and he often fasted to encourage others to resolve their problems.

(G)   Gandhi continued to work for peace and justice for all the people of India and held daily prayer gatherings for his followers. On January 30, 1948, he had arrived for prayers as usual when he was approached by a young member of the Brahman (priest) caste, the highest, most powerful group in the Indian caste system. This young man believed Gandhi's efforts to encourage friendship between Hindus and Muslims were harmful to India. He fired three gunshots at Gandhi and killed the Mahatma. Gandhi died as he had lived, serving others and working for peace.

About the Reading

1. What was Gandhi's family background?

2. How did Gandhi meet his wife?

3. Why did Gandhi commit himself to helping the Indians living in South Africa?

4. How did Gandhi die?

5. What do you think Gandhi was most famous for?

What Do You Think?

Gandhi's philosophy included a strong belief in promoting change through nonviolent ways. What is your own philosophy about promoting change in society?

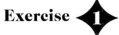

Exercise 1

Scanning. Look back at "Gandhi: Man of Truth," and practice the reading skill of scanning (see Chapter 1, Part Three) to find the information for the following exercise. In the blanks below, write the major events of Gandhi's life which correspond with the dates, time periods, and ages below. Remember, when you are scanning a text, you don't read every word. Move your eyes quickly back and forth across each line until you find the date, time period, or number you are looking for.

1. 1915:

    _____

2. 13 years old:

    _____

3. 1906:

    _____

4. 1948:

    _____

5. 1869:

    _____

6. mid 1920's:

    _____

7. 19 years old:

    _____

Using Details in Biographies

Biographical details enhance the reader's understanding of the person being described. By providing more details about the individual, the biographer offers deeper insight into the person and the story of her or his life.

 **Prereading Activity**

The following essay is an autobiography written by Larme, a student from Cameroon. In his autobiography, Larme not only writes about the major events and time periods in his life, but he also adds details that help his reader better understand the challenges he has faced. While you are reading, note Larme's use of supporting details. Before you begin reading, however, discuss the following questions in small groups, and then review the vocabulary words shown here.

1. Look on a map of Africa, and find Cameroon and Chad. What do you know about either of these countries?

2. Larme was born in a small city in Cameroon, Africa, in 1963. How do you think that his life might be the same as yours? How do you think that it might be different?

✦ *V*OCABULARY *W*ATCH

NOUNS	VERBS	ADJECTIVES	EXPRESSIONS
topography	loot	everlasting	civil war
astronomy	scatter	uncertain	
surveying			

Much Uncertainty

(A)   On April 2, 1963, a baby was born in Foumban, a small city in Cameroon, Africa. That baby was both the second baby and the second boy in the Daniel family. I was that baby, and Larme Daniel was the name my parents gave me. My father was in the military and spent most of his time away from home, so my mother took care of me.

(B)   In 1969, I began elementary school. My older brother and I were both good students because our parents took good care of us; life was very beautiful. Two years later, my father got married to a second wife, then a third wife six years later; our family began to get very big.

(C)   In 1975, after my family had moved from Cameroon back to our native country of Chad, a strange announcement was made on Radio Chad. It was announced that everybody in Chad had to change their name to a traditional Chadian name because the president of Chad had had a disagreement with the French government, and he decided that all Chadians had to abandon their French names. So my name was changed from Larme Daniel to Larme Doumai.

(D)   After this event, my country fell into **everlasting** trouble, which caused a lot of problems among the people by 1979. This is the year **civil war** began. Because of the war, my school was closed, so I had to stay at home every day; even worse, the war came to my city. It was terrible. We had to sleep under our beds at night. The soldiers **looted** our home and took everything that we had. My large family was **scattered** everywhere because we were afraid to stay together in our city where the war made life so dangerous.

(E)   In 1982, the war was over, but my high school had been destroyed, so I moved to Chad's capital to continue my studies at a scientific high school. In 1983, however, I had to live through war again. Again, there was no school. I had to stay at home all day long. I had extra time, so I began to teach myself to play music to pass the long days trapped inside the house when I was unable to be outside or to go to school. My life continued in this **uncertain** state until 1986 because I didn't have any way to continue school.

(F)   Finally, in 1988, I graduated from high school and passed an examination to study **topography** and **astronomy** in a university in France. Two years later, I got my degree in **surveying,** and I worked as a surveyor for two years in France.

(G)   The year 1992 was a very sad one because my younger brother died. In January of 1993, I went back to Chad to see my parents and then left them again on April 29, 1993, to go to the United States to study. Today, I am attending a university where I study English and engineering. My life has been difficult, but I have tried to work and study hard, and most of all, I have tried to be happy.

by Larme

About the Reading

1. Is Larme's autobiography in chronological order?
2. Is each paragraph centered around a main event or time? List the main event or time for each paragraph.
3. Why did Larme's family get so big?
4. Why did Larme have to change his name?
5. Why did Larme finish high school in the capital city instead of his own city?
6. Although Larme had many hardships, he succeeded at many things. Why do you think he succeeded?

What do You Think?

Have you (or anyone you know) ever had to live through war? If so, what were your (or that person's) experiences and feelings?

Exercise 2

Looking for Details.   Using details in your writing can help to develop, explain, or illustrate important events or time periods. These details also make what you write and read more interesting. Practice looking for the details that are used to develop, explain, or illustrate the major events and time periods in Larme's life. List those details next to the dates and years from Larme's life. Two periods have already been completed as examples to guide you.

April 2, 1963: _____

_____

_____

From 1969 to 1975: <u>began elementary school, good students, caring parents,</u>

<u>father marries second and third wife, the family grows</u>

1975: _____

_____

_____

1979: _____

_____

_____

1982: _____

_____

_____

1983: <u>war again, no school, began playing music</u>

From 1988 to 1993: _____

_____

_____

Inferring Information

Even when an author provides the details that are needed to make a biography interesting for the reader, the author often doesn't explain everything. There may be events in a person's life story that are not fully explained, but only suggested. It is then the reader's job to "read between the lines"—to read beyond the text—to figure out the whole story or message the author is trying to communicate. When the author doesn't tell all, the reader must use the skill of *inference:* The reader tries to use the limited information provided in order to make a reasonable guess about the missing information.

For example, in Larme' autobiography, you read that when the war came to his city, his family members had to sleep under their beds. Larme does not give many details to explain why his family had to do this, but you can use your own knowledge to infer or guess the complete meaning of this statement. You can imagine the conditions that would force family members to sleep under their beds, even though Larme did not give you much more information.

In the following autobiography, the author suggests many things without actually writing them down. After you finish reading, draw your own inferences to answer the questions in Exercise 3.

✦ **Prereading Activity**

The following autobiography was written by an American man who relates what it was like growing up in the United States in the 1950s and 1960s and then going to fight in a war. Before you read this essay, discuss the following questions in small groups, and then review the vocabulary highlighted here.

1. What do you know about American society before, during, and after the Vietnam War?

2. In your opinion, when a person writes an autobiography, who is the author's most important reader?

✦ VOCABULARY WATCH

NOUNS	VERBS	ADJECTIVES	EXPRESSIONS
panic	raise	pregnant	standing on tiptoes
tragedy	cower	popular	last a lifetime
	strive for	lasting	drift apart
	relate to	wounded	burned out
	cope with		
	withdraw from		

An American Story

(A)   My earliest memory is of an earthquake in Bakersfield, California. I remember my mother holding my brother Stuart in her arms. At the time, she was **pregnant** with my brother Scott. With things rattling in the house and my mom's general **panic** as she ran out of the house, I got the idea I should do the same. I was just learning to walk, but I thought that I had better forget about walking. Instead, I dropped to the ground and crawled out of the house as fast as I could.

(B)   My next memory is of Sister Mary Charles, the head nun at the local Catholic grammar school. I remember her holding me by the arm and digging her fingernails into the soft part of the back of my arm. She had me **standing on** my **tiptoes.** Because I was only three feet high, it was easy for her to keep me off balance and keep me separated from the other first-grade boy that I had been fighting with.

(C)   I survived the earthquake and Sister Mary Charles, and I actually had a very happy childhood. My mom, my brothers, and I lived with my grandparents on their little farm just outside of Madera, a small farming town in the San Joaquin Valley in California. My friends were the Mexican kids down the street and an old French couple who lived across the road from my grandparents' house. My grandparents **raised** fruit, nuts, and chickens. The farm was like a park with all the orange and almond trees blossoming in the spring and the fresh, sweet oranges, apricots, and plums right off the tree in the summer. It was wonderful to wake up on a quiet spring morning and lie in my bed smelling the scent of blossoms on the breeze that came into my room, along with the hum of the bees outside of my window. In addition to the chickens, lambs, and cows on the farm, there were the occasional **wounded** wild animals that we would nurse back to health: a fox, a tortoise, and wild birds.

(D)   When I started high school, it was a shock. I had spent eight years fighting my way to be the most **popular** kid in the Catholic school student body. I had been a big, tough eighth-grader, and suddenly I was a lowly ninth-grader **cowering** from the big, tough, twelfth-grade seniors who ran the high school. I realized then that it's nice to **strive for** something, but that you also have to enjoy the moment you're in and be happy where you are.

(E)   Rock and roll had always been an important part of my life. I remember as a young child, borrowing my grandfather's radio and listening to Elvis Presley and Buddy Holly. Later, I listened to the Beatles and the Rolling Stones. My friends and I used to drive around until the late hours of the night listening to the music of rock-and-roll legends. During those teenage years, I made friendships that I thought would **last a lifetime.** Most people that age think the same thing, but people **drift apart:** jobs, families, and **tragedies** separate people from those lasting friendships. The tragedy that separated me from my friends forever was the

Vietnam War. A year after I graduated from high school, I left for Vietnam. I came back **"burned out"** and tired, like an old man, as though I had lived ten lifetimes in the short span of 14 months—the 14 months I was in the war. I couldn't **relate to** the friends I had had in high school. They still seemed childish, concerned with childish things that weren't important to me. I was still trying to **cope with** the death, destruction, and evil I had seen in Vietnam. I felt like we had done terrible things to innocent people there and, in turn, I had seen terrible things done to my friends. Nobody won there and everybody lost.

(F)   I **withdrew from** my friends and started college, then I quit college and took many different jobs. I spent a lot of my time and money on alcohol and other drugs. Finally, in an effort to get my life going in the right direction again, I sold everything and took what little money I had and bought myself an airplane ticket to Israel. I went there to study history and archaeology. While I was a student at Haifa University, I met my wife, who was also an American student.

(G)   To make a long story short, I now teach high school back in the United States. I look at my students and see them struggling with so many of the very things I struggled with so many years ago. As their teacher, I try to help them over the rough spots as best I can.

by Steve

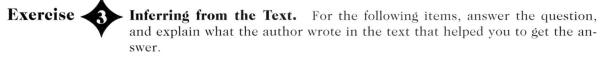

Exercise ◆**3**◆ **Inferring from the Text.**   For the following items, answer the question, and explain what the author wrote in the text that helped you to get the answer.

Example: Did Steve like Sister Mary Charles?

No. The author mentions how Sister Mary Charles dug her nails in his arm, and then he said that he survived the earthquake and Sister Mary Charles. You usually don't like someone who hurts you, and the fact that he said he "survived" the nun indicates that he didn't like her very much.

1. How old was Steve at the time of the earthquake? _____

    _____

    _____

2. Did Steve live with his father? _____

    _____

    _____

3. Was Steve confident in the ninth grade? _____

_____

_____

4. How does Steve feel about the Vietnam war? _____

_____

_____

5. Why do you think Steve became a teacher? _____

_____

_____

Now Revise: Second Draft

Now that you have read several biographies, rewrite the first draft of your autobiography. You should concentrate on making sure you add interesting or important details to your essay. Include not only details that are most important or significant to you, but also those that will add interest for your reader. Use the following Second Draft Checklist to evaluate and make changes to your essay.

When you have finished your second draft, exchange papers with a classmate. Read and discuss each other's essays. Make suggestions for additional changes that will improve the writing.

Second Draft Checklist

✓ Are all of the main events included?
✓ Are the main events listed in correct chronological order?
✓ Does each paragraph contain a main idea, such as a significant event, period, or character trait?
✓ Are there enough details to develop, explain, or illustrate the main events or periods?

Part Three

Refining and Reviewing

In this final section, you will learn about words or phrases that connect ideas. These particular connecting words and phrases work especially well with biographical writing. You will also write the final draft of your autobiography. You worked on the content and organization of your essay in your first and second drafts. In the final draft, you will want to refine and polish your autobiography so that you will have a well-written story of your life. To aid you in refining your writing, you will practice building your vocabulary by figuring out meanings from context.

Chronological Connectors

In biographies (and other time-sequenced stories), *chronological connectors* can signal the sequence of events. These words and phrases help your reader recognize when you are moving from one event to another, or from one period of time to another. These connectors also help link thoughts, themes, topics, and controlling ideas in your writing.

Chronological connectors, which usually appear at the beginning or the end of a sentence, include sequences of events (e.g., "next"), movements from one time period to another (e.g., "later"), and expressions of time (e.g., "June 8th," or "last month"). The following table highlights some useful chronological connectors.

Cohesive Devices: Chronological Connectors		
Uses	**Cohesive Devices**	**Examples**
To show sequences of events	*first, second, third, . . . , next, last, finally*	*First,* I did my homework. *Next,* I did the dishes.
To show movements from one time period to another	*before, then, after, later, until, since, while, during, during that time, eventually*	*Before* I went to France, I finished law school. *While* I was at law school, I studied hard.
To show expressions of time	*yesterday, last night, last year, last week, in 1964, on March 6, the next year, tomorrow, at that time, at night*	*In 1964,* my father died. *The next year,* I left for Washington.

As a writer, look for ways that you can use chronological connectors to help move from one event to the next in your autobiography. As a reader, watch for these signals to help you understand a sequence of events.

Prereading Activity

The following essay is by Vui, a student from Vietnam. Although Vui and Quynh (see "My Journey," page 40) are from the same country, their life stories are very different. In small groups, discuss the following questions, then review the vocabulary words shown here.

1. What do you know about Buddhism?
2. What do you know about the Vietnam War?

✦ VOCABULARY WATCH

NOUNS	VERBS	EXPRESSIONS
monastery	force	approve of
Buddha		
advice		
meditation		
temple		
compassion		
monk		

Escape from Vietnam

(A)   I was born in Nha Trang in the middle of Vietnam in 1951. At that time, I lived with my family. My parents had nine children. I was the second child. My parents were unlucky because five of my brothers and sisters got sick and died because we didn't have enough money or enough medicine, and my house was very far from the hospital.

(B)   I grew up knowing that my parents loved me. They wanted me to become a good student, and they hoped that I would become a wonderful person and be useful to many people in society. They sent me to a Buddhist **monastery** when I was about ten years old. There, I studied the teachings of the **Buddha** and many languages including English, French, Chinese, and Spanish. Sometimes I went home and visited my parents and my brothers because they missed me a lot. Many times they had **advice** for me. They told me, "We want you to study well and practice **meditation** in the Buddhist **temple** so that you will become a good person and have **compassion** for everybody you meet." My parents wanted me to become a Buddhist **monk** and use my life to love and care for people, which I did. I lived in a Buddhist temple for about 24 years.

Read to Write

(C)   In 1975, the Communists captured South Vietnam. My temple was closed so I wasn't able to study anymore. The new government didn't **approve of** my life as a Buddhist monk. Instead, at that time, they sent me to the mountains to cut trees and to build houses for people. I didn't choose this new life far away from the Buddhist temple. The communists **forced** me to change the way I had been living for many years. So, because I wanted to continue to study and to have my freedom, I escaped from my country in 1988.

(D)   During my escape, I felt terrible and often I thought that I would die. I had been able to join some other people who were escaping Vietnam in a small boat. The boat didn't have a captain, so I drove it even though I had never done anything like that before. My boat had 22 people on it. At night on the sea, the sky was very black and the water was dark blue. We didn't always know where we were going, and I worried a lot about food and fresh water because there wasn't enough for everybody on the boat. We were on the sea about three days and four nights. Finally, we met some Filipino fishermen, who put us on their boat and took us to Manila. These good fishermen saved our lives.

by Vui

Exercise  **Identifying Chronological Connectors.** Now that you have read Vui's autobiography, look at his story again, and circle all the chronological connectors Vui used. Then take out a separate sheet of paper, and fold it in half lengthwise. On the left side of the paper, write down eight of the chronological connectors you circled. On the right side of the paper, identify which type of connector Vui used—sequence of events, movement from one time period to another, or time expressions. (You may want to refer back to the chart on page 53, showing examples of each type of chronological connector.)

Exercise  **Adding a Variety of Chronological Connectors.** Look back at the essays by Larme (page 47) and Quynh (page 40), to see how each author used a variety of types of connectors. In addition, note the placement of these connectors, both within paragraphs and within sentences.

Practice adding various chronological connectors in different places in the following four sets of sentences. Remember that no matter which chronological connector you use or where you decide to place it, the purpose is to make the timing and the sequence of events more clear to your reader. To guide you in this exercise, an example is provided. When you have completed your work, ask a partner to give you feedback on how well you improved the short paragraphs.

Example: My parents were married in a small white church in their village. They moved to the island of St. Martin, where my father opened a flower shop. I was born.

Chronological connectors have been added to the preceding sentences, to make the following paragraph.

On Sunday, June the 8th, 1954, my parents were married in the small white church in their village. Three years later, they moved to the island of St. Martin, where my father opened a flower shop. I was born later that same year on October 10, 1957.

1. We ate dinner at a small cafe on the beach. We walked to the highest point on the shore. I asked her to marry me.

_____

_____

_____

_____

2. I studied hard. I graduated with a major in music and a minor in Chinese. I moved to Peru. I write songs and own a small business.

_____

_____

_____

_____

3. Matthew became very ill. He coughed constantly and couldn't sleep. He went to the hospital. The doctors said that they could find no cure. He made an astonishing recovery.

_____

_____

_____

_____

4. Anton left the jail house with no one noticing him. He ran across the fields in the night. He lived off the food he found on the land. He crossed the enemy line. Anton found freedom.

_____

_____

_____

_____

Exercise 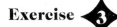 **Using Chronological Connectors in Your Own Writing.** Take out your second draft of the autobiography you are writing. Insert chronological connectors where they may be missing, using a variety of types. Remember, these are meant to help your reader by signaling shifts in time or events.

Finding Meaning from Context

In Chapter 1, Part Three, you were briefly introduced to some ways to learn vocabulary, such as finding meaning from context. In this final section of Chapter 2, you will be able to practice this skill.

The following autobiography has a lot of idiomatic expressions, many of which are two-word verbs (e.g., "look for," "fill out"); they are <u>underlined</u>. As you read, try to discover the meanings of the idioms and phrases from the context in which they occur. After the reading, you will have a chance to do an exercise that uses the idioms and phrases in other contexts.

◆ **Prereading Activity**

The following biography is about a famous early American, Benjamin Franklin. Before you read his biography, discuss the following questions in small groups, then review the vocabulary words highlighted here.

1. What do you know about the United States (the 13 colonies) before the Revolutionary War?

2. What do you know about Benjamin Franklin?

 **VOCABULARY WATCH**

NOUNS	VERBS	ADJECTIVES
diplomat	publish	amusing
tradesmen	invent	vivid
apprentice	negotiate	fatal
colony		household
almanac		extreme
ingenuity		detestable
bifocals		
patents		
delegate		

A Short Biography of the Long Life of Benjamin Franklin

(A)   Benjamin Franklin is one of the most important figures in United States history. He was a printer, writer, scientist, inventor, statesman, legislator, postmaster general, and **diplomat.** As one of the original founders of the United States, Benjamin Franklin helped to write both the Declaration of Independence and the U.S. Constitution. Today throughout the United States there are streets, towns, buildings, schools, and businesses named after this great American.

(B)   Benjamin Franklin was born in the city of Boston in 1706. His family was very large; he was the 15th of 17 children. Benjamin's father and older brothers were all **tradesmen** who worked with their hands, but Benjamin was the last of the ten sons born in the Franklin family, and he seemed special. His father didn't want Benjamin to be a tradesman like the other Franklin men; instead, he wanted Benjamin to go to college and become a minister. For that reason, seven-year-old Benjamin was sent off to school to learn Latin. Benjamin was smart and soon was at the <u>head of his class</u>. But after a year of Latin school, Mr. Franklin decided that being a minister was not a good way for his son to <u>make a living</u>, so he took Benjamin out of Latin school and sent him to a school to learn reading, writing, and mathematics. Benjamin loved to read and write, but he didn't do well in math. Benjamin stayed in school two years before his father finally gave up on the idea of sending his son to college. He decided that Benjamin should be a tradesman like the other men in the family.

(C)   When he was ten years old, Benjamin was <u>taken out</u> of school and began to work in his father's shop, where they made soap and candles. He didn't like the work (especially the smell), so he was <u>turned over</u> to his older brother, James, to become an **apprentice** and learn to be a printer. As an apprentice, Benjamin had to promise to work for James until he was 21 years old. He also had to promise to do everything James told him to do. But Benjamin didn't <u>get along</u> with his older brother; they had many arguments about what Benjamin could and couldn't do as an apprentice. So, Benjamin decided to <u>run away</u>. He left Boston for New York, but when he arrived in New York, he found that there was already a printer in town and not enough work for two printers. From New York, Benjamin traveled to Philadelphia, the largest city in the **colony** of Pennsylvania, not knowing that this city would become his home for the rest of his life.

(D)　　When he arrived in Philadelphia, Benjamin was tired and dirty, but most of all, very hungry. He <u>stopped at</u> the first bakery he saw and bought three large rolls. Benjamin walked through the city with one roll under each arm while he ate the third. When he walked down one street, a young girl standing in the doorway of her house laughed at the sight of the dusty young man and his three giant rolls of bread. This girl, Deborah Read, who found Benjamin Franklin so **amusing** on his first day in Philadelphia, later became his wife.

(E)　　In Philadelphia, Benjamin became a successful printer. His newspaper, the *Pennsylvania Gazette*, became the most important paper in the colonies. <u>From the time</u> he was a boy, Benjamin loved to read and write. He wrote dozens of essays, articles, and pamphlets and thousands of letters. It is believed that during his lifetime he wrote to over 4,000 different people. Benjamin **published** the first novel printed in America. When he was in his sixties, Franklin wrote his life story in **vivid** and often humorous detail. Because no other author had attempted such a detailed account of his or her life, Benjamin Franklin is said to have invented (or at least made popular) the autobiography. Of all the books he printed or wrote, Benjamin Franklin was most famous for his *Poor Richard's Almanack*. His **almanac** was a calendar book <u>filled with</u> advice for farmers and housewives, weather predictions, general information, and clever sayings, such as "No gains without pains," and "Early to bed and early to rise makes a man healthy, wealthy and wise." Franklin's almanac was very popular, selling 10,000 copies a year for 25 years. Benjamin Franklin is considered by many historians to have been the greatest American writer of his day.

(F)　　Although he had only two years of formal schooling, Franklin became one of the leading American scientists and inventors of the 18th century. He was curious <u>by nature</u>—always wanting to find out how things worked. Benjamin Franklin was observant and discovered much of what he knew just by careful examination and observation.

(G)　　Franklin the scientist is probably most famous for his experiment with a kite and a metal key, which demonstrated that lightning and electricity were the same thing. He and his son conducted this experiment in a rain and lightning storm. The kite had a metal rod attached to the back of it, which attracted the electricity in the storm clouds. The electrical current <u>picked up</u> from the storm clouds traveled from the metal rod on the kite down the wet string to a metal key tied to the end of the string. Benjamin suspected that there was "electric fire" in lightning and quickly found out he was correct when he touched the metal key and received a shock of electrical current. Benjamin Franklin survived the shock because he knew to keep the part of the cord he was holding dry and to stand in a doorway out of the rain. If lightning had struck the kite, and the string in Franklin's hand had been wet, it would have been **fatal** for him.

(H)   Whenever Benjamin Franklin the scientist made a scientific discovery, Benjamin Franklin the inventor tried to <u>think of</u> practical ways to use what he learned. For example, after his famous kite and key experiment, Franklin <u>came up with</u> the idea for the lightning rod, a pointed iron rod put <u>on top of</u> a house, which would attract lightning, and then lead it by wire to the ground, where it couldn't do any damage to the house. Franklin's lightning rods became very popular in the 1750s. Benjamin also used his curiosity and **ingenuity** to **invent** musical instruments, furniture, and **household** goods. Among his many discoveries and inventions are the odometer (mileage gauge), the Franklin stove (which is still used to heat rooms today), chemical fertilizer, an electric generator, and a smokeless candle (which burned brighter and longer than the candles of his day). In addition, he made the first copperplate printing press in America and used it in his printing shop. Franklin also invented the eyeglasses we call **bifocals,** which allow someone to see both <u>close-up</u> and across long distances. Although Benjamin Franklin invented many things, he did not become rich from his discoveries and inventions. He didn't apply for **patents** that would have protected his inventions from being copied by others because he didn't seem to mind when other people made money using his ideas and inventions.

(I)   In addition to his leadership in science, Benjamin Franklin was also a great government leader and public servant. In Philadelphia, he organized a volunteer fire department and started the first fire-insurance company. He suggested ways to better light the streets at night, dispose of the city's garbage, and keep the people of Philadelphia from slipping on the ice in the winter. As postmaster of the colonies, he improved mail service and introduced home delivery. Benjamin Franklin helped to open the first American hospital. He also started the first public library so that anyone who wanted to read could borrow books <u>for free</u>. Franklin also began a school that later became the University of Pennsylvania.

(J)   Beginning in 1736, Franklin became active in local and regional politics for the rest of his life. He represented the colony of Pennsylvania in negotiations with Native Americans and worked hard to make sure that Native Americans were treated fairly. Franklin also organized and led local Pennsylvania defense units. Before the American Revolution, there were 13 separate colonies that were ruled by England. In 1754, Franklin wrote the first plan that would have united the 13 colonies under one government. Even though the other colonies and the British rulers of the colonies rejected Franklin's plan, it <u>laid the groundwork</u> for what was later to become the United States of America.

(K)   In 1757, Franklin went to England as a representative of the colony of Pennsylvania to present the colonists' <u>point of view</u> to the king. Franklin remained in England for 18 years, doing his best to <u>keep the peace</u> between England and the colonies. But by 1765, the king's representatives in the colonies were putting **extreme** hardships on the people. The colonists were becoming more and more angry, and Franklin warned the king that the colonists might soon want the British out of their land forever. The king and his advisors didn't like what Franklin told them, and so they ignored his advice. An angry Franklin left England, convinced that the British rulers had to be removed from the colonies <u>once and for all</u>. By the time he reached America, the Revolutionary War between the colonies and England had begun.

(L)   Benjamin <u>served on</u> many colonial committees during the war, including the committee that wrote the Declaration of Independence, the document that explained why the 13 American colonies could not continue to be ruled by England. It is said that, as the members of the committee signed the Declaration of Independence, Benjamin Franklin reminded them of the importance of being unified: "Gentlemen," he said, "we must now all <u>hang together</u>, or we shall most assuredly hang separately."

(M)   Not long after Franklin returned from England, he became a **delegate** to the Second Continental Congress, the group of colonial leaders who met to unite the colonies in their fight against England. Franklin and the other colonial leaders knew that the colonies could not win their freedom from England without <u>outside help</u>. When it was suggested that Britain's enemy, France, was the <u>best hope</u> for this help, Franklin was sent to **negotiate** with the French. Because of Franklin's work in France, the French provided soldiers, arms, and loans to help the colonists defeat the British.

(N)   Franklin spent nine years living in France. For the most part, Franklin enjoyed living in France, and the French people adored him.

After the war, he returned to Philadelphia. He was almost 80 years old, and his wife, Deborah, had died several years before. Benjamin was old and not very healthy, but he was still very active in local and national events. For three years, he was elected President of the Pennsylvanian government. Franklin was also a member of the Constitutional Convention, where he designed the "great compromise" that established two houses of Congress—the Senate and the Congress. At the same time, Franklin was president of a society that worked to <u>put an end to</u> slavery in the United States. Some of Franklin's last writings were attacks against slavery, calling it, "this **detestable** traffic in the bodies and the souls of men."

(O)   At the <u>end of his life</u>, Benjamin Franklin became too weak to leave his bed. However, he continued to read and write everyday. Each afternoon, his granddaughter would come to his bed to practice her school lessons. If she did well, Franklin would reward her with a big spoonful of strawberry jam from a jar he kept by his bed. Benjamin Franklin died in 1790 at the age of 84. His funeral was one of the largest public gatherings to take place in the history of the new nation. More than 20,000 people walked for miles to the cemetery where Franklin was buried. People in the United States and France mourned. Today many historians consider Benjamin Franklin not just one of the outstanding early Americans, but *the* outstanding American of his time.

✦ About the Reading

1. Benjamin Franklin had a long and eventful life. Without looking back at the biography, make a list of all the events you can remember.

2. What are some of the things Franklin is remembered for as a writer, as a statesman, and as an inventor and scientist?

3. Franklin is still remembered for the wise and witty sayings he wrote for his almanac. Following are some of his most popular sayings. As a class, read each saying and discuss its meaning.

   "No gains without pains."

   "One today is worth two tomorrows."

   "A penny saved is a penny earned."

   "Fish and visitors smell in three days."

   "Light purse, heavy heart."

   "Don't throw stones at your neighbors if your own windows are glass."

What Do You Think?

Write a short biography of a famous person in your country's history.

Exercise  **Guessing Meanings of Idioms and Phrases from Context.** Practice guessing meaning from context to figure out the meaning of the following idioms and phrases. Remember to read the words around each idiom or phrase to infer the meaning. Read the following sentences, which come from "A Short History of Benjamin Franklin." (If you want to read them directly from the original text, scan for them, and read the sentences around the idiom or phrase.) Then read the following options, and circle the letter of the definition that best fits.

1. Benjamin was smart and soon was <u>at the head of his class</u>.
   a. the best student
   b. graduated
   c. the teacher

2. Mr. Franklin decided that being a minister was not a good way for his son to <u>make a living</u>.
   a. find a job
   b. live
   c. earn money

3. He was <u>turned over</u> to his older brother, James, to become an apprentice and learn to be a printer.
   a. given
   b. sold
   c. taken

4. Benjamin decided to <u>run away</u>.
   a. stay
   b. leave
   c. hide

5. He was curious <u>by nature</u>—always wanting to discover how things worked.
   a. by learning to be that way
   b. by being born that way
   c. by trying to be that way

6. Franklin <u>came up with</u> the idea for the lightning rod.
   a. sold
   b. thought of
   c. tried

7. Although his plan was not accepted by the other colonies, it <u>laid the groundwork for</u> what was later to become the United States of America.
   a. was the best part of
   b. was the end of
   c. was the beginning of

8. The British rulers had to be removed from the colonies <u>once and for all</u>.
   a. once
   b. forever
   c. now

9. "Gentlemen," he said, "we must now all <u>hang together</u>, or we shall most assuredly hang separately."
   a. die together
   b. disagree with each other
   c. unite and support each other

10. Benjamin was president of a society that worked to <u>put an end to</u> slavery in
    the United States.
    a. stop
    b. promote
    c. start

Final Draft

Now it is time to write the final draft of your autobiography. Before you
write it, use the following checklist to remind you of the things discussed
in this chapter. Also, try to include the suggestions you received from
your classmate after he or she read your second draft. Notice that in the
final draft, you not only want the content to be complete and interesting
and the organization to be clear, but you also want the essay to look
good on the page.

Final Draft Checklist

✓ Are all of the main events included?
✓ Are the main events listed in correct chronological order?
✓ Does each paragraph contain a main idea, such as a significant
   event, period, or character trait?
✓ Has there been enough detail added to develop, explain, or
   illustrate the main events or periods?
✓ Have a variety of chronological connectors been used to signal
   changes in time or events?
✓ Does the paper look clean and neat?
✓ Are the grammar, spelling, and punctuation correct?

Going Further: Idea Generator

Activity  **Important Ages.**   In the United States, there are several important ages in people's lives. For example, at 5 years of age, children begin school. At 16 or 17 years of age, many people get their first driver's license. Most people graduate from high school and become legal adults at age 18. Twenty-one years old is the legal age for drinking alcohol in most states, and most people now look forward to retirement at age 65.

What are the important ages in your culture? How do people mark these special times? How closely has your life followed these important ages?

Activity **2** **Who Is It?**   Choose a famous living person, and do some research on him or her. From your research, choose the 10 most important facts about the person's life. Working in small groups with your classmates, take turns reading your lists to each other, and see whether you can guess each person, based on these important facts.

Chapter 3

Description

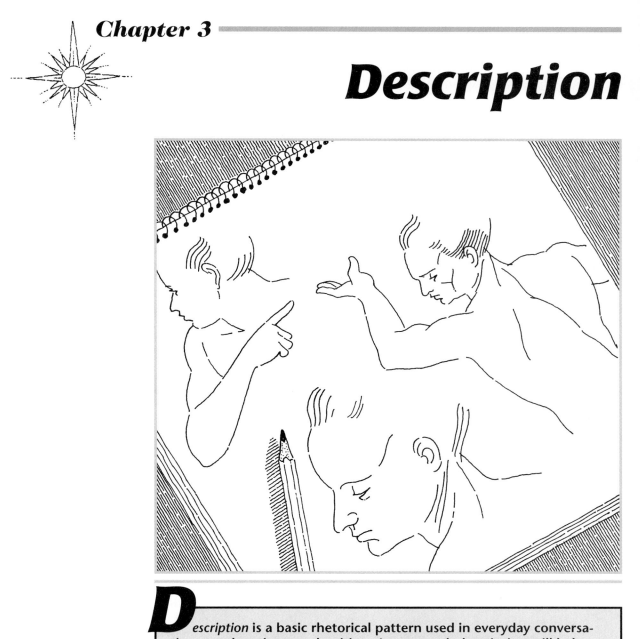

Description is a basic rhetorical pattern used in everyday conversations, explanations, and writing. As you read, description will help you to understand more clearly what the author wants you to know or feel. As you write, the details of your descriptions will present pictures to your readers so that they may better imagine what you are describing. All rhetorical patterns use some sort of description; therefore, learning how to write an effective description will help you in other areas of writing.

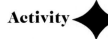

Reading and Writing Description

In this chapter, you will be reading and writing descriptions of objects, people, and places, making use of all or some of the five senses—sight, hearing, touch, smell, and taste. The particular senses on which you focus depend on the images you want your readers to see or the emotions you want them to feel. A good description often helps readers feel as if they are experiencing what is being described.

Activity ◆ **Describing an Object.**   Look at an object that either you or your teacher has brought to class. As you observe the object, write down as many adjectives and nouns as you can which describe the object. Next, use your list to write a paragraph describing the object. Share your description with the class.

Description in the Real World

Description is a very large part of your everyday world. You use description to transmit knowledge from one individual to another and to help others understand your experiences. Some forms of description with which you come into contact regularly are scientific explanations, literature, and advertising. A good writer will use detail in order to catch the reader's eye, to accent the best features of something, or—in the case of advertising—to make something ordinary seem extraordinary. In advertising, the more exciting the description, the more the product may appeal to the customer.

◆ **Prereading Activity**   The following is a description of a home found in a newspaper. The article gives the reader a brief description of the *exterior* (outside) of a house and a more detailed description of the *interior*. (Guess what this word means.) Before you read the description, look at the pictures of the Hopkins home exterior and interior (on pages 69–70). In small groups, discuss the following questions, and then review the vocabulary words highlighted on the next page.

1. How would you describe the exterior?

2. How would you describe the interior?

NOUNS		VERBS	ADJECTIVES
façade	utility room	sweep	contemporary
core	nook	feature	adjacent
suite	vault	nestle	galore
basin	attic		octagonal
bidet			coffered
spa			

Hopkins

(A)   If you are looking for a place to put a porch swing, take a look at the Hopkins. The long, covered porch of this country-**contemporary** home **sweeps** across most of the front **façade** and along one side.

(B)   This plan is designed to please families who want room for both individual and group activities. Gathering spaces, formal and informal, are at the **core,** master **suite** to the right, living and dining area to the left. Secondary bedrooms are on the top floor.

(C)   The spacious master suite is more than just a place to sleep. A fireplace spreads its warmth throughout the suite. The huge, private bathroom **features** a shower, twin **basins,** separate toilet and **bidet,** roomy walk-in closet and a recessed **spa** to erase the tensions of a busy day. A private entrance to the back deck lets you enjoy the sun, weather permitting.

(D)   The family room, with two-story ceiling and fireplace with built-in wood box, is a cozy place for family and friends to watch television or play the latest board game. **Nestled** between the family room and master suite is a handy **utility room.**

(E)   A raised dishwasher, cooktop, freezer, and large walk-in pantry make the walk-through kitchen a dream for the cook in the house. This configuration allows meals to be

Continued

served easily in the recessed breakfast **nook** or in the **adjacent** dining room.

(F)   A small home office, full bathroom, and living room with fireplace and windows **galore** complete the first floor plan.

(G)   On the top level are two modest bedrooms. One is **octagonal** in shape, with **coffered vault** and windows all around. The other, perfect for use as a guest suite, has a private bath. In addi-

tion, there is a sewing room, which could be used as another bedroom. Topping off the home is a skylit, 443-square-foot unfinished **attic**.

(H)   The lowest level houses a two-car garage, with a roomy dark room for the photographer in the family, a half-bath, and extra storage area.

The Deseret News, **August 28, 1994**

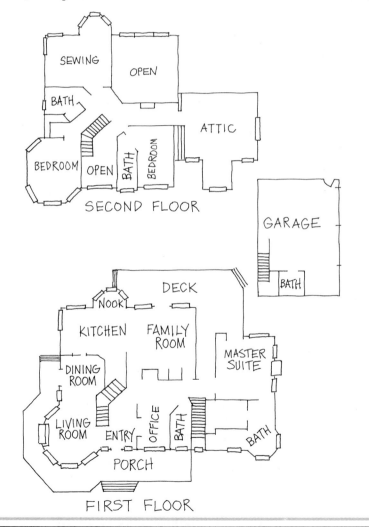

SEWING

OPEN

BATH

ATTIC

BEDROOM   OPEN   BATH   BEDROOM

SECOND FLOOR

GARAGE

BATH

DECK

NOOK

KITCHEN   FAMILY ROOM

MASTER SUITE

DINING ROOM

LIVING ROOM   ENTRY   OFFICE   BATH   BATH

PORCH

FIRST FLOOR

Exercise  **Identifying Descriptive Words and Phrases.** Once you have read the advertisement for the Hopkins home, review it to identify the words and phrases that made this advertisement most descriptive to you. Write those words and phrases on a separate sheet of paper.

Exercise  **Writing Your Own Advertisement.** On a separate sheet of paper, write an advertisement for your own dream house similar to the advertisement you just read. Use at least five of the descriptive words or phrases that you listed in Exercise 1. Be sure to include a description of the inside (use your imagination), as well as the outside, of the house.

Identifying Descriptive Details

In this section, you will read three different essays, each focusing on a different kind of description—an object, a person, and a place. Each uses sensory details to help you sense and feel what is described.

✦ Prereading Activity

In the following essay, the author describes an object that she never wants to throw away. The object is a pair of leather shoes, which brings back memories of her experiences as a teacher in Uruguay. Before you read the essay, think of something you own that you would never throw away. Then discuss the following questions.

1. Why do you want to keep it?
2. Why is the object special for you?

The Shoes

(A)   I look into the old box that holds my memories of my time in Uruguay, and I discover the shoes. They are old, ugly, worn out, having served their owner well. I smell the old leather, and the memories begin coming, taking me back in time. I take the shoes out, put them on the table, and study them.

(B)   They are made of rough, yet beautiful leather. The stitching on the top that once held the sides together has broken and allows the sides of the shoes to fall away. Inside, there is a well-marked heel print, where the bare foot put its weight day after day. The sweat from the heel has left the leather a dark orange color. Forward, on the inside, I see the mark that each toe has left; looking closer, I notice tiny holes where the leather has completely worn away.

(C)   The leather, once new, soft, and flexible, is now old, hard, and stiff, a result of the rains and countless Uruguayan floods. I count what

---

is left of one, two, three, four worn out soles that the shoemaker put on with such care. Each one has a slightly different color—brown, gold, beige, and tan. Looking between the different layers that have shrunken and separated from the rain, I observe the dried mud and tiny little rocks that have been caught between the layers.

(D) Some tell me to throw them away. "They're ugly. They take up too much space." But I ignore them. My shoes are like a couple of good friends who have traveled with me on an unforgettable journey.

(E) With a satisfied heart, I smile and return them to their box.

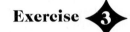

About the Reading

1. Who is the audience for this essay?
2. Without looking back at the essay, what details can you remember?
3. Why does the author keep the shoes?

What Do You Think?

Write a description of an object that has some special memories for you.

Exercise ◆3 **Identifying Similar Meanings.** Review the preceding essay, and find the sentences that are similar in meaning to the following sentences. Then write those sentences on the lines below.

1. The leather is old and hard. _____
2. I look at the shoes. _____
3. The shoes are important to me. _____
4. Many different soles have been put on the shoes. _____
5. My shoes are kept in a box. _____
6. The shoes are torn on the sides. _____
7. The shoes have turned color inside. _____
8. The shoes are old. _____

Next, you will read a description of a person. Frequently, when describing people, you describe their physical characteristics, but you often go beyond describing what they look like. You also try to describe the personality and character traits that make those people unique.

Prereading Activity

In the following essay, the author describes her father. Notice how the author uses detail to express both outer appearances and inner feelings. In small groups, discuss the questions before you read the essay.

1. Think of a person in your life who has influenced you. How has this person's influence affected your life?

2. What characteristics and qualities do you remember most about this person?

My Dad

(A)   My dad is one of the most fascinating people I know. I love to look at him. When I look at him, I first notice his physical characteristics. If I look long enough, however, I can see some of the things that have happened during his 72 years of life.

(B)   My dad has been almost bald ever since I can remember. When I look at him carefully, I see that the top of his round head is smooth and shiny. The little bit of silver hair that circles the bald spot on top will soon be gone. When I was little, he once told me that his brain made his head so big that there wasn't enough hair to cover it. I laughed then, but now that I realize how smart he is, I wonder whether it might be true.

(C)   I really like looking at my dad's face. One side of his face droops a little because of a small accident he had many years ago. When he smiles now, only half of his mouth turns up, as if he is trying to keep the smile from showing. Behind his smile, his teeth are strong, white, and perfectly straight. His bright blue eyes, surrounded by wrinkles of experience, seem to smile more than his tired mouth. They reflect a bright mind that is always busy in thought.

(D)   My father has always been smaller than most men, but he seemed big to me as I grew up. Now his thin body is not quite as tall or as straight as it once was. When he stands, his shoulders droop forward as if they are too tired to hold his head and its heavy thoughts. When he sits, his head and wrinkled neck come out of his shirt collar like the head of an old turtle coming out of its shell.

(E)   Though his body shows his age, his hands still appear strong and youthful. Thick, short fingers make each hard-working hand look square. The skin on his hands is rough, with dark blue veins running through the back of them. It is with these hands, along with his bright mind, that he continues his work. Each day he still spends many hours using his hands to draw pictures of machines that will eventually save his company hundreds or even thousands of dollars.

(F)   After watching my dad for some time, I forget to look at his hands or face or body. Soon I begin to see what I will always remember about him. I see his care, his determination, and even his frustration. I see a man who has survived service in World War II, who has supported a wife and ten children, and who is still finding more to live for each day.

by Laurie Shin

About the Reading

1. What is the thesis statement in this essay?

2. How does the author feel about her dad? How do you know?

3. What details does the author include to make you *feel* and *see* as you read this essay?

What Do You Think?

Write about a person who has influenced your life and how you feel about that person.

Exercise 4 **Reviewing Vocabulary.** The following list of words are from the preceding essay. For each of the following sentences, fill in the blank with the word that best fits. If you don't know a particular word, try to guess its meaning from the context. Use each word only once.

| bald | shiny | determination |
| smooth | eventually | frustration |

1. Her smooth black hair was so _____ that you could see the light in it.

2. I tried and tried to hit the ball, but I couldn't do it right. I was very upset, and my _____ grew with each unsuccessful try.

3. If we study very hard, _____ we will be able to do anything, no matter how difficult.

4. James wouldn't let his injury keep him from running the race. His strong _____ kept him practicing, even when it hurt.

5. As he got older, his hair began to fall out until finally he was totally _____.

6. The frozen lake was as _____ as a piece of glass.

Exercise 5 **Identifying Detail within the Essay.** Get together with a partner to do the following exercise. Write your answers on a separate sheet of paper, then exchange papers with your classmates and compare answers.

1. List some of the words that describe the dad's face.

2. What are some of the features about the dad's hands that make him still appear "strong and youthful"?

3. List some words that describe the dad's body.

4. Draw a picture of the top of the dad's head.

The next essay in this section is a description of a place. In describing places, you can use many of the same skills you used in describing objects and people. Again, a description of a place can include both physical and emotional description. A description of a place sometimes includes descriptions of objects and/or people that may be associated with that place.

Prereading Activity

The following essay describes a neighborhood. However, it is more than a physical description. The author makes the essay more interesting by including details that express feelings about this special place. Before you read the essay, think about the neighborhood you lived in as a child.

1. What do you remember about the place (or places) you lived as a child?

2. What did you like about it?

3. Was there anything that you didn't like about it?

Memory Lane Isn't What it Used to Be

(A)   About this time every year, I get very nostalgic. Walking through my neighborhood on a fall afternoon reminds me of a time not too long ago when sounds of children filled the air, children playing games on a hill, and throwing leaves around in the street below. I was one of those children, carefree and happy. I live on a street that is only one block long. I have lived on the same street for sixteen years. I love my street. One side has six houses on it, and the other has only two houses, with a small hill in the middle and a huge cottonwood tree on one end. When I think of home, I think of my street, only I see it as it was before. Unfortunately, things change. One day, not long ago, I looked around and saw how different everything has become. Life on my street will never be the same because neighbors are quickly growing old, friends are growing up and leaving, and the city is planning to destroy my precious hill and sell the property to contractors.

(B)   It is hard for me to accept that many of my wonderful neighbors are growing old and won't be around much longer. I have fond memories of the couple across the street, who sat together on their porch swing almost every evening, the widow over the fence who yelled at my brother and me for being too loud, and the crazy old man in polyester who drove the forty-year-old Plymouth. In contrast to those people, the people I see today are very old and withered neighbors who have seen better days. The man in polyester says he wants to die, and another neighbor just sold his house and moved into a nursing home. The lady who used to yell at us is too tired to bother anymore, and the couple across the street rarely go out to their front porch these days. It is difficult to watch these precious people as they near the end of their lives because at one time I thought they would live forever.

(C)   The "comings and goings" of the younger generation of my street are now mostly "goings" as friends and peers move on. Once upon a time, my life and the lives of my peers revolved around home. The boundary of our world was the gutter at the end of the street. We got pleasure from playing night games, or from a breathtaking ride on a tricycle. Things are different now, as my friends become adults and move on. Children who rode tricycles now drive cars. The kids who once played with me now have new interests and values as they go their separate ways. Some have gone away to college, a few got married, two went into the army, and one went to prison. Watching all these people grow up and go away only makes me long for the good old days.

(D)   Perhaps the biggest change on my street is the fact that the city is going to turn my precious hill into several lots for new homes. For sixteen years, the view out my kitchen window has been a view of that hill. The hill was a fundamental part of my childhood life; it was the hub of social activity for the children of my street. We spent hours there building forts, sledding, and playing tag. The view out my kitchen window now is very different; it is one of tractors and dump trucks tearing up the hill. When the hill goes, the neighborhood will not be the same. It is a piece of my childhood. It is a visual reminder of being a kid. Without the hill, my street will be just another pea in the pod.

(E)   There was a time when my street was my world, and I thought my world would never change. But something happened. People grow up, and people grow old. Places change, and with the change comes the heartache of knowing I can never go back to the times I loved. In a year or so, I will be gone just like many of my neighbors. I will always look back to my years as a child, but the place I remember will not be the silent street whose peace is interrupted by the sounds of construction. It will be the happy, noisy, somewhat strange, but wonderful street I knew as a child.

by Melia James

About the Reading

1. Choose three paragraphs from the essay, and underline the topic sentence in each one.
2. Write down as many details as you can remember about the essay. Trade your list with a partner, and compare the things you each remembered.
3. Does the author like the old or the new neighborhood better? How do you know?

Exercise 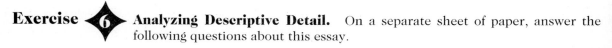 **6** **Analyzing Descriptive Detail.** On a separate sheet of paper, answer the following questions about this essay.

Read to Write

1. In this description, the author compares life on her street now with life as it was in the past. What specific details create this comparison?

2. In paragraph (A), the author describes old familiar sounds that she remembers. Find where she discusses these sounds, and write down some of the descriptive words she uses.

3. The author often adds little descriptive details about each of the characters she describes. Reread paragraph (B), and then list some of the words or phrases she uses to make the following people seem real: the couple across the street, the widow, the crazy old man.

4. In paragraph (C), the author once again uses comparison to illustrate the stark changes around her. She takes time to explain different circumstances of individual people. What are three different things that have happened to her old friends and neighbors?

5. The author uses many visual images in her nostalgic description. Find five descriptive words or phrases that gave you new visual images.

Exercise ◆7 **Adding Descriptive Detail.** Here is another short essay about a place. The writer could have made the essay much more interesting by adding some descriptive details.

Step 1. Read the following essay, then follow the directions in the steps that follow it.

My House

(A)   My house is really nice. We have two floors. On the main floor we have two bedrooms, two bathrooms, a kitchen, and a living room. On the bottom floor, we have three bedrooms, a family room, a bathroom, and a laundry room.

(B)   As a child, my favorite room in the house was the kitchen. There were always lots of people there, and it seemed like my mother was always cooking something.

(C)   I also enjoyed my small bedroom, where I always went when I wanted to be alone. The walls of my room are light green, and the floor is dark brown. When I went there while growing up, I used to lie on my bed and listen to music.

(D)   The outside of my house is just as nice as the inside. It is made of multicolored brick—red, yellow, brown, and beige. The best things about our house are the yards, a big one in the front and a very large one in the back, where we had some nice fruit trees. I think the reason I liked our big yards so much as a child was because all the neighborhood kids used to come to our place to play.

Step 2. The following chart gives examples of details that the writer could have added to paragraph (B) to make the description easier for the reader to imagine. Notice that one detail for each sense has been included.

Smell	See	Taste	Feel (touch)	Hear	Feel (emotion)
burnt toast	green, striped curtains	fresh cookies	warm sunshine	popcorn popping	happiness and love

Step 3. Following is an example of how paragraph (B) of the preceding essay could be made more descriptive by adding the sensory details from the preceding chart. As you read the paragraph, identify the added details.

As a child, my favorite room in the house was the kitchen. I can remember feeling the warm sunshine coming through the green, striped curtains. There were always lots of people there, especially in the mornings. I often smelled the burnt toast that my father made in his rush for work. I remember hearing popcorn popping on Sunday evenings as we gathered around the table to talk. It seemed like my mother was always cooking something. My favorite thing was the fresh cookies my mother made for me to eat after school. Most of all, I remember the feeling of happiness and love I felt in that room.

Step 4. On a separate sheet, make a set of columns similar to the ones shown in the chart for Step 2. Choose a different paragraph from "My House," and use this chart to write details that could be added to that paragraph.

Step 5. Now, on a separate sheet, rewrite the paragraph you selected from "My House," adding the details from your chart.

Getting Started: Brainstorming Sensory Details

In the preceding chapter, you learned the prewriting strategy of making a time line before beginning to write your short autobiography. For the writing assignment in this chapter, first choose something, someone, or someplace you want to describe. The following are a few suggestions for topics, or you can choose a topic of your own.

Objects

- A pet or an animal
- The car you would most like to have
- A special gift you have received

People

- Your best friend
- Your favorite actor
- A leader in your country

Places

- A place where you feel peaceful
- A place where you work or have worked
- A place where you would never like to live (or visit) again

After you choose a topic, brainstorm for sensory details to describe your subject. Don't think about your ideas too much—just write down whatever comes immediately to mind. Later, you can choose exactly which ideas you want to write about.

On a separate sheet of paper, create another six-column chart like the one you used in the preceding activity. Use the chart to record your ideas. For example, if you want to write about a beautiful beach, under **see** in your chart, you might write *the bright sunlight*, under **feel (touch),** you might put *sand on my skin*, and under **hear,** you might have *rushing water*.

Essay Writing: First Draft

Write the first draft of your descriptive essay. Include enough detail to create a full picture of your subject in the mind of your reader. Read over the ideas you wrote on your brainstorm chart. Choose the ideas that best provide a clear picture to your reader, and include those ideas in your first draft.

Before you write your first draft, read the following checklist to help guide your writing. Then, after you have written your draft, look at the checklist again, and make changes that will improve your writing.

First Draft Checklist

✓ Have you used some of the five senses and some emotions to describe your topic?

✓ Have you used specific details in your description?

✓ Will your reader be able to "see, hear, feel, smell, or taste" what you have written?

✓ Does each paragraph have one main idea?

Part Two

Developing Descriptions

In Part One, the focus was on detail used in descriptive reading and writing and on how details make descriptions more interesting. This section focuses on ways that descriptive reading and writing can be organized. Good organization helps the reader better understand the ideas presented. Therefore, as a writer, you should learn techniques such as providing clear topic sentences and supporting details, which will make your writing easier for your reader to follow.

Organizational Style in Descriptive Writing

Much descriptive writing is organized according to how the person, place, or object exists in the real world. For example, a description of a person might focus on different areas of the body, perhaps moving from the head down to the feet. A description of a house might begin with the outside, then move to the inside, and proceed from room to room. When this type of *spatial organization* is used, the main idea of each paragraph focuses on an area or a part of the whole. Organizing descriptive writing according to parts of the whole helps a reader to better visualize the items being described. The previous essays in this chapter have been organized in this manner. For example, "My Dad," on page 73, is organized around the different parts of his body, as follows next:

Paragraph (B): _dad's head_

Paragraph (C): _dad's face_

Paragraph (D): _dad's body_

Paragraph (E): _dad's hands_

Prereading Activity

The following essay describes a child's favorite place to vacation—her grandmother's house. Using the senses, the author describes memorable experiences that took place at her grandmother's house. As you read, notice how the body of the essay is organized around different places in her grandmother's home. Before you read, think of a place that you remember from your childhood, and discuss the following questions with a partner. Following this discussion, review the vocabulary words highlighted on the next page.

1. What made that childhood place memorable?

2. What experiences did you have there?

✦ VOCABULARY WATCH

NOUNS	VERBS	ADJECTIVES	ADVERBS
treat	melt	hideous	immaculately
grandfather clock	chime	ancient	reluctantly
trinket			
hedge			
trim			

Vacation at Grandma's

(A)   I clearly remember when I was a small child, waiting excitedly for our yearly summertime trip to Grandma's house. A few nights before the trip, while I lay in my bed, I would become so excited that I couldn't sleep. In my mind, I could see my grandmother's house. I could hear my grandmother's unclear English, and I could imagine myself rolling down the thick, golden carpet on her stairs. I could hardly wait for the day to come.

(B)   As soon as we got to Grandma's house, we always went to the kitchen. There, Grandma would give us a burning hot bowl of soup. As we drank it down, it felt like fire. The white, round table was crowded with eight bodies. We were so close that I could feel the thick hairs on my grandfather's arms and my grandmother's breath on my cheek. After eating our soup, Grandpa would bring out the **treat** that we all waited for. We each received our own smooth bar of milk chocolate that **melted** in our mouths as soon as it touched our tongues.

(C)   Just off the kitchen was Grandma's living room. The golden carpet in this room looked like piles of sunshine. High on the wall was a **grandfather clock,** which **chimed** a pleasant melody every fifteen minutes. At the far end of the room were Grandma's round end tables, which really weren't tables at all, but short octagonal cabinets with round tops. Grandma polished the deep brown wood on the cabinets until it shone like a freshly combed coat on a horse. Inside were all kinds of tiny **trinkets** that Grandma had brought with her from faraway places. Each one had a special story, and we loved to sit around Grandma and listen to her retell the fascinating history of each piece. Sitting on the floral-patterned couch in the center of the room, you could see into the spacious front yard with an **immaculately** trimmed lawn and **hedge.** Along the hedge, there was a single row of brightly colored tulips: red, pink, violet, yellow, white, and orange.

(D)   Grandma also had a place that made us feel carefree and wild. It was the basement. In the basement, there was always time for adventure. We spent hours jumping on the bed, which seemed to take up a whole room. Our laughter rang throughout the house when we found Grandpa's special hiding place for our treats. It was high up on the shelf in the coat closet that smelled a little like mothballs: high enough so that the candies were never out of sight, but always out of reach. In the corner of the basement, there was a door that was always locked from the other side. The door was an odd shape, shorter and wider than average. We wondered what kind of monsters lived on the other side of the door. We spent countless hours creating **hideous** tales about them.

(E)   Best of all about Grandma's house, however, was the **ancient** building behind the house—the garage. Inside this dark and dusty building were endless rows of cars. Not just regular cars, but wonderful old cars. The cars had smooth wood on the sides and shiny silver **trim** all over them. Their bright green, yellow and red paint made the garage shine. When the engines of those old cars started, they sounded like lions roaring. The garage was like a dreamland, where we pretended that we were rich and famous.

(F)   When the time came to leave Grandma's house, we were always sad. We would miss Grandma's fresh cinnamon rolls in the morning and Grandpa's loud laughter. Sometimes we would hide under Grandma's great big bed, hoping our parents would leave without us. Eventually, they always found us. **Reluctantly,** we'd kiss Grandma and Grandpa good-bye and get into the car to return home. As we drove off, we began planning what we would do during next year's visit.

◆ About the Reading

1. What is the main idea of paragraph C?

2. How did the author feel as she waited to go to her grandma's house?

3. What did she taste at her grandma's house?

4. What different feelings did she have at her grandmother's house? How do you know?

What Do You Think?

Write about a place that has special memories for you.

Read to Write

Exercise 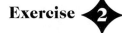 **Identifying Spatial Organization.** In the following blanks, write the spatial areas around which "Vacation at Grandma's" is organized. You will notice that the first paragraph is not necessarily organized around a specific space; rather, it is an introduction to the essay.

Paragraph (A): <u>Introduction</u>

Paragraph (B): _____

Paragraph (C): _____

Paragraph (D): _____

Paragraph (E): _____

Paragraph (F): <u>Conclusion</u>

Exercise **2** **Using Spatial Organization.** Now look at the first draft of your descriptive essay. Have you organized it around the senses or around spatial arrangements? Around what spaces can you organize your essay? Write a list of those spaces on a separate sheet of paper.

Topic Sentence

As you have already learned, each paragraph of a description tells about a particular aspect or characteristic of the person, place, or other being described. One general topic sentence usually gives the main idea of a paragraph. As you learned in Chapter 1, this topic sentence tells the reader what the paragraph is about. The other sentences in the paragraph give specific details that support the topic sentence.

The topic sentence is often, but not always, the first sentence in the paragraph. A good topic sentence should introduce one main idea. It should be neither too general nor too specific. If a topic sentence is too general, it may give too *little* information: The reader will not have a clear understanding of what the paragraph is about. If a topic sentence is too specific, it may give the reader so *much* information that reading the rest of the paragraph is unnecessary.

Prereading Activity

In the following student essay, the author describes her favorite place to go when she wants to relax or to feel peaceful. As you read, try to identify the topic sentence in each paragraph. Before you read, discuss the following questions in small groups, and then review the vocabulary words highlighted on the next page.

1. Where do you go when you want to "get away from it all?"

2. What do you like about this place? Is it peaceful and safe, or is it fun and entertaining—or both?

◆ Vocabulary Watch

Paradise

(A)   I love the garden in my backyard. I love it for many reasons, but most of all because it gives me a peaceful feeling, much like looking at the ocean on a spring morning. Whenever I have special feelings of sorrow, happiness, or loneliness, I sit on a bench at the edge of my garden. I especially like to go to this place when I have argued with a friend or a loved one. I feel that this place can **heal** my wounded heart. While I look at the garden, birds cheerfully sing to me, and flowers speak, telling me, "Be happy with who you are."

(B)   I often work in the garden with my mother and father. While I work, I notice that I love the things that I can see and feel in the garden. I touch the cool earth and enjoy the graceful white lilies, passionate red roses, fresh green plants, and a huge, ancient tree that has watched me, my father, and my grandfather grow and change. While I smell the gentle, sweet-scented flowers, I feel that I am part of nature. My favorite time of all in the garden is on warm summer evenings, when shining fireflies dance before my eyes. These lovely fairies make the garden seem like its own **galaxy.**

(C)   I also love the pond, which reminds me of a cereal bowl for a giant. This pond is filled with carp that swim leisurely through the shimmering water, like noble ladies. Yet, when I stand in front of the pond and offer the carp food, they change and begin to beg like hungry baby birds.

(D)   Perhaps the most pleasant satisfaction that comes from the garden is the sweet-tasting **harvest** in the fall. We harvest nutritious oranges, sweet persimmons, and ripe, warm, soft figs which my mother makes into jam. When we smell the **alluring aroma** of the cooking jam, we can no longer be patient children. We must taste the jam immediately. It burns our tongues, but we don't care because of the heavenly taste. Our smiles after tasting the jam are like those of bears eating honey.

(E)   My garden at home always brings me a happy, peaceful feeling. Even though I don't have a garden now, thinking of my garden helps me to relax and feel at home and at peace anywhere I am.

by Masae

About the Reading

1. Why does the author like her garden so much?

2. Around what spatial area is each paragraph organized?

3. Do you feel as though you can picture the author's garden? How does she help you to see it?

What Do You Think?

The author says that she likes to go to the garden to be alone after she has argued with friends or a loved one. In what situations do you like to be alone and where do you go?

Exercise 3

Identifying Topic Sentences. Remember that the main or controlling idea of a paragraph is usually stated in the topic sentence. Now, go back and underline all the topic sentences in "Paradise." Notice how these sentences are the most general ones in each paragraph.

Exercise 4

Choosing Good Topic Sentences. The topic sentences have been removed from the following paragraphs. Read each paragraph, and then read the three possible topic sentences for each one. Choose the topic sentence that best fits the paragraph, and put a checkmark in the blank provided. The other topic sentences are either too general or too specific. Put a *G* in the blank next to the topic sentence that is too general and an *S* next to the topic sentence that is too specific. An example has been done to guide you.

Example: They can be loyal friends, provide protection for your house, or even act as the eyes for a blind person. We have all heard of how a dog saved someone's life by helping him or her out of a dangerous situation. Not many animals can be both a companion and a lifesaver.

__✓__ Dogs are the most wonderful animals alive.

__G__ Many kinds of animals make good pets.

__S__ Dogs can help the blind.

1. A healthy diet should include fresh fruits and vegetables, bread, pasta, beans, and some fish or poultry. Along with these kinds of foods, a nutritious diet also includes plenty of water—at least eight glasses a day. If you want to be healthy, don't forget to eat the right food.

_____ Food and exercise are important for our health.

_____ Eating nutritious food is one of the best things you can do for your health.

_____ Water is essential for a good diet.

2. Hundreds of years ago, people didn't travel far from where they were born. It was difficult to go very far when you had to walk every place you went. However, as different kinds of transportation, such as horses and ships, became more widely available, people began to move farther away from their homes and villages. As various kinds of transportation have become faster

and more common, people today are able to travel farther than ever. As we travel to new places, we meet new people, learn new ideas, and experience new cultures. Our world has grown smaller as our transportation has taken us farther and farther away from our homes.

_____ Horses have made people move away from their homes.

_____ Transportation has changed throughout history.

_____ Changes in transportation have changed the world.

3. Without good communication, all the other good things a couple may enjoy at the beginning of a marriage may be lost. No matter how attracted they are to each other or how much they love each other the day they get married, if they cannot talk to each other and really share their feelings with each other, they may find it hard to keep their marriage happy.

_____ Marriage is a good idea.

_____ Talking about plans for the future is important for a good marriage.

_____ Good communication is a very important quality in a good marriage.

4. No matter where you go, you'll find that each country has at least one national sport. In the United States, football is popular. In Japan, one of the national sports is baseball. In Europe and South America, the number one sport is soccer. In Africa, rugby is popular. Around the world, the choice of sports may differ, but the way people feel about sports is the same: People all over the world love their national sports!

_____ Sports are an important part of life.

_____ Most countries of the world have a national sport, although the particular sport may differ across countries.

_____ In Europe and South America, soccer is popular.

5. When things are hard and you need someone to talk to, it's nice to have a friend who knows you and is willing to listen to your problems. A best friend is that kind of person. No matter how terrible everything seems, if you have a friend who can give you love, support, and some encouragement, you will be able to survive anything.

_____ A best friend always loves you.

_____ Having a best friend can be a lifesaver during difficult times.

_____ Human beings are social animals who need contact with other people.

Supporting Details

In the preceding section, you learned that a topic sentence introduces the main idea of a paragraph and that the other sentences in the paragraph add supporting details. Supporting details explain, expand, or describe the main ideas of the topic sentence. They also make descriptive writing more interesting because they help the reader to sense, imagine, and feel what is being described.

✦ Prereading Activity

In the following essay, the author uses descriptive supporting details to help the reader imagine the smell of something delicious cooking in the kitchen. Look at the following charts. Each chart contains the topic sentence of a paragraph from "What's for Dinner?"

Step 1. Read each topic sentence. Then, on the lines under Prereading in each chart, write the details you expect to read in the paragraph that follows each topic sentence. After you read the essay, you will fill in the actual supporting details in each paragraph. The first chart is done as an example to guide you in completing your own chart.

Example:

Topic sentence 1: Tired and hungry, I open the door to my small apartment and immediately smell the familiar aroma.	
	Prereading	Postreading
Details:	What the aroma is	
	Why author feels tired & hungry	
	What author does next	

Use the preceding chart as a guide for filling in the following chart.

Topic sentence 2: Slowly, I lift the shiny, silver lid that rests on the deep, black pot.	
	Prereading	Postreading
Details:		

Step 2. On a separate sheet of paper, create two charts similar to the preceding two charts, using the following topic sentences.

Topic sentence 3: I replace the lid on the black pot and turn to the smaller blue pot at its side.

Topic sentence 4: As I hungrily look at the thick, lumpy tomato sauce, my mouth begins to water in anticipation.

Step 3. Now read the following essay, and see whether the topic sentence in each paragraph prepared you for the details in the following paragraphs.

What's for Dinner?

(A)   Tired and hungry, I open the door to my small apartment and immediately smell the familiar aroma. My stomach becomes excited as I breathe in the delicious air. I hurry to the kitchen, where two large pots are cooking on the stove.

(B)   Slowly, I lift the shiny, silver lid that rests on the deep, black pot. Steam rushes out and dampens my face. The long, thin noodles inside are tangled together, making a big ball. I pull on an end of one of the noodles and watch the other end appear out of the tangled mass. I put the hot noodle in my mouth, but find the flavor almost tasteless on my tongue.

(C)   I replace the lid on the black pot and turn to the smaller blue pot at its side. A cloud of various smells drifts up to my nose as I remove the lid from this pot. The tangy smell of tomatoes is mixed with a perfect combination of herbs—oregano, basil, and garlic. Onions, mushrooms, and beef float on the surface of the sauce, surrounded by dark green herbs. Bubbles of heat slowly come to the surface and then noisily explode and disappear.

(D)   As I hungrily look at the thick, lumpy tomato sauce, my mouth begins to water in anticipation. I quickly reach for a fork and a plate. The red sauce, running down the large pile of noodles I put on my plate, reminds me of a volcano that has just exploded. I push my fork into the pile and spin it around and around until the sauce-covered noodles are twisted around the fork. Slowly I raise the fork and put it into my mouth. With satisfaction, I close my eyes to enjoy the wonderful flavor.

(E)   Ahh! Spaghetti!

by Laurie Shin

About the Reading

1. Is this description organized spatially? If so, what areas is it organized around?

2. What details most effectively helped you experience what the author felt?

3. Describe the noodles.

4. How does the author feel while eating? How do you know?

5. What do you think is the meaning of the idiom "my mouth begins to water" in paragraph (D)?

Read to Write

What Do You Think?

Food is a big part of any culture. Write about some of the special foods in your culture and why they are important.

Exercise  **Postreading Supporting Details.** Did you notice how the author used details to support the ideas presented in the topic sentences? Go back to the charts on page 87, as well as the charts you created yourself, filling in the details you expected to find in the essay. Read the essay again, and fill in the details that were actually given to support each topic sentence. An example has been provided to guide you in this exercise. When you are finished, compare the list of what you expected to read with the list of the details that the author actually used.

Example:

Topic sentence: Tired and hungry, I open the door to my small apartment and immediately smell the familiar aroma.		
	Prereading	**Postreading**
Details:	What the aroma is	something from two large
		pots on stove
	Why author feels tired & hungry	doesn't say
	What author does next	hurries to the kitchen

Exercise 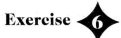 **Writing Supporting Details.** Practice writing supporting details. Use the following example as a guide for building your own paragraphs based on topic sentences. After you read the example, do the following for each of two topic sentences:

a. Write a question about the topic sentence.

b. Write some supporting details that would describe the topic sentence and would answer your question.

c. Organize the details into a paragraph that supports the topic sentence.

Example: Topic Sentence: <u>The sights, sounds, and smells of autumn make it</u>
<u>my favorite time of the year.</u>

a. Question: <u>What are the sights, sounds, and smells?</u>

b. Supporting Details:

<u>what the sights look like</u>
<u>what the sounds sound like</u>
<u>what the smells smell like</u>

c. Paragraph: <u>The sights, sounds, and smells of autumn make it</u> <u>my favorite time of the year. The leaves begin to turn from the</u> <u>bright greens of summer to the rusty reds, yellows, and browns</u> <u>of fall. Piles of fat orange pumpkins and baskets of crisp, deep</u> <u>red apples appear in the fields and roadside markets. In autumn</u> <u>even the sunlight changes, and everything seems to be washed</u> <u>in a golden glow. Th crackling sounds of dry leaves under my feet</u> <u>and the lonely honking of a gray goose flying over my head keep</u> <u>me company as I walk along, breathing in the cool air that hints</u> <u>of cold, white winter days ahead. The cool autumn air is tinged</u> <u>with the smokey smells of pine logs burning in someone's fireplace</u> <u>on a frosty morning. The sights, sounds, and smells of autumn</u> <u>can never last too long for me.</u>

For each of the following topic sentences, write a key question, a list of supporting details, and a paragraph that builds on the topic sentence.

1. Topic Sentence: <u>Riding a crowded bus or train can be an unpleasant</u> <u>experience.</u>

2. Topic Sentence: <u>A cup of hot soup on a cold day does more than</u> <u>taste good.</u>

Now Revise: Second Draft

Rewrite your first draft, paying special attention to organization. Have an area or a specific aspect of what you are describing be the main idea of each paragraph. Also, make sure that each paragraph has a topic sentence that is neither too general nor too specific. Then make sure that all the details in each paragraph support the topic sentence. Use the Second Draft Checklist to evaluate and make changes to your essay.

When you have finished your second draft, exchange papers with a classmate. Read and discuss each other's essays. Make suggestions for additional changes to improve your essays.

Part Three

Refining and Reviewing

In this section, you will have a chance to review how details help support the main idea and how descriptive language can make your writing more interesting to the reader.

Review of Supporting Details

The following essay and follow-up exercise will give you more practice in identifying topic sentences and supporting details. Remember that supporting details explain, expand, or describe the main idea in a topic sentence.

Prereading Activity

We all know people whom we will never forget—sometimes because our experiences with them were so wonderful, or so terrible! In the following essay, the author describes a very interesting school teacher whom he will never forget. Before you read, discuss the following questions in small groups, and review the highlighted vocabulary words.

1. What do you think makes a teacher unforgettable?
2. Which one teacher will you always remember? Why?

VOCABULARY WATCH

NOUN	VERB	ADJECTIVE
witch	shrivel	anxious
highlights	blotch	cackling
frames	twirl	piercing
thunder		
hailstones		

My Unforgettable Teacher

(A)   I'll never forget my eleventh-grade writing teacher. She was unforgettable not because of her great knowledge of writing, her love for teaching, or because she was a wonderful teacher who taught me all about life. The reason I won't forget her is because she was different from anyone that I had ever met before. I will always remember her because she didn't care at all about what others thought about her. She didn't care at all that she was different from absolutely everyone around her.

(B)   When I found out that she was going to be my writing teacher, I was curious because I'd heard so many amazing things about her. I was **anxious** to see whether the stories were really true. Some students described her as a **witch.** Others said that she was completely crazy. Some of us had heard that she was an actress who had never had the chance to become a star. On the first day of class, we all waited anxiously to find out what our teacher was really like. I wondered just what we would learn, or whether we would learn anything at all.

(C)   When she walked into the room, we immediately discovered why students had called her a witch. Her hair was long and black, with grayish-silvery **highlights.** It was completely straight and parted down the middle. Not only was she short, but she was also very thin. She was so thin that the skin on her hands looked as if it had been stretched tightly across her bones. Her fingernails were long and yellowish. She was in her late fifties, but many years in the sun had **shriveled** and **blotched** her skin until her face looked a little like an apple that had been left outside for a few days. However, the thing that completely convinced us that she was indeed a witch was the way she dressed. She wore a black shirt that came up to her chin and down to her wrists. She also wore a long black skirt, which almost touched the floor. From underneath the skirt we could barely see a pair of black high-heeled shoes. Around her neck she wore a silver chain from which hung a round, black watch. On her face was a pair of glasses with thick black **frames.** As she entered the room, I wondered to myself where her broom and black cat were.

(D)   Later, during the year, we learned other reasons why her previous students had called her a witch. Among these were her high-pitched **cackling** laughter and her rapidly changing moods. For example, one day she laughed at my friend Michael for his funny comments in class. However, the next day, when Michael made some more funny comments, she gave him a **piercing** look and commanded him to leave the room.

(E)   We also became convinced that the story that she was crazy was true. Sometimes, she would sneak quietly to the back of the classroom while we were busily writing our essays. We would hear the door quietly open and shut. Seconds later we'd hear the door open again, but this time it would slam shut like **thunder,** and in a whisper she would say, "Class, stand up." We'd all stand, not daring to turn and look at her. Then, from nowhere we'd feel little hard bombs smacking our heads and our backs like a shower of large **hailstones.** She'd cackle again and howl, "Take a break." As we looked around, we would notice that she had been throwing bright balls of hard candy at us.

(F)   On other occasions, she seemed equally as crazy. On one dark, rainy day, she was in the middle of a lesson. Something that she saw through the window seemed to catch her eyes, which began to dance and twinkle. A smile spread across her face, showing her yellowed teeth. She walked carefully to the window. She looked outside for what seemed like forever and then, with all of her strength, she threw open the window. In an opera-like voice she burst out, "Coo-roo-koo-koo-koo-koo-koo-koo, Coo-roo-koo-koo-koo-koo-koo-koo." With her narrow nose she drew in a long breath of air and turned to the class. Calmly she stated, "Oh I do love it when it rains." Then, she turned and gently shut the window, walked to the front of the class, and continued the lesson from where she'd stopped.

(G)   By the end of the year, we were almost all certain that the story that she had wanted to be a Hollywood star was also true. One day when we arrived at class, we saw her sitting alone in the middle of the classroom floor. She had painted her fingernails a bright apple red, and she was using her bony fingers to comb through her hair. Then she arose from the floor and began to sway back and forth; from her lips came a low humming sound. Suddenly, she began to **twirl** wildly on her pencil-like legs and then, like a candle that is suddenly blown out, she stopped dancing and fell to the floor. When she stood up and turned towards us, she slowly smiled and raised her eyebrows. She looked at each one of us and said, "Today, we will learn to dance."

(H)   The year continued this way. We were constantly surprised and amazed at the actions of our unforgettable writing teacher. We were never certain what she would do next and how we should react to her. Although I can't remember anything that I learned in her class, I will always remember my eleventh-grade writing teacher because she was so different.

About the Reading

1. What audience was this description written for?

2. Which descriptive details best help you to imagine what this teacher looked like? Which details helped you to know what she sounded like?

3. Did the author like the teacher? How do you know?

What Do You Think?

Do you think teachers should act or look a particular way? Why?

Exercise  **1** **Identifying Supporting Details.** Following are several topic sentences from "My Unforgettable Teacher." On the lines below, write the supporting details that explain, expand, or describe each topic sentence.

Example: Paragraph (A), Topic Sentence: <u>I'll never forget my eleventh-grade</u>
<u>writing teacher.</u>

Supporting Details: <u>(1) She was different. (2) She didn't care about</u>
<u>what others thought. (3) She didn't care that she was different.</u>

1. Paragraph (B), Topic Sentence: When I found out that she was going to be my writing teacher, I was curious because I'd heard so many amazing things about her. I was anxious to see whether the stories were really true.

   Supporting Details: _____

   _____

2. Paragraph (D), Topic Sentence: Later, during the year, we learned other reasons why her previous students had called her a witch.

   Supporting Details: _____

   _____

3. Paragraph (F), Topic Sentence: On other occasions, she seemed equally as crazy.

   Supporting Details: _____

   _____

4. Paragraph (G), Topic Sentence: By the end of the year, we were almost all certain that the story that she had wanted to be a Hollywood star was also true.

   Supporting Details: _____

   _____

Descriptive Details

When you are reading, pay close attention to the descriptive language the author uses. One of the ways authors use language to help readers capture the desired image is through the use of similes. A *simile* is a comparison between two different things, using the words *like* or *as*. Similes can bring colorful images to the reader.

Exercise **2** **Recognizing Common Similes.** The following are common similes in English. See how many you already know. Many may be the same as or similar to those in your own language. The first two are done for you.

as pretty as <u>a picture</u>   as blue as _____

as quite as <u>a mouse</u>   as loud as _____

as still as _____   as slow as _____

as white as _____   as cold as _____

as red as _____   as sweet as _____

Compare your answers with those of your classmates. What are some common similes in your native language?

Exercise ◆**3**◆ **Identifying Original Similes.**   Sometimes, you can use original similes, which you make up yourself, to add variety and vivid detail to your descriptions. Be careful not to use too many similes, however, as this may make your writing seem unnatural. Each of the following three descriptive paragraphs includes one or more similes. Work in small groups. Identify and discuss the similes in each paragraph. Which similes do you like best? Are there any similes that you don't like? Why?

Jorge

From afar, you can see him in the middle of the crowd, the image of a gentle, smiley snowman. He is not very tall, and his 270 pounds—which are spread mostly between his waist and chest—make him look like a big snowball, no matter from which side you see him. Despite his weight, however, he walks in such a light manner that it is like watching someone dancing a waltz, tiptoeing gently around a hall. His small, narrow eyes are just like two straight slits above the pudgy, pink cheeks, which, with the thin lips of his big mouth, give the idea of a permanent smiling face even when he is not smiling. He always wears a multi-colored butterfly tie, which with his ever-smiling face, makes him seem like a portrait of a happy man.

by Riva

My Dorm Room

My bedroom, in the farthest corner of the basement floor of the dormitory, is big and comfortable. When you open the door and step into the room, the first thing you notice is the feel of the plush carpet, as soft as cotton candy. Directly in front of you, you can see a large window, which allows the twinkling sunshine to come in. Under the window, there is a light-colored oak desk and chair. On the right hand side of the room is a bed, which is as comfortable as a cloud in the sky. The minute I lay down my head, I'm lost in silent slumber. On the wall on the left hand side of the room, there are two pictures. One of them is of majestic Yosemite National Park, and the other is a Monet masterpiece. On the same side of the room is a closet. It has enough space to keep my clothes and many of my other belongings. My room is so big that I think you could play football in it. Because of its spaciousness and peaceful feeling, every time I enter the room, I feel relaxed.

by Sang Kwon

Angela the "Angel"

Angela is the most wonderful woman I have ever met. She is tall and slender, and she looks like a model. Her smooth, tan skin feels good to the touch. She has blond curly hair that looks just perfect on a windy day. Her eyes are blue; when I look into her eyes, I imagine the deepest part of the sea. Her perfect nose accents her beautiful face. She has a small mouth, and her lips are soft, like silk. The best quality of Angela, though, is not her physical appearance, but the way she expresses herself with people around her. She is kind and sweet with the people she loves. Angela is the perfect woman for me.

by Ramón

Exercise  **4** **Using Descriptive Details.** In addition to similes, the three paragraphs used other good descriptive words and phrases. Go back to each paragraph, and underline the descriptions that you found particularly, effective.

Exercise **5** **Creating Your Own Similes.** Complete the following similes with your own comparisons. Be as creative as you can.

1. When I turned the corner, I was startled to see a man as big as _____.

2. The sound of the earthquake was as/like _____.

3. In the summer, the mountains where I live get as hot as _____.

4. The old house looked as/like _____.

5. Swimming always makes me feel as fresh as _____.

6. The sunset outside our large window looked just like _____.

Exercise **6** **Using Descriptive Language in Your Own Essay.** Now, go through your own essay, and add at least two similes. Also, see whether there are places where you can add other descriptive language that would bring vivid images to the reader's mind.

Final Draft

Now rewrite your second draft, concentrating on your use of descriptive language. As usual, on your final draft, you will also be polishing the grammar, punctuation, and form of your writing. (Refer to the Final Draft Checklist in Chapter 1, if necessary.) As you write, review the following checklist to remind you of the things you have worked on in this chapter, which should be included in your essay.

Final Draft Checklist

✓ Have specific details been used in the description?

✓ Will the reader be able to see, hear, feel, smell, or taste what has been written?

✓ Does each paragraph have one main idea?

✓ Is there a topic sentence in every paragraph?

✓ Does each paragraph have supporting details, which further explain, expand, or describe the ideas in the topic sentence?

✓ Has the description been organized well, around a spatial pattern, a specific aspect, or the senses?

✓ Was at least one simile included in the essay?

✓ Are the spelling, punctuation, and grammar correct?

 # Going Further: Idea Generator

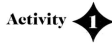 Activity 1 **What Do You Like to Eat for Dinner?** Write a vivid descriptive paragraph about a favorite food. Bring enough of the food to class so that three of your classmates can sample it. Each classmate should also write a description of your food. Share and compare these descriptions.

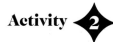 Activity 2 **Noticing Details.** Write a description from memory of a place that is very familiar to you. Then, go to the place with a notepad, and write down at least ten sensory images. Write a second description based on your recent observations.

Chapter 4

Narration

Narration, sometimes referred to as storytelling, is used in everyday life to explain events, preserve history, and to entertain. Descriptive details, which help to make a description clear and interesting, do the same for a narration. Well-chosen details help the reader envision what is being described. Other important elements of a narration that keep the reader interested are inviting introductions and essential story features such as conflict, climax, and resolution.

Reading and Writing Narration

In this chapter, you will read different types of narratives, both fictional and factual. As you read, look at the different ways in which narrative is used, and think about the importance of audience and purpose in this kind of writing.

Activity ◆ **Storytelling.**   In every culture, storytelling is a way for people to share their experiences and history with one another. To prepare you to read and write narratives, get in groups, and practice sharing stories with your classmates. Each person in the group should tell at least one story. Tell about things that have happened to you or to someone you know. For example, tell about:

1. A day when everything went right

2. A day when everything went wrong

3. A true story about an ancestor

4. A favorite childhood memory

5. The most embarrassing thing that ever happened

6. The most frightening thing that ever happened

7. A really big mistake that you made

8. The most difficult choice that you've ever had to make

9. Your greatest accomplishment

10. An event that you will never forget

As you shared stories with your classmates, what were their reactions? Were they entertained, informed? Did they learn something new? Did your classmates react as you expected? If not, why not?

Narrative in the Real World

Every day, people use narratives to communicate with one another. We tell others about our daily experiences, and we share local and world news events. We often share these events to entertain, to share information, to build relationships with others, or to explain and understand our world. In this section, you will read three different examples of how narrative writing is used in our everyday world.

Often, stories are told as part of the oral history of a group of people. In the United States, Native American cultures have used stories, legends, and folktales to explain the creation of the earth, the beginning of human beings, and people's relationships to each other and to their environment. Like other cultural groups, Native American cultures respect good storytellers, whose talents help to preserve each group's stories for future generations.

The following legend comes from the Flathead Indians, who live in the northern part of the United States, in and around the state of Montana. It is a legend that is used to explain a natural phenomenon—willows changing colors in the autumn. This legend is typical of many Native American tales, in that it includes an animal that has special powers. In this story, the animal is a coyote—an animal in the dog family that is something like a wolf. Before you read, discuss the following questions in small groups.

1. Does your culture have stories that help explain events such as the creation of the earth, seasonal changes, or other natural phenomena?

2. Does your culture have stories in which animals have special powers?

3. How do legends and stories benefit a culture?

Why the Willows Are Many Colors

(A)   One cold, autumn day, the old coyote was walking along a grassy river bank where many tall, green willows grew near the water. Suddenly, a terrible windstorm began. It was so strong that it blew the old coyote along the river bank, faster and faster. The old coyote was afraid that he would be blown into the icy, cold river or, even worse, that he would be picked up and carried off by the strong wind.

(B)   Just as the wind began to gather him up and carry him off for good, the old coyote took hold of the willows growing along the river. He held on to the strong, slender willows as tightly as he could until the wind finally died down. If the tall, green willows had not been there, the old coyote would have certainly been blown away and never been seen again. The old coyote was very grateful, and he thanked the tall, green willows for their help by changing them into beautiful shades of red, brown, purple, and yellow.

(C)   And that is why, once every year when the cold, strong winds begin to blow, the willows change into many colors.

A Flathead Legend

About the Reading

1. According to this legend, why do the willows change colors every year?

2. What adjectives are used to describe the willows? From this description, what do you think willows look like?

3. What characteristic(s) of the willows made them able to help the coyote?

What Do You Think?
Write a legend from your culture, or make up one of your own.

Prereading Activity

Legends are a form of narrative that tell about the shared experiences and beliefs of a cultural group. Personal narratives tell about different individual's experiences. The following two narratives tell how spouses met each other during the 1940s. Before you read, discuss the following questions in small groups.

1. Do you know how your parents or grandparents met?

2. How do you think courtship and romance have changed in the past 50 years?

How I Met My Wife

(A)   How did I meet my wife? Well, that's quite a story. My Aunt Suzie and my Uncle Gerald were having a surprise birthday party for my cousin Gerry. They asked me to come to their place for the party. I remember that the weather was awful that night.

(B)   After I got there, my aunt asked me to go to a neighbor's house to borrow some forks and spoons because she didn't have enough. My aunt said that I should take Esther with me because she knew how to get to the neighbor's house. I said, "Sure."

(C)   I had a Ford coupe that my dad had just bought for me. So, in my new car, we drove to the neighbor's house. On the way back to my aunt's house, I said to her, "Hey, can I take you home tonight?"

(D)   She answered, "Oh, I've got a boyfriend coming to the party. His name is Swenson and he works at the railroad. He has to go to work at midnight, so he's going to pick me up at the party at eleven. He'll walk me home, and then he'll go to work."

(E)   "Let him forget that," I said. "Let me take you home." When Swenson came to the party, she asked him, and he said it was all right.

(F)   It was raining hard when I took her home. I pulled my car into her yard because I didn't want her to get wet. I opened her door, picked her up, and carried her to the front door. I gave her a kiss and said goodnight. I didn't know if I'd ever see her again, but I thought she was pretty cute.

(G)   Fortunately, all week long, one of Esther's friends dared her to call me and invite me to a social club dance. She called me and asked me to come and bring a date. I did bring another girl, but after the dance, all of the dates were with Esther.

from the journal of Paul Alexander Dahl

How I Met My Husband

(A)   Suzie had a birthday party for Gerald, and that's where I met my husband Paul. I had really met him before, but I had thought that he was very conceited. I always saw him driving around in his father's red Buick.

(B)   Anyway, the first time we met, we both liked other people. On the night of the party, Paul didn't have a date. However, I had a date with a very nice man, but my date had a meeting and got to the party late.

(C)   Suzie needed some dishes and asked me and Paul to go get some from a neighbor's. While we were at the neighbor's house, he asked if he could take me home. My date was late, and I thought that maybe he wasn't coming after all, so I said that Paul could take me home.

(D)   To my surprise, when we got back to Suzie and Gerald's house, my date was there. I was embarrassed when I had to tell him I was going home with Paul. However, my date was a real good sport, and he said that it was okay because it was raining and he didn't have a car.

(E)   It was raining hard when we got to my house, and Paul picked me up and carried me to the back door and then was on his way. I thought he was a bold young man.

(F)   All that next week, a friend of mine dared me to call Paul and invite him to a Friday night dance. I took the dare, and as a result, I dated him from then on, except for a few times when I went out with Swenson. My mother soon put a stop to that. She said that I could date only one boy at a time, so I chose Paul.

from the journal of Esther Craven Dahl

About the Reading

1. List all the differences in Paul and Esther's stories about how they met.

2. Why do you think there are these differences?

What Do You Think?

What is a story you know about how two people met? Share it with your classmates.

Prereading Activity

The following newspaper article is very different from the two narratives you just read. It deals with life in the world of gang violence in the United States. As you will see, narrative is used here to explain and to analyze two tragic events. In small groups, discuss the two questions and review the vocabulary words highlighted on the next page.

1. What thoughts come to your mind when you read the title of this article?

2. In your opinion, why do young people get involved with gangs?

✦ VOCABULARY WATCH

NOUNS	VERBS	ADJECTIVES	EXPRESSIONS
nickname	prosecute	solemn	open fire
felony	restrain	forbidden	become hysterical
spree		abusive	
tie			
suspect			
arson			
burglary			
probation			
detention			
placement			

Short Life of Crime Ends When 11-Year-Old Appears Murdered by Fellow Gang Members

CHICAGO—His **nickname** was "Yummy." In a short life filled with abuse, he was **prosecuted** at least eight times for **felonies** before police sought him in a shooting **spree** that left one teenager dead and two others wounded.

Officers found Robert Sandifur in a pool of blood beneath a railroad overpass Thursday. He was 11.

Robert's body—not yet 5 feet, not quite 70 pounds—lay about seven blocks from where police believe he **opened fire** Sunday at two different groups of boys, fatally hitting a 14-year-old girl, Shavon Dean, about 10 blocks from her home.

Robert was suspected of having gang **ties.** Two gunshot wounds—one to the back of the head, one to the top—led police to suggest fellow gang members had killed him. Authorities had a **suspect** in the boy's slaying.

Solemn neighbors gathered around the pool of Robert's blood in the South Side neighborhood of neat yards and well-kept homes. Adults showed young children the still-wet blood as a warning.

"This is our problem," Valerie Jordan said. "The authorities and the system have failed. This is our child. The young lady that was killed, that was our baby."

In the last two years, Robert was **prosecuted** for felonies, including robbery, car theft, **arson** and **burglary.** He was convicted twice and received **probation,** although one judge sentenced him to three weeks of **detention** for probation violations.

Robert was no stranger to the state's child-welfare agency, either.

A 1986 investigation by the Department of Children and Family Services found scars on Robert's face, cordlike marks on his abdomen and leg, and cigarette burns on his buttocks.

Continued

Read to Write

Robert was taken from his mother and placed with his grandmother, who nicknamed him "Yummy" for his love of cookies.

Complaints that she was not supervising the boy led to his placement in a juvenile facility in 1993, but he ran away.

In July a judge returned Robert to his grandmother until the boy could be put in an out-of-state detention center that permits locking in or physically **restraining** children, both of which are **forbidden** in Illinois.

"This kid got missed a number of times in the system," said Dr. Elva Poznanski, chief of child psychiatry at Rush Presbyterian St. Luke's Medical Center in Chicago.

"It points out the fact that there is just simply not enough **placement** available for kids."

Poznanski said she's seeing more and more violence among young children, many the products of **abusive** homes.

"If you don't provide some way to raise these kids to be useful citizens you're going to spend a lot of money on the other end," she said.

Robert's grandmother, Janie Fields, **became hysterical** before she shut the door on reporters. "I really can't say what I'm going through. I know my baby's not here anymore and I can't say I love you Robert, anymore."

Associated Press, September 2, 1994

◆ About the Reading

1. Who was the audience and what was the purpose of this narrative?

2. Why did the adults show young children the pool of blood that was still wet?

3. The article stated that two teenagers were wounded and one was dead after the original shooting. According to the author of the article, how many victims were there really?

4. What did Dr. Poznanski mean when she said, "This kid got missed a number of times in the system"?

What Do You Think?

How do you think that this problem—violence among young children—can be solved?

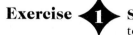

Exercise 1 **Scanning for Information.** Scan "Short Life of Crime" to find the answers to the following questions.

1. How tall was Robert?

2. How old was Shavon Dean?

3. What happened in 1986?

4. What happened in 1993?

5. Who is Janie Fields?

Identifying Audience and Purpose

Some of the many purposes for writing narratives are to entertain, to explain, to teach, to record important events, or to share personal experiences. It is important to be conscious of your audience as you write a narrative because how you tell a story may change, depending on your intended readers. For instance, if you were telling a story to someone who knew about your topic, you would tell it differently than you would to someone who didn't. You might also consider the age and experience of your audience.

Remember, when you write, you want to keep your audience (your reader) and your purpose (why you are writing) in mind. In this section, you will read three narratives. Pay special attention to the audience and purpose of each.

 **Prereading Activity**

This first narrative is by a student from Chile. His narrative relates a personal experience from his childhood. As you read, determine the intended audience and purpose. Before you read his story, discuss the following questions in small groups.

1. What does "unforgettable" mean?
2. What might make a race unforgettable?

The Unforgettable Race

(A) When I was about four years old my hero was my oldest brother Juan. There were fourteen children in my family, and Juan was quite a bit older than I was. As a matter of fact, when we were together, people often thought that he was my father. I loved him and wanted to grow up to be just like him.

(B) Juan was a good athlete. He ran the 800 meter and 1500 meter dashes. He was so good, in fact, that one day he was invited to run races during the intermissions between Chile's national soccer games. He would run one race between the first and second games, and another between the second and third games. His goal was to break his own personal record.

(C) I was excited because Juan decided that he would take me with him to the competition. When we were at the stadium, Juan told me to wait for him outside while he went to the locker room and changed into his running clothes. I waited for a while, but I got bored. I wanted to see everything that he was doing.

(D) Juan lost track of me, but he didn't have time to worry because it was close to the beginning of his first race. When the gun went off, Juan began to run. He completed his first lap in good time, then he noticed that everyone in the stadium was laughing. He looked around to see what they were laughing at, but he couldn't see anything funny, so he continued running. He ran around the track again, and still he saw nothing. However, the fans continued to laugh.

(E)   What Juan didn't realize was that I didn't wait outside for him like he had told me to. Instead, I had followed him into the locker room. Since I always wanted to be just like Juan, I decided that I would run the race, too. Quietly, I watched him take off his clothes, so I took off mine, too. Juan put on his running clothes, but I had no running clothes to wear. At first, I didn't know what to do. Then I decided that it would be better to run the race naked with Juan than to run in my regular clothes. As Juan ran out onto the track, I was right behind him.

(F)   Juan finally decided to stop running. He knew it would make him lose valuable time, but he wanted to know what everyone was laughing at. When Juan turned around, there I was, naked and running behind him just as quickly as I could. Juan instantly knew why the fans were laughing because he was laughing, too.

by Eduardo

About the Reading

1. Who is the intended audience of this narrative?

2. What is the purpose of this narrative?

3. How did Eduardo feel toward his brother? How do you know?

4. Why were all the fans laughing during Juan's race?

5. How do you think Juan felt after he stopped running?

What Do You Think?

Write about a personal experience that would entertain a reader by making him or her laugh.

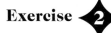

Exercise 2 **Guessing Meaning from Context.**   The following words and expressions in items 1–7 come from the narrative, "The Unforgettable Race." Scan the narrative for the sentence where each word is used. Read the complete sentence; if necessary, also read other sentences around the sentence. Then, for each item, circle the letter of the meaning that best fits the context.

1. Hero
   a. someone who is older than you
   b. someone you want to be like
   c. someone who is your friend

2. Athlete
   a. someone who likes to watch sports
   b. someone with a good sense of humor
   c. someone who is good at sports

3. Break a personal record
   a. to run very fast
   b. do something faster or better than you ever have before
   c. to end a race by breaking the tape at the finish line

4. Locker room
   a. a place to exercise
   b. a place to buy clothes
   c. a place to change clothes

5. Lost track of
   a. not be able to run on the track
   b. not know where someone or something is
   c. not understand someone or something

6. Lap
   a. a running race
   b. the beginning of a race
   c. circling one time around a race track

7. Fans
   a. people in a crowd who cheer for you
   b. the officials at a sports event
   c. people who will also run in the race

<h2>✦ Prereading Activity</h2>

A folktale is an entertaining story that people pass along from generation to generation. These imaginary tales usually teach a lesson. The following folktale (which is sometimes also told as a poem or a song) is no exception. Before reading "Get Up and Close the Door," discuss the following questions in small groups.

1. What do you usually do when you have an argument with someone?

2. What usually happens if both people feel that they are right when they are arguing?

3. If you are arguing and you realize that you are wrong, what do you do?

Get Up and Close the Door

(A)   Once upon a time, there was an old couple who had lived together a very long time. One evening, as they were busily working in their cozy little home—he was fixing a broken chair and she was mixing together a spicy sausage—a cold, strong wind began to blow. Soon the small home was filled with chilly air. The old man looked up from his work on the broken chair and said to his wife, "There is a cold wind outside. Get up and close the door." Well, the old woman was also very busy making the sausage and didn't think she should have to stop her work, so she replied, "I'm up to my elbows in sausage meat. If you want the door shut, get up and close it yourself!"

(B)   Neither the old man nor the old woman would move from their work. Meanwhile, the house grew colder and colder. Finally they agreed that the first one to speak would have to get up and close the door. The sun went down, and the night was dark and cold, but the stubborn old man and woman did not say a word, and neither would get up and close the door.

(C)   Later that night, two travelers were passing the old couple's house and noticed the light coming through the open door. The travelers were tired and hungry. They decided to stop and see what was going on in this friendly home where the door was open even on a cold, windy night. "Hello!" they called as they walked up the path to the open door. "Is this the home of a rich man or a poor man?" they asked as they stuck their heads inside the open door. There was no answer because neither the old man nor the old woman wanted to be the first to speak. The travelers were amazed to see the silent old couple who seemed unable to talk. The travelers tried again. "Good evening to you both," they said, but still no answer came from either of the couple. "How odd," said one of the travelers. "They seem to hear us, but they are unable to speak. Let's take a closer look."

(D)   So the two tired and dusty travelers stepped into the chilly and silent little home. The travelers were hungry and thirsty. "As long as we are here, would it be possible to have a little something to eat and drink?" asked one of the travelers, who was a bit bold. Still nothing but a silent stare from the old couple. "I'll take that silence to mean that we can help ourselves," he said to his companion. The two travelers began to eat and drink whatever they could find. When they began to eat the sausage that the old woman had just made, she was furious, but not wanting to be the first one to speak, she remained quiet as she gave the two travelers her most disapproving look.

(E)   After the travelers had had their fill of food and drink, they were feeling very good and even more bold and daring than before. "We are like two kings in this house. We can do anything we like here!" boasted one of the travelers. "What should we do next?" he asked with a mischievous look. "Here's my knife," he said as he tossed the knife to his friend. "You cut off the old man's beard while I kiss his wife!"

(F)   When the old man heard this last remark, he could not take anymore from these rude travelers. He jumped to his feet and shouted, "First you eat my food and drink my wine, and now you plan to kiss my own wife in front of me! Why I ought to. . . ." But before the old man could finish his threat, his wife jumped to her feet and exclaimed, "Ah-ha, old man! You were the first to speak. Get up and close the door!"

A Folktale

About the Reading

1. Who was the author's intended audience?

2. What lesson do you think this folktale is trying to teach?

3. What can you infer from the folktale about this couple's marriage?

4. Imagine that you are one of the characters in this story. How would you have reacted to the situation?

What Do You Think?

What can you infer about how the author of this folktale feels about arguments? How do you feel about arguments?

Exercise 3

Understanding Meaning from Context.   The new vocabulary words in this story are surrounded by many clues. You can use these clues to discover the meaning of the unfamiliar words. For example, the word *stubborn* in paragraph (B) may be new to you. However, when you read the word in its context, you can begin to get an idea of what it may mean:

> The sun went down, and the night was dark and cold, but the *stubborn* old man and woman did not say a word, and neither would get up and close the door.

Based on this context, what do you think the word *stubborn* means? What part of speech (noun, verb, adjective, etc) is it? What word or words around *stubborn* give you clues to its meaning? Write your own definition of *stubborn* here:_____. Then compare your meaning with that of a partner.

Next, read the following sentences from the folktale. Use the context—the words or sentences around the italicized word in each sentence—to write your definition for each word. The letter in parentheses after each sentence tells you what paragraph the sentence is in. When you finish, share your definitions with a small group of your classmates.

1. The travelers were *amazed* to see the silent old couple who seemed unable to talk. (C)

   _____

2. When they began to eat the sausage that the old woman had just made, she was *furious.* (D)

   _____

3. After the travelers had had their fill of food and drink, they were feeling very good and even more *bold* and daring than before. (E)

   _____

4. When the old man heard this last remark, he could not take anymore from these *rude* travelers. (F)

   _____

5. "First you eat my food and drink my wine, and now you plan to kiss my own wife in front of me! Why I ought to. . . ." But before the old man could finish his *threat,* his wife jumped to her feet. . . .(F)

   _____

Getting Started: Don't Take Your Pen off the Paper!

So far, you have learned two different prewriting strategies—brainstorming with a time line and brainstorming using the senses and emotions. Now, you will learn a very different kind of prewriting strategy; this strategy will get you started in narrative writing, although you can also use it for any type of writing. First, you need to have in mind a very general idea of the story you want to write. Look again at the ideas on page 100 that you used for the storytelling activity at the beginning of this chapter. Choose one of those ideas, or use an idea of your own. Next, take out a piece of paper and a pen or pencil, and begin writing about your idea. Once you begin writing—this is very important—**don't stop writing or take your pen off of the paper for three minutes.** Even if you get stuck and you can't think of what to write next, just keep writing. You can even write, "I am stuck, and I don't know what to write!"

After three minutes, you should stop and take a one-minute break. Then, write for another three minutes without stopping, take a break, and then write another three minutes. The main object of this prewriting strategy is to get ideas flowing onto the page without a lot of analyzing of what you are writing. When you complete this prewriting exercise, you should have some story material to work with as you write the first draft of your narrative essay.

Essay Writing: First Draft

Everyone has experiences that make a good story to tell. Now it is time to begin the first draft of your narrative essay. Be sure to use the material that you produced in your prewriting.

Before you write your first draft, read over the First Draft Checklist to help guide you in your writing. Then, after you have written your draft, use the checklist to evaluate what you have written. Make any changes that will improve what you wrote.

First Draft Checklist

✓ **Who is the audience?**

✓ **What is the purpose?**

✓ **Have the essential events from your prewriting brainstorm been included?**

Part Two

Developing Narratives

In Part One, you focused on audience and purpose. In this section, you will focus on the kind of organization and descriptive detail that is typically used in narrative writing. By understanding the typical organization in narratives, you will become a better reader and writer. In addition, you will see how the use of descriptive detail enhances narrative writing.

Organizational Style in Narrative Writing

Narratives are usually written in *chronological order,* which means that you write or tell the events of your narrative in the order in which they took place. In order to understand the narrative, the reader must know when each event occurred.

There are four essential elements of a story: background, conflict, climax, and resolution. The author usually begins a narrative by giving you the *background* or setting in which the events unfold. Each event then builds on the preceding events and leads to the following events while presenting a problem that must be resolved. This problem is the *conflict* of the story. As the story continues, the conflict is developed through a series of actions. Often, there is a *turning point,* where the story makes a dramatic change. At this point, the reader comes to the *climax* of the story, where the problem in the story is fully developed. A story's climax is usually followed by the *resolution,* where the problem is resolved in some way, or at least the story reaches some kind of end.

Progression of a Narrative

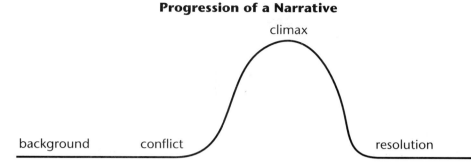

To understand the progression of background, conflict, climax, and resolution in a narrative, imagine yourself on a roller coaster. The car begins to move on a level area at first. This area is like the background: It's where you begin the ride. Then the car begins to move, slowly pulling itself upward as its weight tries to pull it down. This is like a story's conflict. The car keeps moving until it reaches the top. You know that when you are at the very top of a roller coaster, something very exciting is about to happen. That excitement is similar to the feeling the reader has as the story reaches its climax. Then, the car suddenly rushes downward until it finally reaches the bottom again, and you come to a stop. This phase is like a story's resolution, where the problem is finally resolved (taken care of). Sometimes this up-and-down process can happen more than once in a story, just as it can on a roller coaster.

Following is a diagram of the background, conflict, climax, and resolution of the story, "The Unforgettable Race."

Progression of "The Unforgettable Race"

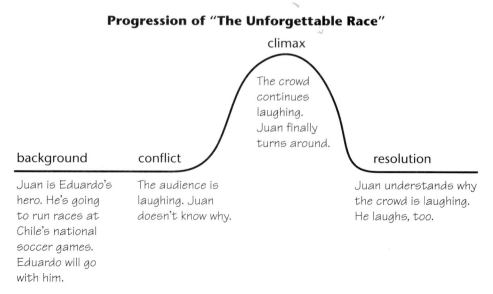

Yung Yu, a student from Taiwan, wrote a narrative about a camping trip that had a great impact on him because of a tragic event that took place. As you read the story, think about the progression of background, conflict, climax, and resolution. Before you read the story, discuss the following questions in small groups.

1. What is one of the most frightening things that has happened to you?
2. How did you react?

Camping with a Wolf!

(A)   When I was 20 years old, I really liked to go camping with my friends. One day, we decided to go on a camping trip, but this time, we had a new plan. We wanted to find a place where nobody lived, so we picked a forest outside of the city. I had once heard someone say that there were a lot of ghosts living in that forest, but we decided to go anyway.

(B)   It was a nice day, and the sun was shining. We prepared everything we needed, and we were so happy because we would have a new experience. When we arrived at this strange place, the sun was going down. Everything looked golden and very beautiful. I was especially excited by the lake, where there were a lot of fish swimming. Soon the sky became dark, and we couldn't see anything except the moon and stars. It was a wonderful night sky.

(C)   By midnight, everyone was asleep. Suddenly, I heard a strange sound from the forest, "Hoooo. . . . Woooo. . . ." The sound reminded me that there were supposed to be a lot of ghosts at this place. I was scared, so I woke my friend and asked, "Do you hear something?"

(D)   He said, "Hey, man, don't be silly, OK?!" and he went back to sleep. But I couldn't sleep anymore, so I went out of the tent.

(E)   I saw a big thing moving very fast in the forest. It was a huge animal. I could also see its eyes—they were glowing, and they seemed so hungry. It looked like a wolf, but I had never heard of Taiwan having wolves. Full of fear, I woke my friend up. I said, "Maybe it will attack us!"

(F)   We tried to find the animal, but as we walked through the dark forest, I was getting more and more scared. Suddenly, the animal appeared; it jumped quickly at us. I took a piece of wood to try to kill this crazy animal. I hit it with the wood. When the animal stopped moving, I could see that my hand was covered with blood. I moved closer to look at this animal that had frightened me so much. To my surprise, I saw that it was a big black dog. It was so strange. Why was there a dog out there? Why did he jump at us like that?

(G)   I felt so sad because I had never killed anything in my life before. I have tried to be kind to animals since that night, and I have sworn never to kill anything again in my life.

by Yung Yu

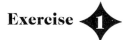

Exercise ◆**1**◆ **Identifying Narrative Elements.** Fill in the narrative elements of the story, "Camping with a Wolf!," in the following diagram.

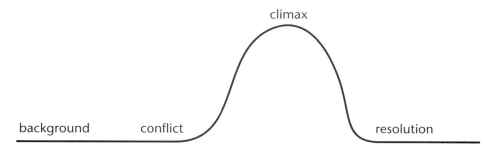

climax

background   conflict   resolution

Adding Detail to Narrative Writing

A narrative may have exciting elements, but it may not interest the reader if the author hasn't included enough detail to fully develop the story. Following are two versions of the story, "The Birthday Heart." The first version has all the elements of a narrative, but it is lacking in detail. The second version offers greater detail.

◆ **Prereading Activity**

These narratives are about a woman's memories of her mother's birthday. The author writes about a time when she was a young girl and she gave her mother a special birthday gift. Before you read the stories, discuss the following questions in small groups.

1. What is the best present you have ever received? What made it the best?

2. What is the best present you have ever given someone? What made it the best?

The Birthday Heart (1)

(A)   One day we decided to have a picnic. I was helping my mom, when my sisters arrived. They said, "Happy birthday, Mom!" and gave her some presents.

(B)   I was sad. I had forgotten it was my mother's birthday. I didn't want her to know that I had not remembered her birthday. I had to find a present that would show my mother how much I loved her.

(C)   I went to my bedroom. I got my bank and opened it. There was one dollar bill inside. I knew that one dollar could buy a lot of candy. I was sure that I could find a present for one dollar, too.

(D)   I went to the store. I looked at everything, and I realized that my dollar wouldn't buy as much as I had thought it would. Then I saw a heart made of plastic. It contained typewriter correction paper. I knew that it would show my mother how much I loved her. It was ninety-nine cents.

(E)   I took the heart to the cashier and gave her my dollar. She said that I didn't have enough money because with tax the heart cost more than a dollar.

(F)   I didn't understand sales tax. All I understood was that I couldn't give the heart to my mom. I went to put the heart back and the cashier asked me if it was my mom's birthday. I nodded. Then she said that she could help me. She put some of her own pennies in the cash register with my dollar and gave me the heart in a bag.

(G)   When I got home, my mother asked me where I had been. "Happy birthday," I said, and I gave her the bag. She opened it and pulled out the heart.

(H)   "What a beautiful present," she said. "It's just what I need." She put me on her lap and told me that she loved the heart and she loved me.

(I)   I don't remember many of the gifts that I have given my mother, but I will always remember the heart that I gave her on that birthday.

The Birthday Heart (2)

(A)   It was a beautiful, warm Saturday in May, and my family had decided to have a picnic. I loved being outside instead of in school. I was helping my mother get the picnic table ready for our lunch when two of my older married sisters arrived.

(B)   "Happy birthday, Mom!" they said as they handed her their brightly colored birthday packages.

(C)   My heart sank. I had forgotten that today was my mother's birthday. I didn't want her to know that I had not remembered her birthday. I looked at the packages from my sisters and decided I had to find a present that would show my mother how much I loved her.

(D)   I quickly went inside the house and ran upstairs to my bedroom. I pulled my bank down from its shelf and opened it. No coins fell out, but as I put my fingers inside, I felt a single piece of paper. It was a one dollar bill. I often walked to the drugstore with my friends, and I knew that one dollar could buy a lot of good candy. I was sure that I could find a beautiful birthday present for one dollar, too.

(E)   I decided to go to the variety store next to the drugstore. Though I had been there many times, I had never been there alone before. It felt strange to walk down the aisles quietly by myself, but I knew I had to look carefully to find just the right present. As I looked at the pretty dishes and other household items, I realized that my dollar wouldn't buy as much as I had thought it would. Suddenly, I saw something out of the corner of my eye. It was a small, pretty pink heart made of plastic. When I picked it up, I saw that it contained typewriter correction paper. It was perfect for my mom! We both loved pink, and I knew that this gift would show her how much I loved her. The best part was that it was just the right price: ninety-nine cents!

(F)   I took my treasure to the cashier and presented it to her with my dollar bill. She picked it up and looked at the price tag.

(G)   "Is that all the money you have?" she asked.

(H)   "Yes," I said. "Just enough to buy this present for my mom!"

(I)   "I'm sorry, dear. With tax, this gift costs more money than you have."

(J)   At eight years old, I didn't understand sales tax. All I understood was that I couldn't give this beautiful present to my mom after all. I felt tears gathering in my eyes; I didn't know what to say. As I picked up the beautiful pink heart to return it to its shelf, the cashier asked, "Is it your mom's birthday?" I nodded. "Well," she said, "you're only short a few pennies. Maybe I can help you out." She reached into her apron, pulled out some pennies, put them in the cash register with my dollar bill, and handed me the beautiful pink heart in a brown paper bag.

(K)   When I arrived home again my mother called me.

(L)   "Laurie, where have you been?"

(M)   "Happy birthday," I said as I handed her the brown paper bag. I watched with excitement as she opened it and pulled out the pink heart.

(N)   "What a beautiful present," she said. "It's just what I need." She pulled me on her lap and continued quietly, "But the best present you could give me is just being you. I love the heart and I love you."

(O)   I don't remember many of the gifts that I have given my mother since then, but I will always remember the pink plastic heart that I gave my mother on that special birthday.

by Laurie Shin

✦ About the Reading

1. What was the conflict in this story? How was it resolved?

2. How do the additional details make the second version of the story different?

3. What would you have done if you had been in the girl's situation?

What Do You Think?

Do you think that gifts can show how much you love someone? Why or why not?

Exercise 2

Identifying Detail. The following sentences are from "The Birthday Heart (1)." The letters in parentheses tell the paragraphs in which the sentences appear. Find the corresponding sentences in "The Birthday Heart (2)," which have the same meaning, and circle them. In the second version, underline the descriptive language that makes the story more vivid. Ask your teacher to help you with any of the idiomatic language that the author used in the second version. On a separate sheet of paper, choose five descriptive words from that version, and write your own sentences.

1. They said, "Happy birthday, Mom!" and gave her some presents. (A)

2. I was sad. (B)

3. I went to my bedroom. (C)

4. I went to the store. (D)

5. Then I saw a heart made of plastic. (D)

6. I took the heart to the cashier and gave her my dollar. (E)

7. She put some of her own pennies in the cash register with my dollar and gave me the heart in a bag. (F)

8. I will always remember the heart that I gave her on that birthday. (I)

Exercise 3

Adding Detail to Your Narrative. Now work on adding detail to your own narrative. First, look for parts of your narrative that you might want to describe more fully. Add as much detail as you can. Then give your narrative to a partner, and have your partner suggest other parts of your narrative that could be improved by adding more details.

Quoted and Reported Speech

A narrative often becomes more interesting to read when a writer uses direct quotations. *Direct quotations* are the exact words a person says when speaking. This type of speech is set apart by quotation marks (" . . . ") and other special punctuation. The words inside the quotation marks are the exact words that the speaker uses. However, speakers are not always directly quoted when a story is told. When the speaker's exact words are not used, but his or her ideas are expressed, the speech is *paraphrased*. When the speaker's words are paraphrased, quotation marks are not used. When someone's speech is paraphrased, it is called *reported speech*. For example:

Direct quotation: Maria said, "I would like some cake."

Reported speech: Maria said that she would like some cake.

Read to Write

The following punctuation rules must be followed when using direct quotations.

Punctuating Quoted Speech

1. Place quotation marks at the beginning and end of the speaker's words.
   Example: The old man looked up from his work and said to his wife, "There is a cold wind outside. Get up and close the door."
2. The first letter of the first word that the speaker says must be capitalized.
   Example: The old woman replied, "If you want the door shut, get up and close it yourself!"
3. If the quotation is within a sentence, a comma should come before the first quotation mark.
   Example: He jumped to his feet and shouted, "First you eat my food and drink my wine, and now you plan to kiss my own wife in front of me!"
4. At the end of the quotation, there should be a punctuation mark inside the final quotation mark. If the quotation ends the sentence, this mark is usually a period (.). If the quotation does not end the entire sentence the punctuation mark is usually a comma (,) before the final quotation mark. Exclamation points (!) and question marks (?) may be used where appropriate.
   Examples: "How odd," said one of the travelers.
   "Hello!" They called as they walked up the path to the open door.
   "Would it be possible to have a little something to eat and drink?" asked one of the travelers.

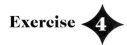

Exercise 4 **Identifying Direct Quotations.** Read the following narrative, "American Mama," and underline each direct quotation.

American Mama

My mother is an expert with an iron. In just six strokes, her shirt looked like—her same old shirt. I hated it.

Then she grabbed her no-color cotton pants.
5 I hated them, too. With each stroke, the cotton seemed to grow thinner. If the pants had a shape, it was that of a box with legs.

"Nadja's mother has a leather skirt," I said.

"She must be young," my mother said.
10 I spoke without thinking. "No. She's your age."

My mother looked at me from the corners of her eyes. "Old?" she asked, slyly.

"Oh, you know what I mean," I protested. "She's not a kid. But . . . she did buy a down
15 jacket."

"Um!" my mother snorted. "Leather and feathers! And when is she going to wear the jacket?"

Continued

American Mama   Continued

20   Now I saw my chance. "I don't know," I said slowly. "She might wear it in the evening. Maybe she'll wear it to the school tomorrow night. It's Parent-Teacher Night, you know."

    "I know," my mother said. "I just don't know why she would wear such an outfit."

25   I hesitated, but spoke anyway. "Maybe . . . she just wants to look like an American mama."

    I waited for my mother to reply. But she didn't. I knew enough to quit for a while.

    My mother is good with an iron, but I am 30 good with a needle and thread. I am also good with a plan. That's why I asked my mother for help.

    "I think my skirt is too long," I said. "Would you put it on while I fix it?"

35   She did, and I fixed the skirt to her size.

    "I wonder how I'll look in the blouse," I said, throwing it over her shoulders.

    "You have a mirror," she said wisely.

    I thought quickly. "But I cannot see the 40 whole outfit," I grabbed the flat slippers from her feet. "With shoes," I added.

    My mother never wore shoes with heels. But she slipped her feet into mine and stared in the long mirror. She looked great! Turning un-45 steadily, she smiled. She was pleased. So was I.

    We said no more about her new look. But the next evening, I left the clothes in her room. I would be happy to greet my American Mama at school.

50   When I arrived at school, I saw my mother sitting in my homeroom. She was sitting there with many other mothers. She was sitting there in her no-color cotton pants, same old shirt, and flat shoes.

55   I stopped at the door. I was going to be embarrassed. My mother did not look like the mother in the jogging suit . . . who did not look like the one in the long skirt . . . who did not look like the mother in blue jeans . . . or the one 60 in the business suit.

    She saw me and smiled. To my surprise, I smiled back. Then I hurried over to kiss her on the cheek.

    I was not embarrassed that her clothes 65 were different . . . just like every other American Mama's.

by Phyllis Fair Cowell, *U.S. Express*, December, 1990

Exercise 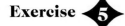 **Using Reported Speech.**   Make two columns on a sheet of paper. Choose five of the direct quotations you underlined for Exercise 4 and write them in the column on the left of the page. On the right side of the page, rewrite each one as *reported speech*.

    Example: "I think my skirt is too   <u>I told my mother that I thought</u>

                  long," I said. (line 33)   <u>my skirt was too long.</u>

Exercise 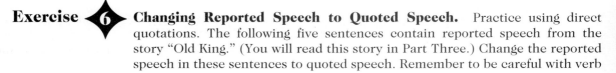 **Changing Reported Speech to Quoted Speech.**   Practice using direct quotations. The following five sentences contain reported speech from the story "Old King." (You will read this story in Part Three.) Change the reported speech in these sentences to quoted speech. Remember to be careful with verb tenses. Although a narrative is usually told in the past tense, quoted speech should be in the tense that the speaker used at the time he or she was speaking. Here are two examples:

Example: My father always warned us that if we didn't take good care of our horses, he would sell them right away.

My father warned us, "If you don't take good care of your horses, I will sell them right away."

Example: I called to my father, and he came riding back through the tall meadow grasses.

I called, "Father, Father!" and he came riding back through the tall meadow grasses.

1. When he listened to Old King's breathing, he decided that it wouldn't be wise to make King go up the last part of the mountain.

   _____

   _____

2. I threw my arms around his sweaty neck and buried my face in his long white mane and begged him to forgive me for making him carry me up this long, difficult trail.

   _____

   _____

3. I promised King that I would never make him go so far from the field again.

   _____

   _____

4. Then I told my sisters that I didn't think that King should race with the younger horses anymore.

   _____

   _____

5. My father felt that this would be a better life for King and promised to find me a younger, stronger horse to take King's place.

   _____

   _____

Exercise  **Using Quoted Speech in Your Own Writing.** Now that you have had some practice changing reported speech to quoted speech, reread your narrative and look for places where you could use quoted speech to make your story more interesting for your reader.

Now Revise: Second Draft

Now, take your first draft and revise it for organization. First, concentrate your efforts on making sure the necessary story elements (background, conflict, climax, resolution) are present in your narrative. Second, make sure enough detail is provided to make your narrative clear and interesting to your reader. Use the Second Draft Checklist to evaluate and make changes to your essay.

When you have finished your second draft, exchange papers with a classmate. Read and discuss each other's essays. Make suggestions for additional changes that will improve the work.

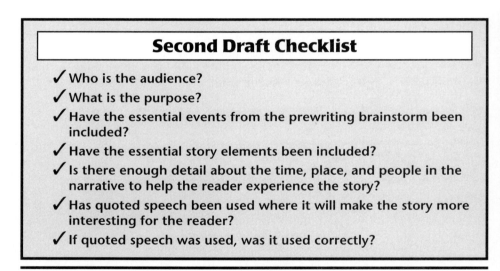

Second Draft Checklist

✓ Who is the audience?

✓ What is the purpose?

✓ Have the essential events from the prewriting brainstorm been included?

✓ Have the essential story elements been included?

✓ Is there enough detail about the time, place, and people in the narrative to help the reader experience the story?

✓ Has quoted speech been used where it will make the story more interesting for the reader?

✓ If quoted speech was used, was it used correctly?

Part Three

Refining and Reviewing

In this chapter, you have learned techniques that will help you to become a better reader and writer of narratives. In this final section, you will learn more about chronological connectors used in narrative writing. You will also review the reading skill of making inferences.

Chronological Connectors as Cohesive Devices

As you learned in Chapter 2, writers use special devices to show the order in which things happen. These *chronological connectors* include words such as *first, then, next, later, afterward,* and *finally.* These connectors help the reader follow the flow of events—that is, they can show that something is beginning, continuing, or ending. Other chronological connectors are used when one event happens in relationship to a specific time or to another event.

Cohesive Devices: Chronological Connectors		
Uses	Cohesive Devices	Examples
To show the beginning of events	*first, first of all, to begin with*	There are three stages in a narrative. *First,* the conflict is presented.
To show the continuation of events	*second, next, then, afterwards, later*	*Next,* we reach the climax of the story.
To show the end of events	*finally, eventually, at last, in the end*	*Finally,* we come to a resolution.
To show a relationship to the specific time of an event	*in September . . . , when . . . , last year. . . , a week ago . . . , a month ago . . . , a year ago . . . , once . . . ,one day . . . , every morning*	Keiko graduated from high school *in 1990.* I broke my leg *when I was two years old. Last year,* our family visited Paris. *One day,* I went to the beach with my friends.
To show a relationship in the order of events	*after . . . , as soon as . . . , before . . . , when . . . , until . . .*	*After Mia finished her homework,* she went to a movie. *As soon as Jim got home,* he went right to bed.

Exercise 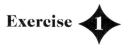 **Brainstorming Connectors.** How many other chronological connectors can you think of? In small groups, brainstorm other chronological connectors that could be added to the preceding charts. Write your group's list on a separate sheet of paper, then compare your group's list with those of other groups.

Exercise ◆2◆ Sequencing. The following narrative is not properly sequenced. Work with a partner and use clues, such as the chronological connectors in each sentence, to put the narrative in the correct order. On a separate sheet of paper, write a narrative paragraph, writing the story in the order in which you think it took place.

1. I was determined that I would begin my new exercise program by running two miles every other day.

2. All that searching for my shoes had made me tired.

3. After looking for the lost shoes for an hour, I finally gave up.

4. It had been a long time since I had worn them, and I couldn't remember where I had put them.

5. I climbed back into bed and fell asleep until noon.

6. I got out of bed, got dressed in my running clothes, and then started to look around for my running shoes.

7. Last Saturday, I woke up early.

8. I decided that I could start my exercise program another day.

◆ Prereading Activity

The following student narrative shows how connectors can make writing more clear for the reader. In this story, the writer tells of a frightening experience she had as a student. In small groups, discuss the following questions before you read the story.

1. Do you believe in ghosts? Why or why not?

2. Have you or someone you know ever thought that you have seen a ghost?

The Ghost

(A)   I know that most people don't think that there are ghosts in the world, especially those people who believe in a religion. However, I had an experience that makes me think that ghosts might exist.

(B)   In 1984, I was a freshman at Hualian Junior College on the east coast of Taiwan. Most of the students, including myself, had to live in the school dormitories because our homes were in other cities.

(C)   I had a habit of washing my face every night before I went to bed. One night I went to the bathroom with my classmate, just as I had done every night. When I finished washing my face, I raised my head. I couldn't believe my eyes. There was a girl's head, floating under the ceiling! She had long hair, but when I looked I couldn't see her face and body. Then my body felt as cold as ice. My classmate,

on the other hand, didn't see anything. As I was about to say something about what I saw, the floating head disappeared. I was so scared that I grabbed my friend's arm and ran out of the bathroom.

(D)   The next day, I talked to my classmates about what I had seen the night before. I discovered that others had had similar experiences in the same place. We were all very surprised. To this day, I am still confused about my experience. I'm not sure whether it was real or just my imagination.

by Li Hua

About the Reading

1. Identify the background, conflict, climax, and resolution of this story.

2. What do you think Li Hua saw? Do you think she really saw a ghost?

What Do You Think?

When have you had—or heard or read about—a strange experience like Li Hua's? Write about it, including the background, conflict, climax, and resolution.

Exercise 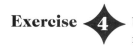 **3** **Identifying Chronological Connectors.**   Go back and underline any word or phrase that is a chronological connector in "The Ghost." You should find at least seven chronological connectors. Can you identify what type of connectors (e.g., connectors that begin, end, show a specific time, or a relationship in the order of events) were used in the story?

Exercise **4** **Using Chronological Connectors in Your Own Writing.**   Read over the narrative draft you have been writing. Make sure that you have made good use of chronological connectors.

Inferring Information in Narrative Text

In Chapter 2, you learned the importance of inferring information. Discovering the message that the writer has not stated directly—but has hinted at or suggested indirectly—is called "reading between the lines" or inferring. Learning to infer meaning that is suggested indirectly will help you to gain a fuller understanding of what the writer is trying to say. The following exercise will help you practice this important reading skill.

Exercise  **Inferring Information.** Read the following paragraphs. In each of the blanks below, write your inference regarding the author's main idea. Remember that the main idea is not always expressed directly.

Example: The 93 year-old woman sits by her window in her rocking chair day after day. As soon as she hears the mail truck drive away, she eagerly checks the mailbox, hoping for some news from her children. When the clock strikes 3:00 in the afternoon, with a longing expression, she watches the happy children as they skip home from school. Every night at 6:00, she eats dinner alone.

Inference: <u>The old woman is lonely.</u>

Example: The man walked to the front of his car and lifted the hood. A cloud of white smoke came out of his engine. He stood there a moment, then slammed the hood down with a loud "bang!" With his face bright red, his fists clenched, he walked to the side of the dead car and kicked the tire as hard as he could.

Inference: <u>The man is angry because his car broke down.</u>

1. As he walked around the corner with the roses in his hands, his knees started shaking, his hands were sweaty, and his heart was in his throat. She should be coming along any minute now. Time stood still. He had waited for this moment forever, it seemed. How would she react? Would she feel the same way, too?

   Inference: _____

2. The father carefully picked up the sleeping baby. He held her close, rocking her softly as he quietly sang her a lullaby and gently kissed her soft pink cheek.

   Inference: _____

3. Mr. Banks had just hid his day's earnings inside the old mattress when he heard a knock at his door. He opened the door to find a small child selling candy for the handicapped children's fund. He stared coldly down at the child's hopeful eyes. He felt annoyed that the child was asking for his hard-earned money.

   Inference: _____

4. Lori rolled over sleepily and opened her heavy eyelids, trying to adjust her eyes to the light coming through her window. Her eyes slowly focused on the time that showed on her clock. She suddenly jumped up, grabbed the first clothes she saw in the closet, hastily threw them on, brushed her fingers through her hair, grabbed an apple, and ran out of the house.

   Inference: _____

5. The girls pulled themselves up and over the last rocky ledge. They could hardly believe that they had finally reached the top of the mountain. They were covered with dust, and they could only keep standing by leaning on each other. As they looked back down the steep mountain slope to the green valley far below, they smiled and patted each other on the back.

   Inference: _____

Now that you have practiced inferring information from individual paragraphs, you are ready to use this skill in answering questions about a lengthier narrative. The following narrative, "Old King," has all of the story elements discussed in this chapter. Read "Old King," and then answer the questions that follow. Some of the answers to the questions are not clearly stated in this story, so you will need to infer these answers.

✧ **Prereading Activity**

In the following story, the author describes childhood memories of home, family, and a very special animal. Before you read, discuss the following questions in small groups, and then review the highlighted vocabulary words.

1. Have you ever had a pet or an animal for which you were responsible? What did you learn from being around this pet or animal?

2. What are the positive and negative things about having a pet or animal to take care of?

3. Do you think it is good for a person to become very attached to an animal? Why or why not?

✧ V**OCABULARY** W**ATCH**

NOUNS	VERBS	ADJECTIVES	EXPRESSIONS
valley	burst	regal	Garden of Eden
grain	wrap		
orchard	tickle		
patchwork quilt	hug		
alfalfa	beg		
waist	suffer		
ramp			
velvet			
hooves			

Old King

(A) I grew up in a small town that was built in a beautiful green **valley** surrounded by tall, rocky snow-capped mountains on one side and a long, deep blue lake on the other side. The town was really just a few streets and shops in the middle of hundreds of **grain** fields and fruit **orchards,** laid out in perfect squares and covering the valley. Years ago, if you climbed a little way up one of the mountains that surrounded the valley and looked at the white, yellow, green, and brown squares of fields and orchards down below, it looked as though a big **patchwork quilt** had been thrown over the entire sleepy valley.

(B) As the town grew, more and more of the fields and orchards were replaced by homes and schools, businesses, and churches. My parents built their house in one of these places that had once been an orchard. For many years, their house was surrounded on three sides by fruit orchards and **alfalfa** fields. I can still remember waking up early on a spring morning and smelling the sweet aroma of the pure white blossoms that covered the large apricot tree just outside my bedroom window. The blossoms filled my room with wonderful smells. As the fruit became ripe, the orchards became our personal **Garden of Eden.** The fruit would be so thick on the trees that the branches of the trees would bend low under the heavy load. We would climb high up into the trees, find a branch to sit on, and eat dark, red sweet cherries or warm, soft golden apricots and peaches until we felt as though we would **burst.**

(C) The orchards were wonderful, but the open fields near my home were even more important. My father's business was buying and selling farm animals, and he spent ten or twelve hours every day driving his big red truck all over the countryside looking for cattle, sheep, or pigs to buy and sell. He would also buy horses of all kinds. Every once in a while, he would buy a horse for us to keep. This is why the fields near our home were so valuable. They made it possible for us to keep our horses nearby. When my father bought each of my two older sisters their own horse, they could see their horses every day as many times as they liked in the field just across the street from our house. They could take their horses a treat such as a fresh carrot or a juicy apple two or three times a day. And when they finished their schoolwork, my sisters could be out of the door and on their horses in just two minutes.

(D) For many years, I was too young to have my own horse, and so I spent most of my time following behind my sisters as they fed their horses carrots or brushed their horses' coats with large brushes. Most of the time, one of my sisters would let me ride with her. I would climb up behind my sister, **wrap** my arms around her **waist,** and let my legs hang down over the horse's broad back and sides.

Read to Write

(E)   One day, my father's old red truck roared to a stop outside of our house, and my father began to call my name. I came running around the side of the house just in time to see him carefully leading a white horse down the truck's **ramp.** "Look what I brought you," he called. The day had finally arrived, I had my very own horse! My father had bought this particular horse for me because the horse was old and very gentle, and I thought that he was the most beautiful horse in the world. He was golden white, the color of thick cream. His tail and mane were long and shaggy. His eyes were like big dark brown pools in the middle of his soft, friendly face. Although he was old, and his head hung down a bit, and his back was not perfectly straight, he still had a very **regal** look about him. He looked wise and even a little proud—like a king who had once been strong and powerful. I decided right then that I would call him Old King.

(F)   Old King joined our other horses in the field. Then, just like my older sisters, I could wake up each morning, stick my head out of my bedroom window, and see Old King without even getting out of bed. I felt so grown up and proud to have the responsibility of taking care of my horse. My father always warned us that if we didn't take good care of our horses, he would sell them right away, so I made sure that Old King got the best carrots or apples in the house. As he ate the carrot or apple out of my hand, Old King's soft mouth and nose felt like **velvet tickling** my fingers. Taking care of Old King became my favorite thing to do each day.

(G)   Because King was old, he was slower than my sisters' horses. When my sisters and I rode our horses into the hills near our home, most of the time, King and I would be behind the others. When we came to the part of the dirt road that ran along the foothills where my sisters liked to race their horses, however, King not only caught up with the other horses—he passed them and won the race! As King raced along the road, I would lean down so that my head was resting near his creamy white neck, and my knees were tightly **hugging** his sides. During those moments, it was as though King and I became one; sometimes, I couldn't tell where he ended and I began.

(H)   After we would run a race, I always let King rest and eat grass for a while. Sometimes, I would jump down off of his old curved back and walk alongside of him when we turned around to go back home. I loved to listen to the thud of his **hooves** hitting the soft dusty road. I loved the smell of the dirt and sweat that mixed together under the leather saddle on his back. My sisters would ride on ahead of me, so Old King and I were left behind to quietly walk along together, enjoying the warm summer breeze on our faces and the sounds of birds singing as they flew over our heads.

(I)   Once or twice a year, we would wake up while it was still dark outside, and my father would load us and our horses in his old red truck and take us to the mountains. We would ride all day long, trying to reach the highest point on the mountain, where the snow never melted. One beautiful summer's day, we were in the mountains, riding through dark pine forests, through mountain streams filled with icy cold clear water and across green mountain meadows filled with tall grasses and red and purple wildflowers. We had ridden since early morning, only stopping long enough to eat sandwiches and fruit near a small mountain lake at lunchtime.

(J)   It was a difficult ride because it was uphill most of the way. Occasionally, the trail we were following would cross a flat meadow or dip down a small hillside, but then it would immediately begin to rise up the side of the next steep slope. After many hours, we came to the last big climb that led to the very top of the mountain. We could see the tall snow-covered mountain top in the distance. As we crossed the last flat meadow before beginning the difficult climb, Old King suddenly stopped. He had been walking very slowly and breathing very loudly. He refused to go another step. I called to my father, and he came riding back through the tall meadow grasses. When he listened to King's rough breathing, he decided that it wouldn't be wise to make King go up the last part of the mountain. King and I would wait in the meadow for the others to return.

(K)   As my father rode off, I began to cry. I cried because I was being left behind, I cried because I wouldn't get to see the top of the mountain and the view of the valley far below, but mostly I cried for my old horse, who sounded as though he was going to die right there in the mountain meadow filled with tall grass and hundreds of wildflowers. I threw my arms around his sweaty neck and buried my face in his long white mane and **begged** him to forgive me for making him carry me up this long, difficult trail. I was worried that my dear, faithful horse and friend would never make the long trip back.

(L)   But he did make it back, and I rewarded him with big bunches of fresh carrots and sacks full of juicy red apples. I promised King that I would never make him go so far from the field again. Then I told my sisters that I didn't think that King should race with the younger horses anymore. I didn't want to do anything that would make King **suffer** again.

(M)   My father didn't think that it was a good idea to keep a horse that couldn't keep up with the other horses, and so he told me one day that he was going to sell Old King. He had found a man in a nearby town who was looking for a gentle horse for his children to ride around their farm. My father felt that this would be a better life for King, and he promised to find me a younger, stronger horse to take King's place. At first I cried and begged my father to let me keep my beloved Old King, but after a while, I knew that my father was right.

(N)   After I brushed King one last time, fed him carrots and apples, and told him goodbye, my father led him up the ramp into the red truck and drove King to his new home. The next morning, when I looked out my window to the field across the street, it looked empty, even though my sisters' horses were still there. For many years, whenever my father met the man who bought Old King, he would ask him how the horse was doing, and then my father would come home and tell me about King and how his new family loved and cared for him. My father did find me a younger, stronger horse just as he promised, but my beautiful new horse never did take Old King's place.

✦ About the Reading

1. What is the background of this narrative?

2. What is the conflict?

3. When does the climax occur?

4. What is the resolution?

5. Who is the author's intended audience?

6. What do you think the author's purpose was?

7. What details helped you visualize this story?

What Do You Think?

Have you ever had a pet or other animal that you became close to? Describe that animal and the feelings you had for it.

Exercise ◆ 6 **Practicing Inference Skills.** Practice the skill of inferring by looking for several ideas in "Old King" that the author shares but doesn't state directly. Read each of the following statements. Decide whether it is true (T) or false (F), depending on information you can infer from the essay. Be ready to discuss the information from the story that helped you draw your inferences. The first statement has been done as an example to guide you.

1.__F__   The author grew up in a busy city. (The author writes, "I grew up in a small town that was built in a beautiful green valley. . . .")

2._____   The valley where the author lived as a child was changing all of the time.

3. ____ The author liked living near orchards and fields.

4. ____ The author thought that the orchards were the best thing about the town.

5. ____ The author did not have a good relationship with the family.

6. ____ It took quite a while before the author learned to love Old King.

7. ____ Racing with the younger horses made Old King tired.

8. ____ The ride in the mountains almost killed Old King.

9. ____ After many years, the author forgot about Old King.

Final Draft

Now you are ready to finish the final draft of your own narrative. Review your narrative one more time. Answer the questions in the Final Draft Checklist to make sure that this will be your best draft.

Final Draft Checklist

✓ Who is the audience?

✓ What is the purpose?

✓ Have the essential events from the brainstorm been included?

✓ Have the essential story elements been included?

✓ Is there enough detail about the time, place, and people in the narrative to help the reader visualize the story?

✓ Has quoted speech been used where it will make the story more interesting for the reader?

✓ If quoted speech was used, was it used correctly?

✓ Does the story use chronological connectors?

✓ Are the spelling, punctuation, and grammar correct?

Going Further: Idea Generator

Activity 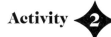 **What Did You See?** As a class, watch a short segment of a story from a television show or a videotape. Practice retelling the story orally, as a group. Then watch another segment and practice retelling the story again, this time in pairs or in small groups. Watch a third segment, and write the events you saw as a short story.

Activity **2** **Adding Details.** Write the story of an important event in your life, using only the facts. In other words, don't add any details that set the mood or heighten the reader's interest. Exchange these stories with a classmate. On each other's papers, mark the places where you would like to see more details. Rewrite your stories, adding these descriptive details.

Chapter 5

Exposition

Expository writing (also termed *exposition*) is used to explain things, processes, or ideas. An expository essay is written to expose an idea or point of view by giving detailed explanations and definitions. What you have previously learned about descriptive writing will also be important in expository writing, as you explain or describe facts and ideas to your reader. As you read expository writing, pay attention to the various facts and ideas the writer presents. Expository writing is meant to inform, so you should be able to clearly identify and understand the ideas the author has attempted to convey.

Reading and Writing Exposition

In this first part of the chapter, you will be reading expository writing and becoming familiar with its features. You will practice identifying the author's purpose, and you will begin to write your own expository essay.

Activity ◆ **Exposing Ideas.** Practice exposing an idea that you have. In small groups, select some information, an idea, or an opinion that your group can share with the rest of the class. For example, perhaps your group has an idea of what makes a good student, a good companion, or a good house guest. Work together, and make a list of the most important things a good student, companion, or house guest does or does not do. Instead, perhaps your group can create a list of the most popular or the most important English slang terms that every student should know. (See the ideas for writing on page 147 for more suggestions.)

After you have completed your list, share your information with the rest of the class. Your classmates may have some additional ideas you will want to add to your list. Give your list an appropriate title, such as "The Ten Most Important Things a Good Student Does," and post your lists where others can read and learn from them.

Expository Writing in the Real World

Expository writing is typically found in newspapers, magazines, textbooks, or pamphlets. Next, you are going to read two newspaper articles. The goal of expository newspaper writing is to present as much fact-filled information as possible in a concise format so that the reader can be informed quickly. Read these articles and do the exercises that follow each one.

 **Prereading Activity**

In the following newspaper article, the writer presents information about the relationship between diplomas and the amount of money a person can earn. Before you read the article, discuss the following questions, and then review the highlighted vocabulary words.

1. In your opinion, what do the words "pay off" in the title mean?

2. Do you think that a diploma is worth the time and money spent getting it? Why or why not?

✦ Vocabulary Watch

Despite Cutthroat Job Market, Study Shows Diplomas Do Pay Off

That college diploma hanging on the wall is worth $1,039 a month in extra pay.

At that **rate,** it takes the **typical** four-year graduate just a little under two years after getting out of school to **accumulate** enough of the extra pay to cover his or her tuition bill.

On average, people with **bachelor's degrees** earn $2,116 a month, a **Census Bureau** study said Wednesday. High-school graduates earn $1,077 a month.

Tuition, books, and **room and board** for four years at a public university averaged $19,880 in 1990, a survey by the College Board found.

The cost of education has since risen to more than $23,000 for the four years.

Prestigious private universities cost far more. Is it worth it?

"As my job search threatens—I've gotten four rejections already—it's kind of depressing, especially considering how much education costs today," said Don Modica, 21, a senior who pays more than $18,000 a year to attend Notre Dame.

Despite the cost, Americans increasingly **prize** a college degree.

In 1990, one American in four had a bachelor's degree or higher, the Census Bureau said.

That's up from one in five in 1984.

But a diploma doesn't always open the doors to high pay and security.

"It isn't like it used to be," said Susan Miller, president of the Annandale, Va., job-placement firm Susan Miller and Associates Inc.

"You **have an edge** to start, but it's not the **guarantee** it used to be."

"People with degrees in engineering, computer science and other technical fields can get well-paying jobs when they graduate," Miller said.

Everyone else is "out there in the job market competing with the high-school grads."

"If someone comes through college and they have no work experience, they're **clueless.**" Miller said.

"We see college grads starting as receptionists."

The universities say the **payoff** comes several years later, as college graduates are promoted past their less-educated colleagues.

"Whatever the field of study, colleges and universities try to teach their graduates to work smarter," said Pat Riordan, dean of admissions at George Mason University in Fairfax, Va.

"We are teaching them a way to **synthesize** and communicate at a much higher level than a student that just graduates from high school," he said.

Continued

"How is your money better spent?" Riordan asked.

"I could have spent the money buying a fancy car and some more vacations . . . but I think **in the long run** spending the money on education is investing in me."

The best-paying bachelor's degree is engineering, worth $2,953 a month, according to the Census figures. Social sciences graduates trail at $1,841 a month, and a liberal arts or humanities degree is worth $1,592 a month in earnings.

But the biggest money goes to people with professional degrees, such as law or medicine. On average, those people earn $4,961 a month extra.

The Associated Press, January 28, 1993

About the Reading

1. What is the overall main idea of this essay?

2. Is there a thesis statement? If so, underline it.

3. What is the purpose of this article?

4. Did reading this article change your opinion about whether diplomas are worth the time and money? If so, how?

5. What types of degrees typically make the most money?

6. When you are choosing a career, how important a consideration is the amount of money you can make in a given career?

7. What audience do you think would be most interested in this essay?

What Do You Think?

What kind of career are you interested in? What things about the career are most important to you? Why?

Exercise  **1** **Finding Details in Expository Writing.** What detailed information helped to expose this topic for you? Use the following example as a guide, and list nine other details from the reading.

Example: A diploma is worth an
extra $1,039/month

_____   _____

_____   _____

_____   _____

_____   _____

 **Prereading Activity**

In the preceding essay, expository writing was used to support a thesis—in this case, that college diplomas pay off financially. Sometimes, expository writing is used to show how something can be done best, how it works, or why it happens. This type of exposition is usually termed *process analysis*. In the next essay, the writer reviews the process of traveling in a foreign country. Here, the author has put together a list of several things you should keep in mind when you are visiting another country. Before you read the essay, discuss the following questions in small groups, and then review the highlighted vocabulary words.

1. What kinds of things do you do to get ready to visit another country or culture?

2. What things make a tourist an unwelcome guest in a country?

3. Make a short list of the dos and don'ts every tourist should know. After you read, compare your list with the list in the essay.

✦ VOCABULARY WATCH

NOUNS	VERBS	ADJECTIVES	OTHERS
lummox	despoil	offensive	in-your-face
enrichment	cultivate	obnoxious	snap-shooting
privilege	reflect	inferior	stand out
		loudmouthed	

Time to Take On Some Travel Manners

Travel is now the No. 1 industry in the world, and with everyone going everywhere, we need to learn some manners. Everyone's seen or heard about the ugly American tourist abroad: the Hawaiian-shirted, shorts-wearing (even though shorts may be **offensive** in the particular culture), **in-your-face, snap-shooting, loudmouthed lummox** trying to order a steak or cheeseburger (instead of the local specialty), who doesn't understand why everyone in the world doesn't speak English.

I remember being in a charming pub in some small English village where some Americans were complaining loudly about the french fries. It made me embarrassed to be American. Americans aren't the only **obnoxious** tourists—though we seem to **stand out** more than others.

Those who know anyone who fits the description above might consider sending them an Earth Day gift subscription to an interesting and informative new magazine called *EcoTraveler* or a copy of the list printed below.

Ever since the term "ecotourism" was invented several years ago, everyone has been trying to define it. Ecotourism includes more than being sensitive about a country's natural environment and not

Continued

---

despoiling it—it includes being sensitive about the cultural environment as well. The premier issue of *EcoTraveler* has listed 11 points of "ethical tourism," which were assembled by the Ecumenical Coalition on Third World Tourism:

1. Travel in a spirit of humility and with a genuine desire to learn more about the people of your host country. Be aware of the feelings of other people, thus preventing what might be offensive behavior on your part. This applies to photography in particular.

2. Cultivate the habit of listening and observing, rather than merely hearing and seeing.

3. Realize that often the people in the country you visit have time concepts and thought patterns different from your own. This does not make them **inferior,** only different.

4. Instead of looking for the "beach paradise," discover the **enrichment** of seeing a different way of life, through other eyes.

5. Acquaint yourself with local customs. What is courteous in one country may be quite the reverse in another—people will be happy to help you.

6. Instead of the Western practice of "knowing all the answers," cultivate the habit of asking questions.

7. Remember that you are only one of thousands of tourists visiting this country and do not expect special **privileges.**

8. If you really want your experience to be a "home away from home," it is foolish to waste money on traveling.

9. When you are shopping, remember that the "bargain" you obtained was possible only because of the low wages paid to the maker.

10. Do not make promises to people in your host country unless you can follow through.

11. Spend time **reflecting** on your daily experience in an attempt to deepen your understanding. It has been said that "what enriches you may rob and violate others."

by Reed Gleen, *Knight Ridder Newspapers*

✦ About the Reading

1. How did your list of tourist dos and don'ts compare with the suggestions this writer gave?

2. Of the preceding points the author listed, which one do you consider most important?

3. Do you think the points that this writer made, such as "acquaint yourself with the local customs," are practical for the average tourist? Why or why not?

4. How do tourists break the cultural rules in your country? Give some examples.

5. Who is the intended audience for this article?

What Do You Think?

Write about your best or worst tourist experience—either one you had with a tourist or one where you were the tourist.

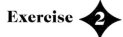

Using Details to Expose a Topic. What detailed information or ideas helped to expose this topic for you? Use the following example as a guide and list more details from the reading.

Example: Ecotourism means being sensitive about the cultural environment.

_____

_____

_____

_____

Identifying the Purpose of Expository Writing

One of the purposes of expository writing is to expose, expound, and explain—in other words, to give a reader detailed information about a specific topic. Good expository writing should have a narrowed topic that is well supported by details, facts, figures, explanations, and so on. Because the second purpose of most expository writing is to inform the reader in a concise manner, the reader should be able to identify the narrowed topic easily. The following exercise will give you practice identifying the narrowed topic.

Analyzing Essay Elements. Look back to the two previous articles. In small groups, discuss the following questions about each one. You might want to select a spokesperson for your group, who will share the results of your group's discussion with the rest of the class.

1. What is the main idea for each essay?

2. What part(s) of each article helped you identify the main idea?

3. To whom (what audience) was the writer of the essay writing?

In the following expository essay, the main idea is introduced in the title. Did you find that the titles in the previous expository essays also helped you to identify the main idea? A well-chosen title can act as a hook that will catch a reader's attention and will interest him or her in your topic.

◆ Prereading Activity

In the next essay, the writer encourages her readers to recognize the examples of goodness all around them. Further, she urges the readers to promote even the smallest acts of goodness every chance they get. As you read the essay, notice how the author uses the first paragraph to develop the topic. She quickly gives the background or purpose for the article—that we all have some goodness we can share with the rest of the world. Then she uses the remaining paragraph to expose her topic by giving detailed descriptions and examples of the different types of goodness. Writers of expository essays often use this technique of *classification* to make their points easier to follow. Before you read, discuss the following questions as a class:

1. How do you define *goodness?*

2. Is goodness something that we are born with, or do we learn it?

◆ VOCABULARY WATCH

NOUNS	VERBS	ADJECTIVES	EXPRESSIONS
fanfare	contort	bonding	ticker-tape parades
vulgarity	cherish	rude	
alleviation	shroud	destitute	
	perpetuate	unheralded	
	salve	overwhelming	
	underestimate		

You're Full of Goodness: Spread it Around

(A)   "In an age **contorted** by violence, I have no doubt whatever that people are born to kindness as a wind is born to movement," reflects Neil Millar. "After all, if tenderness were rare instead of normal, wouldn't the newspapers give it headlines? MOTHER **CHERISHES** FAMILY—BLIND PERSON HELPED ACROSS STREET—PRISONERS VISITED—DESTITUTE PEOPLE CARED FOR—BOY SHARES HIS LUNCH WITH PUPPY—BUSY SCHOOLGIRL TAKES TIME OFF TO TEACH FATHER HOPSCOTCH—and on and on. But such events are not news; they are as common and as beautiful as dandelions."

Read to Write

(B)   In an age contorted by violence, there is still goodness abounding among us—goodness **shrouded** at times by noise, **fanfare,** bright lights, **vulgarity,** or by the shock of evil across the TV screen or in newspaper headlines—but nevertheless goodness that is there for us to find and celebrate. There is, after all, a common soul in man that reaches toward the common good, toward the **alleviation** of pain, and toward the lifting of the human spirit. And that goodness is there for us to **perpetuate,** for our own benefit as well as for others, for, as Henry David Thoreau has reflected, "Goodness is the only investment that never fails."

(C)   Goodness comes in many forms:

(D) • It comes in the form of *love,* the **bonding** emotion of human beings. Love is what happened in the instance of a 5-year-old boy who was asked to bring "something that you love" to the next Sunday School class for St. Patrick's Day. All the other children wore the usual green hats and clothing, but this particular boy entered the class with his 4-year-old sister—dressed in green—trailing behind.

(E) • Goodness comes also in the form of *caring* for others, of which Mother Teresa is the eminent model. On July 20, 1969, the day man first walked on the moon, one of the sisters in Mother Teresa's home for the **destitute** in Calcutta asked her: "Do you think you will ever go to the moon?"

(F)   "If there are poor and unwanted people on the moon, I will surely take my sisters there," replied Mother Teresa.

(G) • Goodness can be further found in the form of *kindness.* "Some time ago without warning, I suddenly was crippled by a painful attack of sciatica. Never mind the details," relates a man.

(H)   "After years of independence, I found myself dependent upon others. My role around the house is to be helpful, but for several weeks I was mostly helpless. It was, as they say, a learning experience. It was also humbling.

(I)   "I have rediscovered the essential kindness of people. Time after time, when I would be struggling with the wheelchair, a total stranger would stop by my side. 'May I give you a push?' There's a motto for the nation. It's something all of us can do: we can give our fellow man a little push."

(J) • In discovering goodness, one can also find it in the form of *respect* for others. "When you meet someone with good manners, you can't know immediately if you're meeting a good person," observes Owen Edwards. "You may not know for years, or ever. But you will know instantly that something is right about the person. The world is well supplied with **rude** people spouting high moral positions about human rights, but it is noticeably lacking in those who worry about the human being waiting in line behind them at the automated-teller machine while they balance their checkbooks."

(K) • Finally, goodness may be found in the form of the *courage* to do what is right. "Courage is not limited to the battlefield or the Indianapolis 500 or bravely catching a thief in your house," says Charles R. Swindoll. "The real tests of courage are much deeper and much quieter. They are the inner tests, like remaining faithful when nobody's looking, like enduring pain when the room is empty, like standing alone when you're misunderstood."

(L) There is no limit to the goodness we can find if we just look to it, rather than to the superficial and artificial creations of man. We will find goodness in honesty, truth, effective habits, work, encouragement, appreciation, patience, family and friends, neighbors and brotherhood, and a host of other areas. And if we look for such goodness, it will **salve** our souls.

(M) It is to our advantage to create and add to goodness wherever we go. "The majority of us lead quiet, **unheralded** lives as we pass through this world," relates Leo Buscaglia. "There will most likely be no **ticker-tape parades** for us, no monuments created in our honor. But that does not lessen our possible impact, for there are scores of people waiting for someone just like us to come along; people who will appreciate our compassion, our encouragement, who will need our unique talents. Someone who will live a happier life merely because we took the time to share what we had to give.

(N) "Too often," he finishes, "We **underestimate** the power of a touch, a smile, a kind word, a listening ear, an honest compliment, or the smallest act of caring, all of which have the potential to turn a life around. It's **overwhelming** to consider the continuous opportunities there are to make our love felt."

by Jo Ann Larsen, D.S.W.

About the Reading

1. What are Dr. Larsen's main points?

2. Choose three paragraphs, and tell what the main idea of each paragraph is.

3. What do you think Dr. Larsen's definition of *goodness* might be? How does it compare to the definition your class produced?

Read to Write

4. What specific types of goodness does Dr. Larsen mention? What examples does she give for each?

5. What audience do you think this essay was written for?

6. Think about a person you know who spreads the most goodness around. What specific ways does he or she spread goodness?

What Do You Think?

When has there been a small act of goodness (either done by you or someone else) that deeply affected your life?

Exercise  **Guessing Meaning from Context.** In this exercise, you will be asked to find a word in the essay, "You're Full of Goodness: Spread It Around" that matches the meaning given. For example, "What word in paragraph (B) means 'covered' or 'hidden'?" Reread the second paragraph, and locate the word that means "covered" or "hidden," and then write it here: _____

The word in paragraph (B) that means covered or hidden is "shrouded."

Now, scan the reading to find the words that match the following meanings. Write the words on the lines.

1. What word in paragraph (B) means to "promote, continue, or preserve"?

   _____

2. What word in paragraph (D) means "connecting something or bringing people together"?

   _____

3. What word in paragraph (E) describes "people without money, food, or homes"?

   _____

4. What word in paragraph (J) means "without good manners, impolite"?

   _____

5. What word in paragraph (L) means "to ease or to soothe"?

   _____

6. What word in paragraph (M) means "not noticed or seen by others"?

   _____

7. What word in paragraph (N) means "ability"?

   _____

Getting Started:
Brainstorming by Mapping

Mapping means drawing a diagram of an essay. It can be useful to both the reader and the writer. As readers, mapping the topic and the supporting details used in an essay can help you better understand the essay's ideas. For example, if you were to map the ideas you read in the essay, "You're Full of Goodness: Spread It Around," your map might look like the following figure.

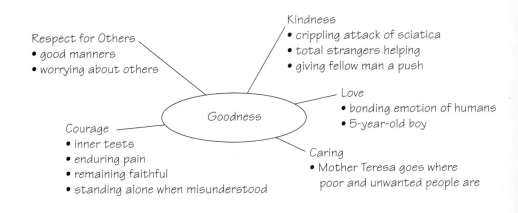

 **Mapping an Essay.** Choose an essay from Chapter 4. On a separate sheet of paper, draw a map of the essay you chose. Think about how the map can help you better understand the writer's ideas.

In addition to helping you in your reading, maps can help you in your writing. A map can guide you to develop and organize your ideas. By creating a map while you brainstorm your topics, you will begin organizing your essay. You can also quickly check to see that all of your supporting details contain ideas and information that help to support the topic of the essay.

 **Choosing a Topic.** Select a topic you want to expose for your reader. Use the list on the next page for possible ideas, or choose your own topic. Try creating a simple map, such as the one you made in Exercise 5, as you brainstorm for ideas you can use in your expository essay. Write as many ideas associated with your topic as possible. You can choose your best ideas after you have finished mapping. No matter what shape your map takes, remember that through-

out the entire process of writing an essay, there is always the option of changing an idea or something you have written.

Ideas for Expository Writing

1. What every visitor to the U.S. should know
2. How to get over a disappointment
3. What a person should consider as he or she selects a career
4. What makes a perfect day
5. What makes a person attractive
6. How to make good decisions
7. What a person needs to be happy
8. How to relieve stress
9. What to do in an emergency
10. What a person should consider when he or she selects a mate

Essay Writing: First Draft

You have discussed the purposes of expository writing, and you have had a chance to read and discuss several expository essays. In addition, by using a map to brainstorm for ideas, you may have thought of several points you could use to explain your topic. You may also have a general idea of how you want to organize your ideas.

Before you write your first draft, read over the First Draft Checklist to help guide your writing. Then, after you have written your draft, use the checklist to evaluate what you have written. Make any changes that will improve your writing.

First Draft Checklist

✓ Was a map used to brainstorm for ideas to use in the essay?
✓ Is the main idea of the essay clear?
✓ Does each paragraph have one main idea?

Part Two

Developing Exposition

In Part One of this chapter, you read essays that were written in expository form, and you practiced using a map to identify and organize main ideas. In this section, you will learn how the supporting ideas in expository essays can be ordered effectively. You will also learn the importance of both an introduction and a conclusion. An effective introduction will help your readers to anticipate the information in the essay. A well-written conclusion will provide your readers with a summary of the essay, briefly stating its controlling ideas or thesis.

Organizational Style in Expository Writing

In an expository essay, your purpose is to explain, so your organization should be quite straightforward. There are basically three ways to organize an expository essay: You can arrange your key points in order of

- Importance
- Familiarity
- Equal value

Order of Importance. One way to write an effective expository essay is to save the best points for last. In writing, you can build the reader's interest gradually by beginning with the least important supporting information and then moving toward the most important. Although all the ideas that you choose to include in your essay should be important, you should save what you consider the most important supporting information for last. For example, if you were discussing different ways you could help to stop air pollution, you might begin with the least important things you could do, such as not using aerosol sprays. Then, you might end with the most important, such as lobbying your elected representatives. By using this style of organization, your reader is left with a greater impression. When you are reading essays by other writers, being aware of this style of organization will help you to determine the most essential information the writer wants you to know.

Order of Familiarity. Another effective way to organize an expository essay is to go from the known to the unknown. Consequently, the first supporting information you would want to include in your essay would probably be

148   Read to Write

whatever would be most familiar to your readers. You would save for last the information that would be less familiar to them. For example, if you were discussing popular sights to see on a vacation to Hawaii, you might begin by discussing those that most tourists are already familiar with, such as Waikiki Beach, and end with those that are less known, such as some of the art galleries and museums.

Order of Equal Value. Sometimes, there really is no one piece of supporting information that is considered more important than another; and, sometimes, depending on how knowledgeable your audience is, there may not be information that would be particularly familiar to your readers. In these cases, each piece of information is equal to the others in supporting the thesis statement of your essay. It is up to you to choose their specific order. For example, you may decide to write about different ways people can learn a foreign language successfully. None of your specific points may be more important or more familiar than any other.

✧ Prereading Activity

Many studies have been conducted, to determine similarities and differences between people based on their *birth order,* the order in which they were born into a family. The following essay discusses some of the characteristics associated with particular birth orders. Before you read this essay, discuss the following questions with your classmates. Then review the highlighted vocabulary words.

1. Do each of the children in a family usually have different personalities?
2. What do you think determines a child's personality?
3. Do you think that the birth order has anything to do with any of the personality traits you or your family members have?

✦ VOCABULARY WATCH

NOUNS	VERBS	ADJECTIVES		EXPRESSIONS
personality	influence	conscientious	spoiled	an only child
theory	tease	picky	carefree	
sibling		outgoing	self-centered	
		motivated	relaxed	
		rebellious	shy	

Birth Order

(A)   Are you the oldest child, a middle child, the baby, or perhaps the only child in your family? Have you ever thought that the order that you were born might have an effect on your **personality?** If you have, you are not the only one. Many people believe that *birth order*, the order that children are born into a family, can influence their personalities. Those who believe that birth order influences personality think that oldest children share personality traits with each other, that middle children share with other middle children, and that youngest children also share traits with other youngest children. This belief is called birth-order **theory.**

(B)   According to birth-order theory, what are oldest children like? It seems that most oldest children are serious and are often high achievers. They are also reliable and **conscientious.** Further, oldest children are more likely to work in high-status professions. For example, lawyers, doctors, and scientists are often oldest children. Many oldest children are **picky** and demanding—they want everything to be perfect.

(C)   Why are oldest children this way? Perhaps it is because for the first part of their lives, their parents had a lot of time to spend with them. As a result, these children probably felt their parents' excitement over their every action or accomplishment, and they wanted to keep their parents' attention. So, first-born children may develop a greater desire to achieve.

(D)   What about middle children? Middle children are the hardest children to put into a general group. They can be quiet or **outgoing, motivated** or lazy. The personality of middle children may depend on how they feel about their older brother or sister. If they want to be like their older **sibling,** they may also become high achievers. On the other hand, if they don't like the oldest child or feel as though they aren't getting enough attention from their parents, they might try to be exactly *not* like their older sibling. As a result, some middle children are **rebellious.** Further, middle children generally seem to have a lot of friends and good social skills. According to some birth-order researchers, this might be a result of not receiving a lot of attention at home. Rather than fight for their parents' attention, middle children will often look for attention in other places.

(E)   The baby of the family, the youngest child, is quite different from the older children. Often, the youngest child is the **spoiled** child of the family. Typically, youngest children are funny and **carefree,** but they are also more likely to be **self-centered** and insecure.

(F)   Why are youngest children this way? The birth-order theory explains that by the time youngest children are growing up, their parents are often older and more **relaxed.** As a result, rules for this child might not be as strict as for the other children. Youngest children are also often teased by their older brothers and sisters. As a result, they sometimes become insecure. Older brothers and sisters also often treat youngest children as though they don't know anything. This might be the reason why many youngest children decide to choose careers that are not thought of as success careers, such as art and entertainment.

(G)   What about an **only child,** the child who is the oldest, middle, and youngest child all in one? Only children seem to be motivated and to feel good about themselves. Only children might also be **shy.** Both of these traits might be the result of spending a lot of time around adults. Because they receive a lot of attention from adults, they are motivated to achieve. However, not having any brothers or sisters might cause only children to be shy around other children. Further, only children are sometimes seen as selfish, perhaps due to the large amount of attention that their parents are able to give them.

(H)   Birth-order theory could possibly explain why you are the way you are. Think about yourself and others you know, and then decide. Do you believe that birth order affects your personality?

✦ About the Reading

1. What is the essay's thesis statement?

2. Does each paragraph have one main idea? Indicate it for each paragraph.

3. In which way has the author ordered the support for the essay (in order of importance, familiarity, or equal value)?

4. What are the personality traits of a first child? How does birth-order theory explain the traits of a first child?

5. What are the personality traits of a youngest child?

6. How does birth-order theory explain the personality traits of an only child?

7. What is your birth order? Do your personality traits match those described by birth-order theory?

8. Do you agree with birth-order theory? Why or why not? Can you think of people who do or do not fit the traits described in birth-order theory?

9. What are some reasons other than birth order that may contribute to a person's personality?

What Do You Think?

What do you think makes you the way you are?

 **Exercise** **Birth-Order Vocabulary.** Many of the new vocabulary words that you read in the preceding reading are related to personality traits. Read the following sentences, and decide what the word in bold letters means from the context of the sentence. If necessary, look back to the sentence where the word appeared, and read it in context. (The letters in parentheses tell the paragraphs where the bold words appear.) Then use the word to write a sentence about someone you know who has that personality trait. Write your sentences on the lines.

1. My sister is **picky.** It's hard to find anything she will like. (B)

   _____

2. My neighbor is **outgoing.** She talks to everyone she meets and is comfortable meeting new people. (D)

   _____

3. My best friend is **motivated.** He gets up at 6 o'clock every morning to run 5 miles because he wants to lose weight. (D)

   _____

4. My sister-in-law is **rebellious.** She doesn't like to do the things that people tell her she has to do. (D)

   _____

5. My nephew is **spoiled.** He gets everything that he wants; as a result, he is sometimes not very nice. (E)

   _____

6. I wish that I were more **carefree.** I always worry too much about everything. (E)

   _____

7. My daughter is often **self-centered.** Sometimes she thinks only about herself. (E)

   _____

8. Sometimes I feel **insecure.** I worry that other people will think that I am stupid and will not accept me. (E)

   _____

9. My boss is very **relaxed.** She is never nervous and is very casual with all of her employees. (F)

   _____

10. Sometimes I feel **shy.** I'm afraid to talk to people whom I don't know. (G)

   _____

Read to Write

Introductions

Often, a writer will briefly introduce or suggest a topic in an essay's title and then will more fully explain the topic in the introduction. As you read, the introduction lets you know the general topic, and then the thesis statement specifies exactly what you can expect the author to discuss in the rest of the essay.

Because the introduction is the first part of the essay to be read, it must be clear, and it must entice the reader to continue. One way to interest the reader is to start with something other than your thesis statement. Instead, introduce the general topic, and then gradually narrow it down to exactly what you want to say. In this book, you will learn three different ways to write introductions. In this chapter, you will discuss the most common and logical type of introduction—the *funnel* approach. In Chapter 7, you will learn two other types of introductions: the *surprise* and the *dramatic* introduction.

The Funnel Approach

A *funnel* is an instrument that is used to pour liquid into a narrow opening; it is wide at the top and narrow at the bottom. Similarly, a funnel introduction is general, or wide, at the beginning and specific, or narrow, at the end. The writer first introduces the topic and then gradually narrows it down to the thesis statement.

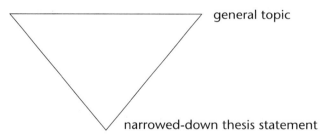

general topic

narrowed-down thesis statement

Exercise 2 **Analyzing Introductions.** Following are three introductions. Each uses a funnel approach. Notice how each begins generally and narrows down to a specific statement about the topic. Read each introduction, and then analyze with your classmates how the funnel approach has been used. The first introduction has been analyzed for you.

1. Throughout history, volcanoes have been feared by people, and for good reasons. Even though a dormant volcano seems to be just a hill or a mountain, inside it, a great amount of heat is waiting to get out in the form of lava, ash, and steam. In the past 10,000 years, at least 500 volcanoes have produced more than 600 volcanic eruptions. These eruptions have had a great effect on the world, changing the climate, damaging agriculture, and causing disasters that have killed countless people.

In the first sentence, the author introduces the topic of volcanoes and the fact that they have been feared by many people. In the second sentence, the author explains what is dangerous about volcanoes. Then, in the third sentence, the author gives some general information about volcanoes that have erupted. In the fourth sentence, the thesis statement, the author observes that these eruptions have had a great effect on the world, specifically stating three major effects.

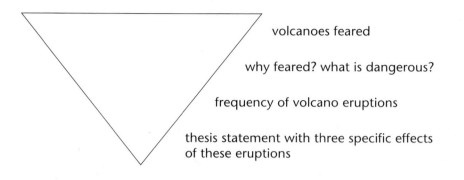

volcanoes feared

why feared? what is dangerous?

frequency of volcano eruptions

thesis statement with three specific effects of these eruptions

Next, analyze and diagram the next two introductions.

2. Divorce is a fact of modern life. A great number of people simply decide that they do not wish to stay married to their spouse. A divorce is not a tremendously difficult situation unless there are minor children born to the couple. If there are no minor children, you simply divide the assets and debts. But you cannot divide a child. The child needs to be placed with the appropriate parent.

3. America has a problem. The number of gang-related crimes is rapidly increasing. So far, we have not found a way to stop this problem, which has become out of control. If we don't find a way soon, we may find the problem is too large to stop. Understanding the causes of this problem is a first step in ending it. If we can understand why youths become gang members, perhaps we can find a way to lead them in a different direction.

The next essay also begins with an introduction that uses the funnel approach. As you read it, see how well it introduces the topic and then narrows down to a specific aspect of that topic.

✦ **Prereading Activity**

The following essay is written as an exposition, yet the author uses good descriptive writing to make her country sound very appealing. Before reading, discuss the following questions with your classmates in small groups.

1. When choosing a place to visit, what factors do you consider?

2. If you could choose one place from your country that would most attract tourists, what place would it be, and why?

Read to Write

Beautiful South Korea

(A)   Many people don't really know much about my country. They think South Korea is just one of many small countries in Asia. Some people even say South Korea is so small that there couldn't be very much to see there. This is not true. I can tell you proudly that my country has many interesting and unique architectural and natural sights.

(B)   In the capital, Seoul, there are some beautiful and important examples of Korean architecture. Many years ago, Koreans used to have kings, and the people attached great importance to the authority of the royal family. Consequently, they made majestic and splendid palaces. They also thought that architecture should fit in well with nature, so the palaces were located near the most beautiful landscapes. Along with their beauty, there are other points of Korean architecture you should not miss. For example, old Korean houses, including the palaces, were put together without nails; nevertheless, they are strong and perfect. Further, the curve of the Korean roof and the various colors under the roof are amazing. The curve of the roof is shaped like a wing of a big bird or a skirt being lifted slightly. If you are interested in architecture, you would probably be delighted while visiting these homes and palaces.

(C)   Kongrung is one of the best examples of Korea's natural beauty. In Kongrung, which is one hour by plane from Seoul, there is a resort area that provides fine scenery, enjoyable activities, and fresh seafood. First of all, if you hike to the top of the mountain, you can see the beautiful blue sea. If you are lucky, you can see the rising sun in the early morning. In the summer, many people visit Kongrung for swimming and sunbathing. Soft sand, clean water, and the hot sun are the pride of Kongrung. In addition, you can eat fresh seafood anytime at several fine restaurants. The quality is excellent, and the prices are reasonable.

(D)   Finally, in the southern part of Korea, there is warm and inviting Jeju Island, known for its many unique qualities. There is no snow there, and it is warm all year long. This island is warm enough to grow bananas and broad-leaved trees. Because it is so very different from other places in South Korea, Jeju Island is also a favorite place for honeymoons. Many newly married couples leave there with romantic memories. Jeju Island is really like another country. Even some words that people in Jeju use are totally different from the standard Korean language.

(E)   South Korea is small but has great natural scenery. In Korean architecture, you can see a harmony of natural and man-made beauty. If you travel to South Korea, I am sure you will agree that my country has some of the most beautiful sights found in any country, large or small.

by Suki

About the Reading

1. How did the author narrow down the topic?

2. What is the thesis statement? What is the controlling idea?

3. In which way has Suki ordered the support for her essay (in order of importance, familiarity, or equal value)?

4. What do all the sights in the second paragraph have in common with each other?

What Do You Think?

Suki has written a beautiful description of her beloved South Korea. If you were to explain the aspects of your country that would draw tourists to it, what would they be? Describe three of these places, and explain what makes them so attractive.

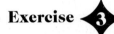 **Writing Introductions.**   Following are five thesis statements. The introductions haven't been written. Choose three statements from the list, and use the funnel approach to write the introductions. Place the thesis statement at the end of the paragraph.

1. Traveling is always better in groups than alone.

2. Managing money is no easy task.

3. Getting to know other cultures is essential in order to maintain world peace.

4. Although there are many advantages to being educated formally, the education one receives at home is the most important at all.

5. Entertainment need not be expensive to be enjoyable.

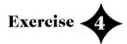 **Writing Your Own Introduction.**   Now, look at the introduction to the first draft of your expository essay. Does it introduce the topic generally, and then narrow down to a specific thesis statement at the end? If not, rework it now, using the funnel introduction style.

Conclusions

Now that you know some of the things that make a good introduction, it's time to focus on what makes a good conclusion. The purpose of the conclusion is to tie together everything that you have said in your essay. Generally, there are three methods used in concluding: (1) *Restate the thesis statement in different words;* (2) *summarize the main points that you have given as your support;* and (3) *make an overall comment on what has been said.* Of course, any of these three methods can also be combined. Occasionally, you will see a new idea presented in a conclusion, such as a suggested solution. Generally, however, it is not a good idea to present any new information in the conclusion.

As a reader, the conclusion will help you to grasp the main idea of an essay. You have learned that skimming involves reading the title, perhaps the introductory paragraph, the first one or two sentences of each paragraph, and the conclusion to help you quickly capture the main idea of a text. You may want to use this skill not only as a way to preview new text, but also as a technique for reviewing text you have already read. Often, by just reading the concluding paragraph(s), you can get a good idea of the thesis of the essay.

The length of a conclusion that you write yourself will depend on the length of your essay. In this book, your essays will generally consist of four to six paragraphs, so your conclusion will probably be only one paragraph. However, if your writing is longer, your conclusion may be more than one paragraph.

Exercise 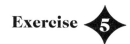 **Determining Types of Conclusions.** The following three paragraphs are conclusions taken from essays in this book. You may wish to look back to the original essays and, after skimming them, determine whether these conclusions restate the thesis, summarize the main points of the essay, or give an overall concluding comment (or a combination of any of these). On the lines, write the method (restatement, summary of main points, or overall comment) used in each conclusion.

1. South Korea is small but has great natural scenery. In Korean architecture, you can see a harmony of natural and man-made beauty. If you travel to South Korea, I am sure you will agree that my country has some of the most beautiful sights found in any country large or small. (page 155)

   What method/s is/are used to conclude?_____

2. There was a time when my street was my world, and I thought my world would never change. But something happened. People grow up, and people grow old. Places change, but with the change comes the heartache of knowing I can never go back to the times I loved. In a year or so, I will be gone just like many of my neighbors. I will always look back to my years as a child, but the place I remember will not be the silent street whose peace is interrupted by the sounds of construction. It will be the happy, noisy, somewhat strange, but wonderful street I knew as a child. (page 75)

   What method/s is/are used to conclude?_____

3. The year continued this way. We were constantly surprised and amazed at the actions of our unforgettable writing teacher. We were never certain what she would do next and how we should react to her. Although I can't remember anything that I learned in her class, I will always remember my eleventh-grade writing teacher because she was so different. (page 92)

   What method/s is/are used to conclude?_____

Prereading Activity

The following essay discusses a topic that we are all familiar with—crying—for it is part of being human. Before you read, discuss the following questions in small groups, and then complete Exercise 6.

1. For what reasons do you cry?

2. How do you feel about crying, both in private and in public?

3. How does your culture view crying, especially for men?

Exercise 6

Predicting a Conclusion. The following essay has an interesting conclusion. Read the essay, but *don't read* the conclusion, which has been separated from the body of the essay. Write a conclusion that you think would be appropriate for this article. Then, read the original conclusion, and see how yours is similar to or different from the author's. Before you begin reading, however, review the vocabulary words highlighted here.

◇ VOCABULARY WATCH

NOUNS	VERBS	ADJECTIVES	EXPRESSIONS
irritation	investigate	enduring	a loved one
stress	secret	interpersonal	going over the edge
ulcers	evoke	prevalent	cultural conditioning
colitis	attribute	drastic	
license			
gland			
fluid			
fatigue			
episode			
puberty			

Why Do We Cry?

(A) Like detectives newly arrived at the scene of a crime, researchers today are picking up clue after clue toward the solution of one of life's **enduring** mysteries—the meaning of human tears. Consider just a few aspects of tearing now being **investigated**:

(B) • Tears have a more complex chemical composition than was imagined, raising the likelihood that they might act as one of the body's waste-disposal systems.

(C) • Emotional tears are chemically different from those caused by **irritation,** and may contain larger quantities of substances the body manufactures when under **stress.**

(D) • People generally feel better after crying. And those who cry more frequently and have better attitudes about crying may be less prone to such stress-related diseases as **ulcers** and **colitis.**

(E) • Women cry more often than men do. This may have to do with body chemistry, as well as the greater **license** to cry that our society grants women.

(F) Incredibly, many of these issues were not raised until recently. While the physical functions of tears—washing and protecting the eyes—were perhaps too obvious to arouse much scientific interest, the relationship between emotions and tears was generally left to poets and psychiatrists.

(G) Researchers began to understand the tearing process only in the past 15 years or so. The eye is covered by a three-layer film—an inner mucoid layer that enables tears to spread evenly over the cornea, a middle watery layer that keeps the surface of the eye wet and optically smooth, and an oily outer layer that is believed to retard evaporation. The inner layer comes from cells on the eye's surface; the outer layer is **secreted** by tiny **glands** located primarily in the lid margins, or edges; the watery layer we think of as tears comes from the lacrimal glands in the upper part of the eye socket.

(H) By blinking an average of 16 times a minute, the eyelids sweep contaminants to the inner corner of the eye, where they exit with a small amount of tear **fluid** through tiny drainage channels. When, however, the lacrimal glands are responding to eye irritation or inward emotion, they can flood these channels to the point where fluid both drains into the nose and overflows the lids onto the cheeks.

(I) Why, apparently alone among all forms of life, do human beings produce tears in response to emotional stress? This question began to intrigue William H. Frey II in 1972. A doctoral candidate in biochemistry at Case Western Reserve University in Cleveland, Frey became interested in how body chemistry relates to mental and emotional changes. It seemed logical that emotional tears might tell him something. It wasn't until 1979, when he became director of the Psychiatry Research Laboratories of the Ramsey Clinic in St. Paul, that Frey had time and funds to pursue his hunch.

(J) Frey confirmed an earlier discovery that emotional tears are chemically different from irritant tears, producing a greater concentration of protein. As Frey delved deeper into the content of tears, he began to develop his own theory about their function in relieving emotional stress.

(K)   To measure how often people cry, what prompts them to cry, and what crying seems to do for them, Frey and his colleagues at the Ramsey Clinic recruited 331 volunteers, ages 18 to 75. They asked these volunteers to fill in a detailed crying diary for 30 days. The women recorded an average of 5.3 episodes of crying in response to emotional stress over the 30 days; the men averaged 1.4 episodes. Significantly, 85 percent of the women and 73 percent of the men reported generally feeling better after crying. (Only 6 percent of the healthy women and 45 percent of the healthy men didn't cry in a 30-day period.)

(L)   More than the statistics, individual diaries reveal the part that crying plays in people's lives. A young mother's diary recorded 16 crying episodes. These included watery eyes from happiness while watching one of her daughters swim, sobbing when she left her husband for a two-week visit to her parents, and a "good cry" from **fatigue** and frustration while getting dinner. In spite of, or because of, all her crying, the woman checked the most positive responses to a test on her general feelings about life—she felt hopeful about the future, knew that she was useful, and considered her life "pretty full."

(M)   A young man cried twice—upon learning of his aunt's death and during a movie that **evoked** thoughts of "the agony of war." (Interestingly, men's reactions to various media—such as radio, television and movies—seemed as likely to make them cry as did their reactions to their **interpersonal** relationships.)

(N)   These cases illuminate some of Frey's general findings. For instance, the leading cause for crying in women involved interpersonal relationships, often separation from a loved one. The main emotions involved in female crying **episodes** were sadness (49 percent), happiness (21 percent), and anger (10 percent). And while almost all the women gave tears as one of their responses to anger, virtually none of the men did.

(O)   Frey's investigation of crying was picked up on by Margaret T. Crepeau, a Milwaukee psychotherapist. In her research at the University of Pittsburgh, Crepeau chose people with no health problems to compare with others who had ulcers or colitis, two of the most **prevalent** stress-related diseases. The responses from 137 people to her questionnaire indicate that healthy men and women cry more often, and feel better about tears, than do the sick ones.

(P)   One of Crepeau's subjects, a 40-year-old woman with ulcers, wrote: "My intellect tells me it is healthy to cry, but I have been brought up to be ashamed of my own tears. I feel weak, out of control and unstable when others see me cry, and I sometimes give in to depression if I allow tears to come." But a healthy 29-year-old woman wrote: "Emotional tears enable me to relieve feelings of sadness, depression and anger. This prevents me from **going over the edge.**" One of Frey's healthy criers covered a lot more ground in a single phrase about crying—"Good for the soul."

(Q)   The difference in crying between men and women has long been **attributed** to **cultural conditioning** ("Big boys don't cry," etc.). Men have a higher incidence of stress-related disease, in which the inability to cry may be a factor. In situations when they feel they might be moved to tears, men often find it easier to distance themselves from their feelings than to fight back the tears. This is why, in Frey's view, many men don't like to be around women who are crying; dealing with a loved one in distress requires that they then deal with their own emotions.

(R)   Now this traditional thinking is getting a severe shaking. Frey was pointed in the direction of what may be his most significant discovery to date—the importance of prolactin, a hormone associated with the production of breast milk. One recent study found no difference in crying patterns between boys and girls up to the age of **puberty.** "Then between the ages of twelve and eighteen," says Frey, "women develop *sixty-percent higher* levels of prolactin than men do, and they start crying nearly four times more often." There may be a connection Frey believes.

Write your own conclusion here.

_____

_____

_____

_____

_____

_____

_____

_____

_____

_____

Now read the conclusion provided by the author.

(S)   Evidence from tear research may warrant a drastic change in our thinking about crying. Although there is such a thing as people weeping to excess, crying in response to various emotions is a natural physical process that we should not be ashamed of.

(T)   Indeed, if we can learn to let the tears flow, we may be able to throw away some of our medicines. As Charles Dickens had Mr. Bumble say in *Oliver Twist:* Crying "opens the lungs, washes the countenance, exercises the eyes and softens down the temper. So cry away."

by Samuel A. Schreiner, Jr.

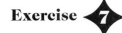
1. What method does the author use to conclude the essay?

2. Who and what are the audience and purpose of this essay?

3. What are the four new aspects of crying that are being investigated?

4. What was the question about human tears that interested William H. Frey II enough that he did research to find the answer?

5. According to the studies cited in this essay, what are some general differences in the reasons men and women cry?

6. What have the differences in men's and women's crying long been attributed to?

7. How is crying, or not crying, related to stress?

What Do You Think?

Every culture has its own tradition and feelings associated with crying. So do all individuals, perhaps depending on their culture or their upbringing. When do you cry, and why?

Exercise 7 **Making a Good Conclusion for Your Own Writing.** Look at your own essay and make sure that it has a good conclusion. If it does not, write one now, which either restates the thesis or summarizes your main points.

Now Revise: Second Draft

Now it's time to write the second draft of your essay. If you've been making changes along the way during this section, you may not have much work to do. Use the following checklist to evaluate and make changes to your essay.

When you have finished your second draft, exchange papers with a classmate. Read and discuss each other's essays. Make suggestions for additional changes that will enhance the writing.

Second Draft Checklist

✔ Was a map used to brainstorm for ideas to use in the essay?
✔ Is the main idea of the essay clear?
✔ Does each paragraph have one main idea?

Continued

✓ Is the support in the essay organized according to importance, familiarity, or equal value?

✓ Is the introduction written in a funnel style, from general to specific?

✓ Is the introduction interesting?

✓ Is the thesis statement narrowed, with a strong controlling idea?

✓ Does each paragraph have a topic sentence with a clear controlling idea?

✓ Does the essay have a conclusion that restates the thesis statement, summarizes the main points of the essay, or gives a general comment, suggestion, or solution?

Part Three

Refining and Reviewing

In this part, you will learn and review skills that will help you to become a better reader and writer of expository writing. Recall that in Chapters 2 and 4, you learned about chronological connectors, one of several types of cohesive devices. In this chapter, you will be introduced to some additional cohesive devices, which indicate the separate expository points and examples in an essay. You will also have the chance to use these devices in your own writing. In addition, you will explore important reading skills, such as observing special highlighting of words and phrases, and reading carefully.

Cohesive Devices: Identifying Important Points

In this section, you will learn about cohesive devices that signal a new point in an essay. These cohesive devices will also help you as a reader to easily identify the most important points. For example, if you read "first, . . . " you know a point will be made which will be followed by "second, . . . " By using these devices as a writer, you will help your reader to anticipate what follows, and you will make your points clear to him or her.

The following table explains the cohesive devices that can be used to show specific points in expository writing.

Cohesive Devices: Expository Connectors		
Uses	**Cohesive Devices**	**Examples**
To show that a new specific point is being presented. These devices are followed by a comma.	Sequence of Points *first, second, third, . . . to begin with, next, then, finally, last,*	There are several things I do to improve my English. *To begin with,* I listen to music in English. *Second,* I read English books. *Next,* I try to speak only English. *Finally,* I write letters in English.
To introduce additional information about a point already presented When these devices begin a sentence, they are followed by a comma.	Added points *moreover, in addition, additionally, further, furthermore, besides, also,*	The country was becoming an undesirable place to live because the cost of living was rising. *Moreover,* crime was increasing.
To introduce a specific example. They are followed by a comma.	Specific Examples *to illustrate, for example, for instance,*	I like to eat chocolate. *For example,* I like chocolate ice cream with chocolate cookies.

To see an example where a variety of these cohesive devices are used, go back to page 155 and reread the essay, "Beautiful South Korea."

Exercise ◆1▶ **Using Cohesive Devices.** The following paragraph is missing cohesive devices. Rewrite the paragraph, adding cohesive devices where you think they are appropriate.

Although I enjoy my job as an electrical engineer, there are several things that I would change about my working conditions if it were possible. I often feel too much pressure to meet deadlines and perform well. Last week, I had to spend 75 hours at work in order to finish a project on time. By the end of the week, I felt tired and stressed. I wish that I could decide for myself what to do rather than having my boss tell me. Often, I have great ideas that I would like to explore. However, because they are not related to what the company is working on, I cannot study and experiment with these ideas. I would like to have a more flexible work environment. It would be nice to work at home. I would like to have more flexible hours. It would be ideal to work four days a week for ten hours a day rather than five days a week for eight hours a day. Except for these things, I really enjoy my job.

Exercise 2 ◆ **Adding Cohesive Devices.** Take the second draft of your expository essay and add some cohesive devices to clarify your specific points and examples for your reader.

Recognizing the Use of Italics, Boldface, and Underlining

It is not always necessary for writers to use the cohesive devices from the previous chart to indicate their most important points or to make transitions between these important points. Sometimes, authors highlight parts of their text in special ways—for example, by using *italics*, **boldface**, or <u>underlining</u>—to emphasize their main points. These special treatments of text can serve the same purpose as cohesive devices. Learn to notice these highlighting treatments as you read.

The author of the following essay uses only a few cohesive devices listed in the chart. Instead, he uses one of the special treatments for highlighting text explained in the preceding paragraph to indicate his main points. As you read the essay, watch for the way he highlights these main points.

◆ **Prereading Activity**

Marriage is never easy. However, some people have figured out how to make marriage work and continually grow. The following essay presents some ideas on how to maintain a happy marriage. Before you read, discuss the following questions with your classmates, then review the highlighted vocabulary words.

1. What do you think it takes to make a good marriage?

2. How do you think you could make a good marriage even better?

◆ **V**OCABULARY **W**ATCH

NOUNS	VERBS	ADJECTIVES	EXPRESSIONS
idiosyncrasy	flourish	marital	a knack for
	cultivate	intimate	green thumb
	enrich	arcane	far-fetched
		sympathetic	take for granted
		vital	broach the subject
			trade-off
			take stock of

Do You Have a "Green Thumb" for Marriage?

(A)   When gardeners have **a knack for** making plants grow, we say they have a **green thumb.** Similarly, some husbands and wives have a green thumb for marriage—a skill that makes their partnership bloom and **flourish.**

(B)   "The analogy is not **far-fetched**" says Selma Miller, a New York City **marital** therapist. "An **intimate** relationship faces the same challenge nature puts to all things—grow or perish."

(C)   Fortunately, the ability to make a marriage thrive is not an **arcane** art, known only to a lucky few. "Almost any couple can **cultivate** a green thumb for marriage," Miller claims. "What you have to do is adapt some of the basic rules for successful gardening." For example:

(D)   *Provide a nourishing environment.* On his wedding day, Alan Loy McGinnis, co-director of the Valley Counseling Center in Glendale, Calif., wrote a letter to his bride. He spoke of his love, his feelings about marriage and his hopes for their future. Each anniversary since then, he has written another letter. He tells of the times that have meant the most to him and of the growth of his love.

(E)   "Just as a gardener **enriches** the soil with minerals and nutrients, so a spouse should nourish the emotional ground in which a marriage is rooted," says McGinnis. "I've seen too many marriages wither, simply because the partners did not provide enough loving enrichment to keep it alive."

(F)   Offering emotional support is one way spouses can nurture growth. "This can be shown in a variety of simple ways," says Nancy Badgwell, a family therapist in Dallas. "Sometimes a spouse only wants the comfort of physical closeness—a hand clasp, an embrace. Or a person may need a **sympathetic** listener or someone to 'be there.'"

(G)   Another approach is to talk together about the qualities you value in each other. "Bob and I always **took for granted** that we were in love," a wife says. "But when we actually told each other how we felt, and what our marriage means to us, we found our love was deeper than we'd thought."

(H)   Experts also suggest that you have *fun* together. Don't let the pressures of daily life turn your marriage into a series of chores and worries. Remember the things you enjoyed doing together when you were courting and start doing them again. Nourish your marriage by supporting your spouse's efforts and ideas. A woman in her 50s thought her husband would laugh when she said she wanted to get her teaching credentials. "But," she recalls, "when I got up the nerve to **broach the subject,** he said, 'If that's what you want to do, go for it.'"

(I)   *Know your partner.* "One secret of green-thumbers," says Ann Hendrickson, whose Los Angeles garden is the envy of the neighborhood, "is to learn all the **idiosyncrasies** of your plants. Which ones require extra water? Which like the sun or shade?"

(J)   Few of us know our spouses as well as good gardeners know their plants. Experts say that even couples who lived together happily for years do not know as much about each other as they think they do. Yet mutual self-disclosure—of hopes and goals, concerns and values—is a key to marital growth.

(K)   The most productive way to find out about one another is to ask questions that open up significant areas. For example: What would you miss if it were lost? What makes you feel loved? What are you most proud of? Worried about?

(L)   "There are no 'right' or 'wrong' answers," cautions Judith Davenport, a family therapist in Santa Monica, Calif. "Don't press for quick responses. An experiment in growth-producing conversation may continue over days, months, even years."

(M)   *Adapt to change.* The green-thumb gardener takes advantage of the changing seasons. Couples can do likewise. "Nothing that's truly **vital** remains the same," says David Mace, a marriage counselor in Black Mountain, N.C. "That's why change in either of you can be a powerful catalyst for growth."

(N)   A middle-aged sales executive quit his high-pressure job in New York City to open a consulting business in his hometown. His wife was worried that their income would drop and her husband would regret his decision. But a year later the woman admitted that the change had done wonders for them. "Charlie is so much more relaxed now," she said. "We have more time for each other and the children. And, though he does earn less, we actually live better."

(O)   "We often spoil dreams for other people by being too concerned with our own needs, or by lacking faith in a partner's vision," says Rockville, Md., counselor Michael Abrahams. "But a marriage cannot flourish if one partner changes and the other resists."

(P)   The late psychologist Sidney Jourard urged couples to "re-invent" their marriage from time to time. Many of us do that without realizing it. "I have been wed to the same man for thirty-three years," says Valerie Hartshorne, who runs a catering business in Blawenburg, N.J. "Yet he has had several different wives in that time—a bride, a friend, a lover, a colleague, a mother, a businesswoman. I wonder if he knows how our marriage has grown with each change in my role."

(Q)   *Deal promptly with minor problems.* No gardener worth his spade allows the first sign of blight to go unchecked. But many couples make the mistake of trying to ignore minor irritants. The resentment triggered can escalate over time.

(R)   The simplest way to smooth minor frictions is for both partners to use consideration and common sense. You can also try **trade-offs** ("I'll remember to put gas in the car if you'll stop leaving things all over the house") or reward systems ("If you fix that leaky faucet, I'll cook your favorite dinner").

(S)   Small annoyances take on significance when they are symptomatic of a bigger problem partners have been refusing to confront. Thus a wife who mildly protests when her husband watches TV sports all weekend may really be quite angry, yet unable to say what really troubles her: "Why don't you pay more attention to me?"

(T)   "Bringing the issue into the open may provoke a temporary crisis," says Neville Vines, a psychologist in Portland, Ore. "But if that crisis sparks frank talk, it helps a couple develop the skills and insights to deal with future conflict. Each time a couple overcome a problem, it strengthens their marriage—for they learn they *can* resolve differences."

(U)   *Give each other room.* Just as a gardener does not put plants too close together lest their roots choke one another, spouses must maintain some distance in their lives. There is a basic human need to have some part of your being that is *not* always shared. By being alone occasionally, your spouse's sense of self will grow—and so will yours.

(V)   At an exhibit of Chinese art, a man studied a large canvas and wondered aloud why the painter had drawn only one small bird on a single branch of a tree. "Because," said his wife, "had the artist filled up all the space, there would have been nowhere for the bird to fly." Like the bird, each of us needs room to spread our wings.

(W)   Being separate does not mean keeping a partner at arm's length. Giving each other room to grow can be as simple as having a private place or a time for private thoughts. Maryland teacher Susan White used to deluge her husband with conversation the moment he came home from work. Eventually he told her that after spending all day listening to problems at the office he needed some time alone. "Now when my husband comes in the door," Susan says, "I take a walk or work in the garden a bit, until he has time to unwind. Then he usually comes looking for me!"

(X)   *Plan for the future.* The rose vine that frames the porch railing or the tree that shades the patio would not be there today had not the gardener planned them years ago.

(Y)   "So it is with marriage," says Alan Loy McGinnis. "I know a couple who sit down together each New Year's Day and talk about what they want to be doing in three years. Discussing their plans gives this couple a sense of permanence."

(Z)   Looking *backward* from time to time is also a way to build for future growth. Therapists suggest that a couple **take stock of** their marriage annually by considering such questions as: Do we give and get enough emotional support? Is it easy for us to agree on decisions? Do we always reveal our true feelings? These questions can serve as a starting point for discussion of areas important to marital growth.

(AA)   *Acknowledge your commitment.* I recently asked a friend the secret of her success in growing exotic orchids. "There's no secret," she said. "You've just got to keep tending them. Otherwise they'll die."

(BB)   Much the same kind of commitment is essential for marriage. As one man puts it, "It is a promise that will always be there. We are not going to be happy all the time. That's when commitment counts most."

(CC)   Partners can define commitment in different ways. Sarah Piehl, a Brentwood, Calif., woman in her mid-30s, thinks of it as continuity: "When Joel and I were planting a garden for our new home," she says, "I looked at him, all grimy and sweaty, and thought how we were creating something we would always share. That garden is a symbol of our commitment. As long as it keeps growing, we do too."

by Norman M. Lobsenz

✦ About the Reading

1. How is this essay organized?

2. How many specific points did the author state regarding how to make a better marriage? What were the specific points?

3. Choose three specific points, and list all the examples Lobsenz provides for each.

4. Which special text highlighting did the author use to signal that a new, important point was being made?

5. What is the thesis statement of this essay?

6. Which of the specific points in this essay do you think is most important? Why? Where did the author place this point?

7. What are some other points that you think the author should have added to this essay?

8. How does Lobsenz make use of direct and indirect quotation in this essay?

9. Evaluate the author's conclusion. Was it effective? Why or why not?

What Do You Think?

This essay talks about what it takes to make a good marriage. Think of someone whom you know who has a particularly good marriage. Write about what makes that marriage good.

Reading Carefully

In this section, you will review some of the important reading skills you have learned up to this point. Thus far, you have focused on the importance of understanding the main idea. Although comprehending the main idea is always essential, it is often also important to pay close attention to the details that support the main idea, whether they can be found directly or indirectly (by inference). A few of these important reading elements and skills are reviewed here.

Techniques for Careful Reading

Identifying the Main Idea: Recognizing the general idea of a text, which explains the main point(s)

Finding the Supporting Details: Looking for the facts, examples, and so on, which further expand, explain, or describe the main idea

Guessing Meaning from Context: Determining the meaning of a word, using the words around it as clues

Making Inferences: Discerning a meaning that is not actually written in the text but is suggested or implied

Scanning: Moving your eyes quickly back and forth over text, in order to find a particular piece of information

---

 **Prereading Activity**

Many people like listening to music for personal enjoyment. In addition, the following essay shows that listening to music may have other benefits. Before you read, discuss the following questions with your classmates in small groups, and then review the highlighted vocabulary words.

1. What type (or types) of music do you enjoy listening to?

2. In what ways do you think that music can affect your mind?

3. Beyond personal enjoyment, what are some other possible benefits of listening to music?

❖ VOCABULARY WATCH

NOUNS	VERBS	ADJECTIVES
neurobiology	hum	substantial
IQ	resonate	intricate
neuron	lubricate	vibrating
genre		

Music Soothes the Savage Brain

(A) *Hmm, hmmmm-humm, humm.* That's the start of Mozart's *Sonata for Two Pianos in D Major* and, according to a new **neurobiology** study, if you **hum** along, you could be a couple of **IQ** points smarter by the time you finish this magazine. The study, published last week in the British science journal *Nature,* found that listening to Mozart could actually increase your intelligence, at least temporarily. Thirty-six college students listened to the sonata, a relaxation tape, and nothing, and then took three different IQ tests. The post-Mozart scores showed a **substantial** boost: an average of 119, as opposed to 111 for the relaxation tape and 110 for silence. Though the brain buzz seems to last only for 15 minutes, researchers say that exposing children to the music at an early age may have longer-lasting effects.

(B) What's the magic in Mozart's flute? One theory is that the **intricate** musical structures may **resonate** the brain's dense web, **lubricating** the flow of **neurons.** Gordon Shaw, a University of California, Irvine, physics professor involved in the research, says neural structure includes regular firing patterns that build along the surface of the brain like bridges. Mozart's musical architecture may evoke a sympathetic response from the brain the way that one **vibrating** piano string can set another humming.

(C) Shaw suspects that other music may have a similar effect, and he wants to take on **genres** like rock and roll and jazz. His guess is that Louis Armstrong and Axl Rose will fire up the intellect as well as the imagination. Both seem to move the hips.

by Joshua Cooper Ramo, *Newsweek*

Exercise 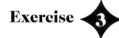 **3** **Reading Carefully.** Answer the following questions. Circle the letter that most accurately answers the question. You may refer to the preceding essay. This exercise incorporates all the reading elements and skills discussed previously.

1. The study has shown that listening to Mozart appears to
   a. increase your intelligence
   b. increase your IQ by at least two points
   c. increase your intelligence temporarily
   d. have a long-lasting effect on your intelligence

2. After listening to the Mozart sonata,
    a. students scored 119 on the IQ test
    b. students scored an average of 119 on the IQ test
    c. students scored 110 on the IQ test
    d. students scored two points higher on the IQ test

3. Which of the following is not *specifically* mentioned in the article?
    a. the effect of jazz on the brain
    b. the effect of classical music on the brain
    c. the effect of Mozart on the brain
    d. the effect of Axl Rose on the hips

4. The word *boost* in Paragraph A could be replaced by the word
    a. *drop*
    b. *similarity*
    c. *rise*
    d. *number*

5. Which of the following is *not* part of the theory to explain the effect of Mozart's music on the brain?
    a. Neuron firing patterns build along the surface of the brain.
    b. The intricate musical structures resonate in the brain's web.
    c. The way Mozart's music is constructed causes a reaction in the brain.
    d. The vibrating piano strings in Mozart's music cause the neurons to vibrate in the same way.

6. Which of the following can be inferred from this essay?
    a. Listening to relaxation tapes lowers the intelligence score on an IQ test.
    b. Further studies will be carried out to test this theory.
    c. Studying the life of Mozart will increase your intelligence.
    d. Louis Armstrong and Axl Rose also increase the intellect and the imagination.

Final Draft

Now that you have practiced using some new cohesive devices, you are ready to write the final draft of your essay. As you rewrite your essay, make sure that cohesive devices have been added to make specific points and examples clear to the reader. Answer the questions in the Final Draft Checklist to ensure that this will be your best draft.

Read to Write

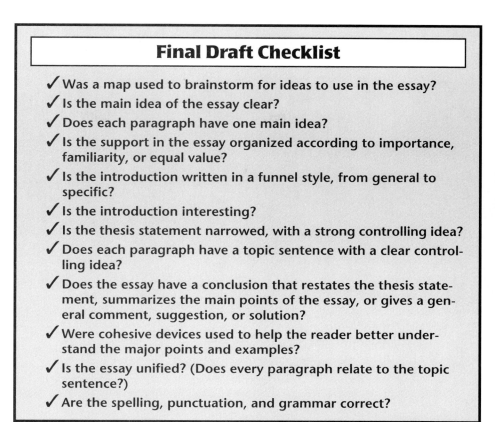

Final Draft Checklist

✓ Was a map used to brainstorm for ideas to use in the essay?

✓ Is the main idea of the essay clear?

✓ Does each paragraph have one main idea?

✓ Is the support in the essay organized according to importance, familiarity, or equal value?

✓ Is the introduction written in a funnel style, from general to specific?

✓ Is the introduction interesting?

✓ Is the thesis statement narrowed, with a strong controlling idea?

✓ Does each paragraph have a topic sentence with a clear controlling idea?

✓ Does the essay have a conclusion that restates the thesis statement, summarizes the main points of the essay, or gives a general comment, suggestion, or solution?

✓ Were cohesive devices used to help the reader better understand the major points and examples?

✓ Is the essay unified? (Does every paragraph relate to the topic sentence?)

✓ Are the spelling, punctuation, and grammar correct?

 # Going Further: Idea Generator

Activity **1** **Surveys.** Often, the information for expository writing comes from surveys or studies. Divide your class into groups of three students each. (Try to work with classmates from different cultures.) Choose a topic about which you are all interested (studying English, how Americans perceive other cultures, the best way to find a good place to live, etc.), and create a survey that you can give to people outside your class. Each of you should give your survey to at least three people. When you all have your results, get together and write an expository essay that will explain the results of your survey.

Activity **2** **Silly Statements.** This activity can be used to get you thinking about how to expose even the most obvious or silly statements. Begin with the following statement: "There are three good reasons why cows don't fly." Write an expository paragraph. Together, the class can suggest other statements. Try to write about a few. It will be good practice for you to come up with and explain supporting details.

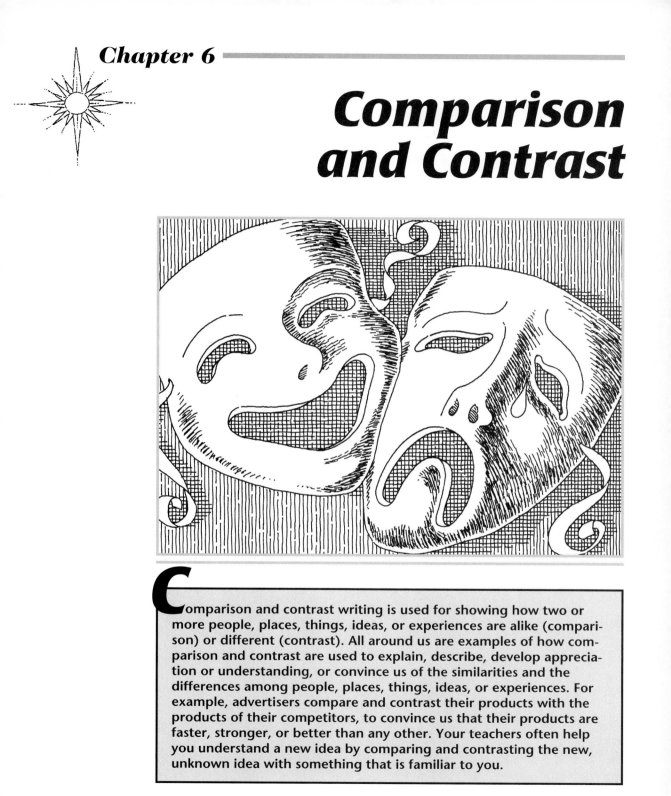

Chapter 6

Comparison and Contrast

Comparison and contrast writing is used for showing how two or more people, places, things, ideas, or experiences are alike (comparison) or different (contrast). All around us are examples of how comparison and contrast are used to explain, describe, develop appreciation or understanding, or convince us of the similarities and the differences among people, places, things, ideas, or experiences. For example, advertisers compare and contrast their products with the products of their competitors, to convince us that their products are faster, stronger, or better than any other. Your teachers often help you understand a new idea by comparing and contrasting the new, unknown idea with something that is familiar to you.

Reading and Writing Comparison and Contrast

In this section, you will read several essays that point out the important differences between two things. By making these differences clear, you can evaluate and understand more about the two items. As you read, think about *why* the author has compared the two items (the purpose) and why he or she has chosen the points of comparison and contrast included in the essay.

Activity ◆ **Identifying Similarities and Differences.**   Following are two pictures. You will notice that although the two are similar, each picture differs slightly from the other. With a partner, make a list of 10 similarities and 10 differences that you observe about the pictures.

Comparison and Contrast in the Real World

Artists and advertisers are not the only ones who recognize the value of using comparison and contrast to inform or to influence people. Writers often use comparison and contrast to explain or to clarify what may be difficult to understand (such as human nature), or to help readers choose among things. The first two of the following three essays use comparison and contrast to discuss societal issues. In the third essay, the author uses comparison and contrast as a means for persuading his audience.

✦ Prereading Activity

The following article explores how men and women are remembered differently after they die. Before you read, discuss the following questions in small groups, and then review the vocabulary words highlighted here.

1. How would you like to be remembered after you die?

2. Do you think people's actions affect how they are remembered after they die?

3. Do you think a person's *gender* (male or female) affects how he or she is remembered after death?

✦ VOCABULARY WATCH

NOUNS	VERBS	ADJECTIVES	EXPRESSIONS
obituary expertise	perceive	indefatigueable entrepreneurial surviving faithful gender-stereotyping	dearly departed rest in peace

Grave Injustice

Men and women who hold the same job while alive are often **perceived** very differently after they die. **Obituaries** published in four European newspapers during the years 1974, 1980, and 1986 described **dearly departed** male managers as intelligent, **indefatigueable,** experienced, and **entrepreneurial,** reports psychologist Erich Kirchler of the Johannes Kepler University in Linz, Austria, in the *European Journal of Social Psychology* (Vol. 22). Women, on the other hand, were remembered by **surviving** colleagues as adorable, **faithful,** and likeable in 1974 and 1980. By 1986, they were portrayed as committed and courageous—though still lacking in knowledge and **expertise.** If obituaries reflect the soul of **gender-stereotyping** society, today's working women may never **rest in peace.**

from *Psychology Today,* January/February 1994

Exercise ◆**1**◆ **Identifying and Expanding Descriptive Language.** In comparison and contrast writing, it is important to use a variety of descriptive words to make the comparisons and/or contrasts clear, and to add interest. To become more aware of the variety of words that can be used, make a list of the words used to describe both men and women in "Grave Injustice." Then write a synonym (word with a similar meaning) and an antonym (word with an opposite meaning) for each word. Use the charts below to write your words.

1. Identify the adjectives used to describe male managers in 1974, 1980, and 1986.

Words from passage	Synonyms	Antonyms
_____	_____	_____
_____	_____	_____
_____	_____	_____

2. Identify the adjectives used to describe women managers in 1974 and 1980.

Words from passage	Synonyms	Antonyms
_____	_____	_____
_____	_____	_____
_____	_____	_____

3. Identify the adjectives used to describe women managers by 1986.

Words from passage	Synonyms	Antonyms
_____	_____	_____
_____	_____	_____
_____	_____	_____

Like the preceding essay, the following essay is intended to describe some differences between men and women—particularly, in their communication styles. Notice that the authors of these essays do not try to explain *all* similarities or differences between men and women. Rather, they choose only those points that they feel represent important differences. In writing a comparison and contrast essay, it is important to remember to narrow your topic.

Prereading Activity

The following excerpt was taken from a chapter in a book written by a linguist who has studied the similarities and differences in the way men and women speak and how they use language. In this excerpt, from the book, *You Just Don't Understand: Women and Men in Conversation,* the author is discussing the question, Who talks more—men or women? Discuss with your classmates the following questions, and then review the vocabulary words highlighted here.

1. Who do you think talks more—men or women?

2. Are you more comfortable talking in a large group or with a few close friends? Why?

✦ VOCABULARY WATCH

NOUNS	VERBS	ADJECTIVES	EXPRESSIONS
rapport	capture	contradictory	reconciled by
status	negotiate	hierarchical	stand out
	impart		holding center stage

Rapport-Talk and Report-Talk

(A)   Who talks more, then, women or men? The seemingly **contradictory** evidence is **reconciled by** the difference between what I call *public* and *private speaking.* More men feel comfortable doing "public speaking," while more women feel comfortable doing "private" speaking. Another way of **capturing** these differences is by using the terms *report-talk* and *rapport-talk.*

(B)   For most women, the language of conversation is primarily a language of **rapport:** a way of establishing connections and **negotiating** relationships. Emphasis is placed on displaying similarities and matching experiences. From childhood, girls criticize peers who try to **stand out** or appear better than others. People feel their closest connections at home, or in settings where they *feel* at home—with one or a few people they feel close to and comfortable with—in other words, during private speaking. But even the most public situations can be approached like private speaking.

(C)   For most men, talk is primarily a means to preserve independence and negotiate and maintain **status** in a **hierarchical** social order. This is done by exhibiting knowledge and skill, and by **holding center stage** through verbal performance such as storytelling, joking, or im-

parting information. From childhood, men learn to use talking as a way to get and keep attention. So they are more comfortable speaking in larger groups made up of people they know less well—in the broadest sense, "pubic speaking." But even the most private situations can be approached like public speaking, more like giving a report than establishing rapport.

from *You Just Don't Understand:*
Women and Men in Conversation
by Deborah Tannen

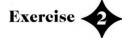

About the Reading

1. What is rapport-talk? How is it used? Who seems to use it most?

2. What is report-talk? How is it used? Who seems to use it most?

3. What is the *purpose* of this essay?

What Do You Think?

Do you agree with Tannen's theory about the differences between men's and women's speech? Why or why not?

Exercise 2

Comparing Major Points. Both of the preceding two essays discuss how men and women are viewed in society. In pairs or in small groups, make a list of all the ways in which each of the articles presents the differences between men and women.

Prereading Activity

In the following essay, a student uses comparison and contrast writing to explain the differences between private companies, those owned and run by private individuals or corporations, and public companies, those owned and run by the government. Before you read, discuss the following questions together as a class, then briefly review the vocabulary words highlighted on page 181.

1. Have you worked for a public company? If so, what were the benefits and the disadvantages?

2. Have you worked for a private company? What were the benefits and the disadvantages?

Read to Write

NOUNS	VERBS	ADJECTIVES	EXPRESSIONS
capability diligence productivity stability	impose	enhanced subtle	take risks

Public Companies vs. Private Companies

(A)   I had to study economics and have a few real-life experiences before I realized there are significant differences between private and public companies. There is no doubt that both types of companies are necessary to meet all the needs of a developed society. However, whatever the benefits for the general population may be, for a professional person, there are several differences that make working for a private company much better than working for a public one.

(B)   The first difference is the system of salaries and rewards. In a public company, after being hired, one's salary will be raised according to the number of years he or she has been in the company. In contrast, in a private company, the most important thing is what one can give in terms of returns to the company. According to this system, one's salary can be as big as one's **capability** and **diligence.** Also, specific rewards for achieving target goals can be distributed to the employees in a private company.

(C)   The second difference between the two systems is the possibility of professional growth. In a public company, everyone must follow a specific pattern of training, which is seldom changed. Also, management's expectations of the employees are most often beneath the employee's true capability. In contrast to this, in a private company, the competitive market **imposes** fast improvements in training programs, which bring enormous benefits to good professionals. Management's expectations of each employee's development and performance are demanding. In private companies, good professionals are challenged to look for new markets and are encouraged to develop a greater willingness to **take risks.** These attitudes bring such positive benefits as improved employee **productivity, enhanced** product quality, and increased customer satisfaction.

(D) The most important difference between the two systems is too **subtle** for the majority of workers to view as a benefit. In public companies, it is very common to have a degree of job **stability,** which gives the employees the feeling they don't need to worry about unemployment. The private company won't offer the promise of job security that a public job may, but with the higher risks of a private company also come higher rewards. In the end, as a result of living with the risk of unemployment, the best professionals in a private company receive personal advantages, in the form of bigger salaries, and of personal and professional victories.

(E) Both systems are very important to the society in general. However, from an individual point of view, for the motivated worker, one system is much better than the other. Undoubtedly, if a worker is interested in his or her own career and personal development, the best system is the private one.

by Rivadávia

About the Reading

1. What are the three differences that the author identifies between private and public companies?

2. According to Rivadávia, how is one's salary raised in a public company, in contrast to a private company?

3. How is professional growth in private and public companies different, according to the author?

4. What is the purpose of this essay? Who is the audience?

5. What is the thesis statement?

What Do You Think?

Compare your own work experiences in public or private companies with the author's conclusions in this essay.

Identifying Similarities and Differences

In order to write and understand comparison and contrast essays, you must first be able to identify the significant similarities and differences between the things you are discussing. In this section, you will practice identifying the significant similarities and differences authors use in describing or explaining a topic or concept.

In the following essay, a student from Japan compares and contrasts Japanese and American baths (how they are used, their purpose, etc.) in order to show the advantage of one over the other. Before you read the essay, discuss the following questions in small groups.

1. Often, when people go to live in a new culture, they miss things from their own native culture. What would you miss if you had to leave your country for a long period of time?

2. What did you think of when you first saw an American bathroom?

Japanese and American Baths

When people ask me what I miss most about my country, I first think about my family and the wonderful meals my mother used to cook for me. Then, I think about my bathtub. I know that may seem strange to someone who has never had a Japanese bath, but when I get homesick and stressed out from living in this new country and culture, I think about my bath.

Japanese and Americans use their bathtubs for different purposes, and as a result, their bathrooms are quite different. The American bathtub is used primarily to get one's body clean. Japanese people, on the other hand, like to use their bathtubs as a place for relaxation. A warm bath at the end of the day helps them to unwind and get rid of stress. When I take a bath, it usually lasts one hour or more, and I use that time to think.

Because of the different purposes of American and Japanese bathtubs, they are quite different physically. American bathtubs are long and shallow. They are made out of porcelain or fiberglass, and they come in many colors, but they are usually white. American baths are most often in the same room as the toilet, and there is usually a shower above the bathtub. A shower curtain pulls across the front of the tub so that water won't get on the floor while someone is showering. Japanese bathtubs are very deep and can be made from many different types of materials. Some are made from porcelain or fiberglass, just like American tubs. However, others are made from tile and wood. Unlike Americans, we wash ourselves off before we enter the bathtub. We stand outside of the tub when we do this and let the water we pour over ourselves run down a drain in the floor. A toilet would get wet if it were in the same room as the tub, so our toilets are always in a separate room. Further, because we don't have to worry about getting the floor wet, there is no shower curtain around the tub.

Sometimes Americans do like to use their tub to relax. It seems like they do this when they have extra time or have had a really bad day. When Americans take a bath they like to add lots of special soap, which often smells good and makes a lot of bubbles. Unlike Americans, most Japanese use their bathtubs to relax every night. However, Japanese never add bubbles to their baths. Rather, they sometimes add special powders, which have minerals in them that are good for the skin and make the bath seem like a natural hot spring.

Finally, when Americans take baths, they use a tub of clean water for every person. Maybe they do this because their bathtubs don't use a lot of water and to fill a tub is not too expensive. In contrast, filling a Japanese bath is very expensive. As a result, everyone in the family uses the same water.

Japanese and American baths are very different in the way they look and the ways they are used. Although both kinds of tubs serve their purpose, for me, it is difficult to really relax in an American bathtub. So when I think of the things that I really miss from home, I think about my Japanese bath.

by Masae

◆ About the Reading

1. What does the author feel are the most important differences between Japanese and American bathtubs?

2. What is this author's purpose for writing? Who is this author's intended audience?

3. Did the author convince you that one type of tub is better than the other? If not, what else could the author have done to convince you?

What Do You Think?

This essay illustrates one way that two different cultures relax. What are some of the common ways people relax in your culture?

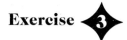

Exercise ◆**3**► **Identifying Similarities and Differences.** Practice identifying similarities and differences in "Japanese and American Baths" by putting a check in the appropriate boxes in the following table. Then, discuss why these similarities and differences were significant to the author, and which differences were most important to her.

	Japanese Baths	American Baths
are used primarily to get one's body clean.		
are used primarily as a place for relaxation.		
are made of fiberglass or porcelain.		
are used for relaxation.		
are often in the same room as the toilet.		
are very deep.		

◆**Prereading Activity** This article explores the differences and similarities in the emotions of envy and jealousy. Before you read the article, discuss the following questions in small groups.

1. Do you think there is a difference in word meaning between *envy* and *jealousy*? If so, what is it?

2. What things are you envious of or jealous about?

Envy vs. Jealousy: A Devastating Difference

Long lumped together by ordinary folks and scholars alike, envy and jealousy are not a single, formless, "super emotion." On the contrary, they are distinct, with different components, and are in fact elicited by completely different situations and in completely different settings.

According to Georgetown University psychologist W. Gerrod Parrott, Ph.D., envy occurs when a person lacks another person's superior quality, achievement, or possession, and desires it—or wishes that the other person lacked it.

Jealousy, by contrast, occurs in the context of a close relationship when a person fears losing an important other to a rival—in particular,

losing a relationship that is important to one's sense of self.

For all their distinctiveness, envy and jealousy sometimes occur together, Parrott reports in the *Journal of Personality and Social Psychology* (Vol. 64, No. 4). For instance, when a romantic partner gives attention to an attractive rival, a person may feel both jealous of that attention and envious of the rival for being so attractive. And since jealousy involves the loss of a personal relationship, it's usually more intense than envy.

from *Psychology Today*, January/February 1994

Envy versus Jealousy

Here's how envy and jealousy stack up:

Envy

- Feelings of inferiority
- Longing
- Resentment of circumstances
- Ill will towards envied person, often accompanied by guilt about these feelings
- Motivation to improve
- Desire to possess the attractive rival's qualities
- Disapproval of feelings

Jealousy

- Fear of loss
- Anxiety
- Suspicion or anger about betrayal
- Low self-esteem and sadness over loss
- Uncertainty and loneliness
- Fear of losing an important person to an attractive other
- Distrust

 **About the Reading**

1. What is the thesis statement in this essay? Underline it.
2. List five supporting details from the essay.
3. What is the purpose of this article? Who is the intended audience?
4. According to the article, what is the major difference between envy and jealousy?
5. When you become very envious or jealous, what do you do?

What Do You Think?

Think of a very strong emotion (love, fear, hate, joy, etc.). Write about some of the different situations that cause you to feel that emotion.

Exercise 4 **Determining Vocabulary Meaning from Context.** The words in the following exercise have been taken from the essay, "Envy vs. Jealousy." In the essay, it isn't possible to determine the meaning of all of the words from the context. In this exercise, the words have been written in a context that will help you discover their meaning more easily. Based on the context here and in the essay, try to write the meaning of each italicized word.

Example: Raj has a very poor sense of self. He never feels that he is as intelligent as his classmates, and he never thinks his work is as good as theirs.

<u>the image or feeling a person has about himself or herself</u>

1. Water is made of two basic *components*—hydrogen and oxygen.

2. Anna worked very hard in her English class all semester long. When she received an A for her final grade, she was happy and proud of her *achievement.*

_____

3. Tova loves her *possessions:* Her sports car, her condominium on the beach, and her beautiful designer clothes seem to be the most important things in her life.

_____

4. Unfortunately, some people show prejudice and stereotype others according to perceived social categories. For instance, they *lump together* all Asians—Japanese, Koreans, Chinese, and so forth.

_____

5. Although they seem the same, envy and jealousy are *distinct* emotions. Each has its own qualities, which makes each different from the other.

_____

6. My teacher tries to *elicit* creative responses from his students. He does this by asking creative questions.

_____

7. The soccer game was going to be very exciting because the two big *rivals* were playing against each other. The competition was going to be tough.

_____

Exercise 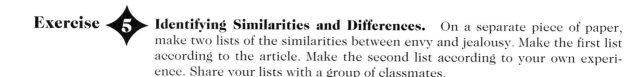 **5** **Identifying Similarities and Differences.** On a separate piece of paper, make two lists of the similarities between envy and jealousy. Make the first list according to the article. Make the second list according to your own experience. Share your lists with a group of classmates.

Getting Started: Brainstorming a Topic

In general, before writing any essay, it is important to think of many possible topics that you could write about. When you are ready to choose a topic, you should keep several things in mind:

1. Choose a topic that is interesting to you. If it is not interesting, you will not be motivated to write.

2. Choose a topic that you know about. You cannot write an accurate and informed essay if you are unfamiliar with your topic.

3. Choose a topic that your intended audience would be interested in investigating.

Exercise 6 Brainstorming Topics with a Partner. Practice generating some topics that you could use to write a comparison and contrast essay. There is a saying in English, "Two heads are better than one." This means that two people can come up with more ideas than can one person alone. Work with a partner to write down as many things as you can think of to compare and contrast.

Exercise 7 Brainstorming for Similarities and Differences. When writing comparison and contrast essays, it is important not only to brainstorm for a topic that is interesting to you and your intended audience, but also to choose a topic that has enough similarities or differences to accomplish your purpose. With your partner, choose two items from your list and write down all the similarities and all of the differences between the two items. Once these have been listed, you can select those similarities and differences that are most important and group them together into logical paragraphs. For example, following is an example of how you might brainstorm the article, "Envy vs. Jealousy."

List of similarities:	List of differences:	
Envy and Jealousy	**Envy vs. Jealousy**	
feeling	desire other's qualities	fear of losing someone or something
emotion	longing	
makes you feel bad	resentment	anxiety
can be felt in a romantic relationship	ill will	anger
overcoming is positive	guilt	suspicion
common feeling	want to improve	low self-esteem
natural feeling		sadness
sometimes have same definition		loneliness
often used as synonyms		

Exercise 8 Brainstorming the Topic for Your Essay. Now that you have practiced brainstorming the similarities and differences between two things, it is your turn to brainstorm for your own comparison and contrast essay. Choose a topic from the list you created with your partner, or choose a topic from the following list, "Ideas for Comparison and Contrast Writing." On a separate sheet of paper, write your topic at the top of the page. Fold the sheet in half. Write "Similarities" at the top of the left column, and write "Differences" at the

Read to Write

top of the of the right column. Next, write down all the similarities and differences you can think of between the two items you chose. Remember, while you brainstorm, you should not worry about whether you will use all of your brainstorming ideas. You can decide which ideas are best after you have finished brainstorming.

Ideas for Comparison and Contrast Writing

1. two products
2. members of your family
3. two friends
4. how you are today and how you were five or ten years ago
5. the food in the United States and the food in your native country
6. two famous leaders
7. two cars
8. two actresses and/or actors
9. your hometown and where you live now
10. two seasons
11. two jobs you have had

Essay Writing: First Draft

Now you are ready to write your first draft. Use the following checklist to help you get started. Then refer to it again after your draft is completed, to evaluate what you have written.

First Draft Checklist

✓ Was brainstorming used to develop a list of similarities and differences?

✓ Did you use the most interesting similarities and differences related to your topic?

✓ What is the purpose for comparing and contrasting the two items in the essay?

✓ Who is the intended audience for this essay?

Part Two

Developing Comparison and Contrast Essays

In Part One of this chapter, you learned how to identify similarities and differences in comparison and contrast writing. You also focused on brainstorming for ideas. In this section, you will work on how to organize comparison and contrast writing. You will also practice finding support within a text.

Organizational Style in Comparison and Contrast Writing

There are several ways that comparison and contrast writing can be organized. Two common methods are described here next.

Method 1: All A, All B. In this method, the thesis statement introduces the two subjects (**A** and **B**), which will be compared or contrasted. In the supporting paragraphs that follow, **A** is completely described first, followed by a complete description of **B**. The comparing and contrasting of the two subjects takes place in the minds of the readers as they draw inferences from the two separate descriptions. This style of organization is appropriate when writing about broad subjects, such as government, education, or emotions.

Look back at the essay "Envy vs. Jealousy," on page 185, which is organized in this way. Here is a diagram of the organization, where **A** is *envy* and **B** is *jealousy*.

Paragraph 1.   Introduction

Paragraph 2. | All A: Envy |

Paragraph 3. | All B: Jealousy |

Paragraph 4.   Conclusion

Method 2: AB/AB/AB. In this method, the topics are also introduced in the introduction and the thesis statement. However, unlike in the All A, All B method, each supporting paragraph discusses a different aspect of both subjects. Within each paragraph, details of comparison or contrast are limited to the particular focus of the paragraph. This method is an effective way to compare and contrast the finer details of two subjects.

Look back at the essay, "Japanese and American Baths" on page 183. Here is a diagram of its **AB/AB/AB** organization:

Paragraph 1.   Introduction:

Paragraph 2. | Purpose of bathtub: American/Japanese |

Paragraph 3. | Physical design of bathtub: American/Japanese |

Paragraph 4. | Ways to take a bath: American/Japanese |

Paragraph 5. | Bath water: American/Japanese |

Paragraph 6.   Conclusion

When you write a comparison and contrast essay, you will need to decide which method of organization will be the most effective way for you to present the information to your readers.

Whichever method you choose, it is important to give approximately equal treatment to each subject you are comparing and contrasting.

Exercise ◆**1** **Determining Method of Organization.** Look back at the other essays in this chapter, and determine which method is used in each. Choose one essay, and make a diagram of its organization. When you finish, work with a partner and compare your diagrams.

The following essay has two versions. The content is basically the same in each version, but it is organized two different ways. After you have read each version, discuss as a class which method of organization you think worked best for this particular topic.

◆ **Prereading Activity**   These essays were written together by two students who compare and contrast the activities surrounding the birth of a baby in their native countries of Taiwan and Mexico. Before you read, discuss the following questions with your classmates.

1. What are the traditions surrounding the birth of a baby in your country?

2. When the baby arrives, who takes care of it? Who takes care of the mother?

3. How is the baby's name selected?

The Birth of a Baby (1)

(A)   Every country has its own unique traditions surrounding important events. However, no matter what country you are in, the birth of a baby is always a great event. The countries of Taiwan and Mexico have similar activities associated with the celebration of a new baby, but they differ in the ways these activities are carried out.

(B)   Traditionally, both Taiwan and Mexico have parties to celebrate the birth of new babies. In Taiwan, the celebration takes place after the baby is born. In Mexico, on the other hand, the party is thrown before the baby is born. The people invited to these parties are also different, depending on the country. In Taiwan, entire families come to the parties; however, in Mexico, only the women gather together to have the party. No men are invited. The purpose of these parties in both countries is to give the family gifts that the new baby will need, such as bottles, clothing, diapers, and toys. In Taiwan, besides these gifts, the baby also receives money and gold things.

(C)   Because having a baby is not easy, the baby's grandmother often comes to help her daughter when the baby is born. While grandmothers in Taiwan arrive to help about a week before the baby is born, grandmothers in Mexico arrive just a day or two before the baby is due.

(D)   Finally, choosing a baby's name is very important because the name has a lot of meaning for the new child. The way that a name is chosen for the baby also differs in these countries. In Taiwan, the baby's name traditionally is chosen by the grandparents. In the past, Mexican babies' names were often chosen this way, too; however, now in Mexico, this rarely happens, and more often, parents choose names that they like for their babies.

(E)   Although the birth of a baby may be celebrated differently, a new life is precious in both of these countries. No matter where a baby is born, it is a cause for great celebration.

by Shu-Fang and Erika

The Birth of a Baby (2)

(A)   Every country has its own unique traditions surrounding important events. However, no matter what country you are in, the birth of a baby is a great event. The countries of Taiwan and Mexico have many similarities and differences in the way their people celebrate the special event of a baby's birth.

(B)   Special parties, help for the new mothers, and naming rituals are all important aspects of a baby's arrival in Mexico. Mexican women have parties for new babies before the baby is born; no men are invited. The purpose of these parties is to give the family gifts that the new baby will need. Guests bring such gifts as bottles, clothing, diapers, and toys. Also, before the baby is born, the baby's grandmother usually arrives early, maybe a day or two before the baby is due, to help her daughter. Finally, when the baby arrives, a name must be given. A baby's name is very important and often has a lot of meaning for the new child. In the past, Mexican babies' names were often chosen by the grandparents; however, now this rarely happens, and parents are free to choose a name that they like for their baby.

(C) Arrivals of babies are just as exciting in Taiwan as they are in Mexico. As in Mexico, people in Taiwan have parties for new babies. However, in Taiwan, the party takes place after the baby is born, and whole families come to the parties, not just women. Taiwanese guests give gifts similar to those given by guests in Mexico, but they also give additional gifts, such as money and gold things. As in Mexico, grandmothers come early to help their daughters, but in Taiwan, they usually come about one week early. Finally, in Taiwain as in Mexico, the baby's name is very important. Naming the baby is still often done traditionally, by the grandparents.

(D) Although the way a birth is celebrated is different in these countries, a new life is precious in both Taiwan and Mexico. No matter where a baby is born, it is a cause for great celebration.

About the Reading

1. Which method of organization was used in each essay? Which method do you think was more effective to deal with this topic? Why?

2. According to the two essays, which are the *similarities* between the birth of a baby in Taiwan and in Mexico? What are the *differences*?

3. Underline the topic sentences for each paragraph in the two essays.

What Do You Think?

Think of a major life event in your country (death, birth, marriage, etc.). Get together with a classmate from another country, and talk about how this event is dealt with in your different cultures. Make a list of the similarities and differences, then write a comparison and contrast essay describing the custom in both cultures.

Outlining

An *outline* is a list of the main points discussed in your essay. You can either make your outline before you write (after brainstorming), or you can do it after creating your first draft. Making an outline before you write may guide you in your organization during the process of writing. Making one after you write helps you check your organization. While making an outline is not always necessary, it can help you make sure your essay is unified and has plenty of support. As a reader, it is sometimes a good idea to outline the main points in a text you read, so that you can grasp the main ideas and supporting details. To give you an idea about the structure of an outline, "The Birth of a Baby" (1) is outlined here.

I.   Thesis statement: The countries of Taiwan and Mexico have similar activities associated with the celebration of a new baby, but they differ in the ways these activities are carried out.

II. Traditionally, both Taiwan and Mexico have parties to celebrate the birth of new babies.
   A. When parties take place
      1. Taiwan
      2. Mexico
   B. People invited to party
      1. Taiwan
      2. Mexico
   C. Gifts given at the party
      1. Taiwan
      2. Mexico

III. Because having a new baby is not easy, the baby's grandmother often comes to help her daughter when the baby is born.
   A. Taiwan
   B. Mexico

IV. Finally, choosing a baby's name is very important because the name has a lot of meaning for the new child.
   A. Taiwan
   B. Mexico

V.   Conclusion: Although the birth of a baby may be celebrated differently, a new life is precious in both of these countries.

Exercise  **2 Outlining.**   Following is the partial outline of the second version of "The Birth of a Baby." Fill in the missing information.

The Birth of a Baby (2)

I.   Thesis Statement: The countries of Taiwan and Mexico have many similarities and differences in the way their people celebrate the special event of a baby's birth.

II. Special parties, help for the new mothers, and naming rituals are all important aspects of a baby's arrival in Mexico.
   A. Special parties
      1. When parties take place
      2. _____
      3. _____

B. _____

    1. _____

C. Naming Rituals

    1. _____

    2. _____

III. _____

_____

A. _____

    1. _____

    2. _____

    3. Special gifts given

B. Grandmothers

    1. _____

C. _____

    1. _____

IV. Conclusion: Although the way a birth is celebrated is different in these countries, a new life is precious in both Taiwan and Mexico.

Exercise  **Outlining Your Essay.** Make an outline of the first draft of your comparison and contrast essay.

How Examples Are Used to Support the Thesis Statement

The outline that you just made is only the frame of your essay. Support, given in the form of details and examples, makes your essay complete. Support is also essential for illustrating the controlling idea found in your thesis statement. The supporting paragraphs contain the main information that is meant to convince the reader of the point made in your thesis statement.

Prereading Activity

The following is a comparison and contrast essay about two different schools, which at first seem similar, but are actually quite different. The essay is an excellent example of clear organization, with many supporting examples. Before you read, however, discuss the following questions in small groups, and then review the vocabulary words highlighted here.

1. What do you think makes high school education successful?

2. How can parents best help their children succeed at school?

3. What role should teachers have in the discipline of high school students?

◇ VOCABULARY WATCH

NOUNS	VERBS	ADJECTIVES	EXPRESSIONS
graffiti	exude	parochial	have input in
subsidy	chaperon	infinitesimal	have a stake in
curriculum	glean	accelerated	
valedictorian	resign	obnoxious	
quest	buttress	headstrong	
sinew	oblige	bizarre	
	proselytize	extracurricular	
	vie	rigorous	
		trendy	

Tale of Two Schools

Two schools—one public and the other parochial—stand just four blocks apart in the crime-ridden St. Louis neighborhood of Walnut Park. Both boast dedi-
5 cated, no-non sense principals and inte-grated faculties. Both student bodies are 100 percent black.

At Northwest High, the public school, I found no litter or **graffiti,** heard no holler-
10 ing in the halls. The youngsters rushing up and down the long corridors seemed in-tent only on pursuing their studies.

At Cardinal Ritter College Prep, cruci-fixes and religious portraits adorned the
15 walls, and all the students wore uniforms. In other respects, its atmosphere was exactly the same as Northwest's: no distractions, a low noise level and a seriousness of purpose evident on the kids' faces.

20 Yet when it comes to results, the two schools are quite different. At Northwest, the average daily attendance rate is 77 per-cent, and over a four-year period an estimated 45 percent of its students drop out. Of the 58
25 seniors who graduated last May, only 19 plan-ned to attend college this year. Northwest's staff numbers 100, its annual budget is $3.7 million, and its cost per student is $7,800.

At Ritter, daily attendance averages 97
30 percent. Juniors and seniors scored nearly 75 points higher on their SATs than North-west students. The dropout rate is **infini-tesimal.** And of the 55 seniors who re-ceived diplomas in May, *all* went on to
35 college. Twenty-five even won academic scholarships. Ritter employs a full-time staff of just 31, its budget is $924,042, and its cost per student is $3,409.

Read to Write

How could the public school be achieving less while spending so much more?

Northwest and Ritter may seem similar, but five important differences leaped out once I dug into what goes on at the two schools.

1. *Parents who get involved.* Last November 19, a concerned grandmother came to Northwest to address the topic "Parents: What You Can Do About Drug Abuse." There were 14 people in the audience.

One morning last spring, Marquita Norman, a guidance counselor at Northwest, telephoned the home of a 15-year-old girl who had missed three weeks of school. The mother said she would bring her daughter in the next day. Neither showed up.

Northwest Principal Carl C. Landis, a former math teacher, is an exceedingly polite man whose calm voice **exudes** authority. Yet anguish creases his brow when he discusses his efforts to involve parents with their school. "If we get 15—of 500—to a parents' meeting," he says, "then we have *really* been successful."

At Ritter, parents run concession stands at games, work as tutors, **chaperon** field trips, paint hallways, repair bleachers, volunteer time in the library. They **have** a strong **input in** preparing the school handbook and determining the dress code. Principal Carmele U. Hall tells parents, "You're going to be involved. If not, maybe your children shouldn't be here." Last spring so many parents attended the induction of new Honor Society members that Hall ran out of chairs.

One reason Ritter's parents participate is that they feel they **have a** financial **stake in** the school's success. Because of a $250,000 church **subsidy** and an additional $150,000 **gleaned** through fund raising, no parent need pay the full $3,409 it costs to educate each child. But the average family still must come up with at least $2,000 per student. For low-income parents, that represents a real sacrifice.

Delores Green, a 36-year-old single mother of three, earns just $13,000 a year. Yet she sends all three of her daughters to Catholic schools, paying $2,085 tuition to Ritter for April, 15, the oldest. The total bill exceeds $5,000. "It's very painful," she says. "There's a lot we have to do without. But I'm determined. If my dad did it with 11 children, I can do it with three."

Green works a split shift at her job, arriving at 5:30 each morning, leaving three hours later and returning in late afternoon to toil through the dinner hour. Her parents take care of the girls when she is gone. On an average day, she is free between 9 A.M. and 3 P.M., and she spends that time at her daughters' schools. "When it comes to education," she explains, "I don't want them to say I didn't try."

2. *High expectations.* Northwest opened its doors in 1964 as part of a district-wide program to place gifted students on an **accelerated** academic track toward college. The district's program has long since ceased, however, and the school's college-prep **curriculum** has been "de-emphasized."

Still, traces of excellence remain. Northwest students took 12 top prizes—more than any other general school—in the Greater St. Louis Science Fair competition this year. French teacher Bob Bullwinkel raises enough funds to send at least one of his charges on a month-long trip to France or Spain each year. Leander Spearman, the 1991 **valedictorian,** was the most outstanding graduate in years—president of Northwest's National Honor Society, star of the debate team, math whiz and basketball captain. He is now attending Tuskegee University in Alabama. Seniors Dan Yelle McBride and Natasha Maiden both hope to become doctors someday.

Yet despite these accomplishments and dreams, enrollment has fallen below 500, and fewer than half the students are enrolled in the college-prep curriculum. "Students are not as motivated as they were a few years back, and I can't tell why," Principal Landis says. "Many don't do their homework or even bring their books to class." Sometimes it's hard to get *them* to class. During my visit to Northwest, 23 percent of the students were absent.

Until 1979, Ritter was known as Laboure, a financially struggling archdiocesan school for girls. Then Sister Mary Ann Eckhoff (now Superintendent of Education for the St. Louis archdiocese) gathered a task force of parents. She asked them: "What kind of school would you send your kids to?"

"We need something we can be proud of," task-force members agreed, "an institution dedicated to academic excellence."

Going co-ed wasn't difficult. Nor was stiffening the curriculum. And after the U.S. Department of Education cited Ritter as "exemplary" in 1984, the school was on its way. But the real key to Ritter's success has been the development and constant repetition of the school's goal: to enroll low-income kids who often test below grade level and then diligently prepare them for college. "There's a firm commitment to that mission," says teacher Leon Henderson. "It has never been debated."

Few students had more trouble making the adjustment to Ritter than Andrew "Smokey" Evans. Until 1988, he had attended a suburban public school where teachers made no demands and coaches seemed interested only in his ability to play basketball. At 15, he'd never been told to study, never been held accountable for his actions.

Sensing that Smokey was lost, William J. Vollmar, an Anheuser-Busch Co. manager, a volunteer basketball referee in the Catholic Youth Organization and a legal foster parent, invited Smokey to live with him. He then offered to pay Smokey's tuition if he attended Ritter. Smokey agreed, but his troubled emotional life was evident at school. His grade point average was a depressing 1.7, and his attitude was **obnoxious.**

"He had no respect for education," says student-services director Preston Thomas. "He was a street kid, very aggressive and **headstrong.** He would talk to me, but he wouldn't *listen.* We expect all our students to achieve, but he just wanted to play basketball."

At the end of his first semester, Smokey told Vollmar, "I'm not going back. It ain't for me. All we do is schoolwork."

Vollmar held firm: "Without an education, you're nobody. Stay at Ritter, and you can succeed."

Slowly, Smokey began to apply himself. He asked for and received extra tutoring. He got off academic probation, played varsity basketball and even made the honor roll. But what instructors remember most is his leadership.

A new Spanish teacher was absent frequently, and his sophomores were learning little. One day Leon Henderson walked into the school office and saw Smokey typing a lesson plan. Later, Henderson poked his head into the class, and Smokey was drilling them on vocabulary. "That moment," says Henderson, "showed me that everything we're doing is really paying off."

3. *Authority to make decisions.* A few years ago, Northwest's Landis realized he had to do something about a veteran custodian whose behavior was becoming increasingly **bizarre.** One day he padlocked the building where the cheerleaders practiced. They had to summon help by phone.

But Landis's hands were tied. In order to dismiss an employee of the St. Louis public schools, a principal must submit a series of negative fitness reports. If the

staffer protests, the process can take
220 years.

The custodian maintained his innocence, and Landis had to keep him on staff. Eventually, Landis won his fight, but the incident underlined the limits of his authority. At
225 Northwest, the principal can't select or dismiss members of his staff. He can't even determine the extent of discipline that can be imposed on an unruly student. School-system bureaucrats have final say on his budget,
230 choice of textbooks and school equipment. "Those decisions are made downtown," Landis concedes. "I have to go along."

At Ritter earlier this year, Principal Hall had two teachers who weren't making the
235 grade. "I don't want you here for the next semester," she told the first. "I'm asking you to **resign.**" The woman objected, but when she saw that Hall would not back down, she agreed to leave.
240 The second teacher was more difficult because he had tenure. Patiently, Hall explained that he wasn't meeting expectations, produced her evidence, and then **buttressed** her case by encouraging par-
245 ents to tell him how unhappy they were with his performance. He, too, got the message and resigned.

Hall sought no one's approval for these decisions. She had authority to act on her
250 own. That's a key difference between public and parochial schools. Though Hall often consults with teachers and parents as well as with Sister Mary Ann Eckhoff, *she* has the final say on admissions, curriculum, budget,
255 and the hiring and firing of staff.

There are limits, of course, to Hall's authority. She'd like to offer more electives and modernize her chemistry labs, but she can't afford that. Then there's the problem
260 of salaries. The teachers at Ritter earn an average $21,800—26 percent below the comparable figure at Northwest. Hall hopes to close the gap, but few leave Ritter because of low pay. There are six applica-
265 tions for every vacancy.

4. *An emphasis on basics.* Northwest students need four years of English, three years of math, science and social studies, and at least one year of a foreign language
270 to graduate. No one with less than a C average can participate in sports or **extracurricular** activities.

That's as it should be. But not all the school's courses are **rigorous.** Some of the
275 more popular last year were "Housing and Interior Design," "Personal and Family Relations" and "Sports," in which students learn the basic rules of four different sports.

Because they can't afford such **trendy**
280 nonessentials, schools like Ritter stress basics. There are far fewer electives for students to choose, and some of them, like pre-calculus, are hardly an easy ride. Yet more than 50 percent of Ritter's seniors
285 enroll in that demanding course.

In their **quest** to keep religion out of the classroom, America's public schools have ignored the spiritual **sinews** that make any society strong. Catholic schools have not.
290 At Ritter, every morning begins with a prayer, religion fills one of seven class periods each day, and every student is **obliged** to take part in religious services. But because 68 percent of the students are not Catholic,
295 the school makes no attempt to **proselytize.** Instead, it stresses the importance of faith in a Supreme Being.

The values these youngsters learn in the classroom motivate what they do when
300 they're not in school. Ritter requires each student to perform 20 hours of community service each year. Working as a volunteer at Jewish Hospital, 1991 graduate Katrina Hubbard logged over 80 hours. Marion Bal-
305 ton answered phones and typed letters at Blessed Sacrament Church.

Roschelle Williams was a volunteer usher at the St. Louis Black Repertory The-

ater. Then there was Courtney Benson, who
310 organized a youth rally against gangs, visited juvenile-detention centers and talked to youngsters about the dangers of drugs.

These "student ambassadors" help Ritter stand out "as a beacon in our commu-
315 nity," and Hall is proud of them. "We stress values, and we're really involved in the community," she says. "But all we're really doing is extending what most of our parents have already started at home."

320 5. *Maintaining discipline.* The neighborhood around Northwest is awash in drugs, rival gangs **vie** to recruit new members, and police radios crackle with reports of knifings and shootings. To keep students
325 safe, Northwest employs four security guards and an assistant principal whose duties include maintaining discipline.

During the 1989–90 school year, Northwest suspended 24 students—more than
330 any other high school in the city—for infractions including assault and possession of weapons or drugs.

At Ritter one morning last May, three parents assembled in Carmele Hall's office.
335 Their daughters had cut classes a few days earlier, and now they listened as the soft-spoken principal explained what would happen next.

"There are rules here, and there are
340 consequences," she said. "Your kids will have detention. They'll be here at 7 A.M. to write essays about appropriate behavior. On Saturdays they'll clean the building or rake the leaves."

345 That seems to be the extent of the "discipline" problem at Ritter. The school employs no security guards or head honchos for discipline, and there were no suspensions for bad behavior last year. "You
350 don't have violence or drugs at Ritter," Sister Mary Ann Eckhoff insists. "The kids themselves control that."

"The seniors set the tone," student-services director Thomas adds, "they've learned
355 to respect themselves and to respect others, and our freshman pick up on that. Every year they get stronger in their beliefs."

As we walk along the main corridor, Thomas points to the framed photographs
360 of recent graduates on the wall. "Look at these people," he says: "Police officer, engineer, accountant, Naval Academy graduate. They're people of *accomplishment.*"

Because they had finished all their
365 classes, Ritter's seniors were excused from school in the week leading up to graduation last May. Yet when I stopped by that week, I found Smokey Evans sitting with Carmele Hall in the library, talking to parents consid-
370 ering sending their kids to Ritter.

Smokey had played on Ritter's state-championship basketball team, finished the year with a sparkling 3.8 grade point average and won a scholarship to Arkansas
375 State University.

"There are support systems here," Smokey began. "People who chastised me when I needed it, people who encouraged me when I was down, people I knew I
380 could always depend on." Smokey paused. "This school gave me a sense of who I am."

by Trevor Armbrister

About the Reading

1. What is the method of organization of this essay?
2. What are the attitudes of each of the school's principals?
3. What are the main problems at Northwest High School?
4. Why do you think that parents are so dedicated at Cardinal Ritter College Prep?

Read to Write

5. What is the author's purpose in comparing the two schools?

6. What accounts for the big difference in daily attendance between the two schools? What are some of the other major differences and the reasons for them?

7. In your own words, compare the discipline problems in the two schools.

8. How does the author use quoted speech in this essay? How does it make the essay different from using reported speech?

What Do You Think?

What is the school system like in your country? How does it compare with the schools described in the essay?

Exercise 4

Finding Support from the Text. The essay you just read is rich in support. In the seventh paragraph, the author gives his thesis statement, "Northwest and Ritter may seem similar, but five important differences leaped out once I dug into what goes on at the two schools." The author gives the five reasons, providing ample support in the form of facts and actual experiences for each one. Use your scanning skills to find the specific details that are used to support the thesis statement. For each of the following points, list what you think are the three most impressive examples that the author uses to support his point.

1. Parents who get involved
   a. _____
   b. _____
   c. _____

2. High expectations
   a. _____
   b. _____
   c. _____

3. Authority to make decision
   a. _____
   b. _____
   c. _____

4. An emphasis on basics
   a. _____
   b. _____
   c. _____

5. Maintaining discipline
   a. _____
   b. _____
   c. _____

Exercise ◆**5** **Identifying Idiomatic Expressions.** Armbrister's essay contains many idiomatic expressions. Use your scanning skills to locate the following expressions, then discuss them with a classmate, and write a definition for each. Be prepared to share your ideas with the whole class.

no-nonsense	dug in	creases his brow
concession stand	split shift	math whiz
co-ed	have one's hands tied	make the grade
back down	have an easy ride	head honcho

Exercise ◆**6** **Adding Support.** Now, read through your own essay. Add support where necessary, by way of either factual (objective) or personal (subjective) examples.

Now Revise: Second Draft

Organize your first draft, using one of the organizational styles you learned about in Part Two. Use your outline to help you. Then use the Second Draft Checklist to evaluate and make changes to your essay.

When you have finished your second draft, exchange papers with a classmate. Read and discuss each other's essays. Make suggestions for additional changes that will improve the essays.

Second Draft Checklist

✓ Was brainstorming used to develop a list of similarities and differences?

✓ Were the topic's most interesting similarities and differences used?

✓ What is the purpose for comparing and contrasting the two items in the essay?

✓ Who is the intended audience for this essay?

✓ Is the essay organized in one of the styles presented in this chapter?

✓ Was an outline of the essay created to check its organization?

✓ Has enough strong support been provided in the supporting paragraphs?

✓ Does each paragraph have one main idea?

✓ Does each paragraph have a topic sentence?

Part Three

Refining and Reviewing

In this section, you will focus on two things: (1) cohesive devices used in comparison and contrast writing, and (2) paragraph unity.

Cohesive Devices: Comparison and Contrast Constructions

In *comparison constructions*, one thing is compared with another, and the similar characteristics are emphasized. However, *contrast constructions* emphasize differences. They signal to the reader that the ideas connected by the construction differ in some way.

Comparison Constructions. The following chart shows some comparison constructions and how they can be used in different sentences.

Cohesive Devices: Comparison Constructions		
Uses	**Cohesive Devices**	**Examples**
Before a noun followed with *and*	*both . . . and*	*Both* the bus *and* the subway have many stops around the city.
In a verb phrase	*is comparable to*	The telephone *is comparable to* television; they are both popular forms of communication.
	is the same . . . as	His bag *is the same* color *as* mine. They are both bright red.
	is similar to	*His* jacket *is similar to* mine. We both have black leather motorcycle jackets.
Before a noun	*like*	*Like* whales, fish need water to survive.
Before adjectives	*as . . . as*	Isabel is *as* intelligent *as* Tomoe. They both get straight A's.
To introduce an independent phrase	*similarly*	My whole family gets together for Thanksgiving dinner. *Similarly,* we get together at Christmas for dinner.

Exercise  **1**   **Identifying Comparison Constructions.**   Look back at "Birth of a Baby," on page 191, and "Public Companies vs. Private Companies," on page 181. Scan the essays and underline the comparison constructions you find. Compare your findings with those of a partner.

Exercise **2**   **Using Comparison Constructions.**   Using comparison constructions can help your reader see the relationship between the things you are comparing. Rewrite the following pairs of sentences. Use comparison constructions to combine the sentences and clarify the relationship between the items. (The comparison constructions are shown in parentheses.)

Example: <u>Math is a difficult subject for me. Chemistry is a difficult subject</u>

<u>for me. (like)</u>

<u>Like math, chemistry is a difficult subject for me.</u>

1. My sister is attending a university. My brother is attending a university. (Both)

_____

2. Meechat's test score was 95. Genisette's test score was 95. (is . . . same as . . .)

_____

3. It rains a lot in Brazil. It rains a lot in Taiwan. (is similar to)

_____

4. Food from Korea is very spicy. Food from Mexico is extremely spicy. (is comparable to)

_____

5. Omar reads 225 words per minute. Jonnice reads 225 words per minute) (as . . . as)

_____

6. Cantaloupe is a melon. Honeydew is a melon. (like)

_____

Contrast Constructions. Like comparison constructions, contrast constructions can be used in various ways in a sentence. Some act as verb phrases, some act as only a part of a phrase, others become complete sentences, and some come only before a noun. The following chart shows some examples.

Cohesive Devices: Contrast Constructions

Uses	Cohesive Devices	Examples
In a verb phrase	*contrast(s) with*	The art of Michelangelo *contrasts with* the work of da Vinci.
	differ(s) from	My ideas about romatic movies *differ from* Raul's.
	is different from	Soccer *is different from* American football.
As part of a phrase	*although* *even though*	*Although (even though)* he had good grades, he didn't win a scholarship. I think basketball is boring, *whereas* Raul feels it is exciting. *While* United States, soccer is popular in many other countries around the world.
football is popular in the	*whereas* *while*	
To introduce an independent phrase	*however*	I love ice cream; *however,* I don't like to eat it in cold weather.
	on the other hand	Mangos are sweet. Lemons, *on the other hand,* are sour.
	on the contrary	Some people believe that airplanes are more dangerous than cars. *On the contrary,* airplanes are safer than cars.
	in contrast	Americans usually eat a large breakfast. *In contrast,* Europeans usually eat a light breakfast.
Before a noun	*unlike*	*Unlike* fish, dogs can be noisy pets.
	contrary to	*Contrary to* what I heard, John is quite a gentleman.
	in contrast to	*In contrast to* Canada, Mexico is usually warm, even in winter.

Note: Each contrast construction has a slightly different meaning, so it is not always possible to use a particular word or phrase in place of another word or phrase in the same category. For example, *however* can be used instead of *in contrast* in the following example, but *although* cannot be used:

A biography is the true story of someone's life. A tall tale, *in contrast (however)*, is not true.

♦ **Prereading Activity**

The following essay shows how contrast constructions can be used to help make differences more clear. As you read the essay, look for constructions such as those listed in the previous chart.

One of the areas in which customs may differ greatly from culture to culture is in the practice of dating. In small groups, discuss the following questions before you read the essay.

1. What are the dating customs of your culture?
2. Are the unstated rules for dating different for women and men in your culture?
3. Have you ever dated someone from another culture? If so, what was it like?
4. Have you ever lived in a country where the dating customs are very different from those in your home country? If so, in what ways are they different?

Dating Customs

(A)   Dating is a very important custom to people all over the world since it can lead to beautiful friendships and sometimes to marriage. Some form of dating is found in all cultures; however, dating customs vary from country to country. Since I have been in the United States, I have noticed differences between dating customs in my country, Mexico, and the United States. The greatest differences seem to be how many men a woman can date at one time, who pays for a date, and who asks for the date.

(B)   A girl's freedom in dating is one of the main differences I see between the two countries. For example, the girls I have met in the United States can have many male friends. They can even date a different boy every night. In Mexico, however, that kind of freedom is very uncommon. Mexico is much more traditional in that dating is very formal and serious. A girl can go out with only one guy, and usually he must be her steady boyfriend in order to date her.

(C)   From what I have observed, the person in charge of the date in Mexico also differs from the one in the United States. For instance, although in the United States, the boy usually pays for the date, the girl can also pay if she wants to. Unlike American customs of dating, in Mexico the boy always pays. In fact, in Mexico if the girl wants to pay, it is very insulting to the boy and he will not let her.

(D)   The main difference between the two countries' dating customs is the difference in who asks for the date in the first place. Even though in the United States it's okay for girls to ask guys out, this is very unusual in Mexico. The boy wants to be the one with the responsibility.

(E)   These are just some of the general differences I have noticed between dating in the United States and dating in Mexico. I think there are differences because we have distinct attitudes and expectations in the two countries. These few dating custom differences remind us that it is very interesting and important to know about the customs from other cultures, especially as more and more cultures come in contact with each other.

by Alina

Exercise  **Using Contrast Constructions.** The following sentences, taken from Alina's essay, all use contrast words. Try using different contrast constructions by substituting a construction you find from the same category in the preceding table, "Contrast Constructions." Use the following example as a guide.

Example: <u>From what I have observed, the person in charge of the date in</u>

<u>Mexico also differs from the one in the United States.</u>

<u>From what I have observed, the person in charge of the date in</u>

<u>Mexico also is different from the one in the United States.</u>

1. In Mexico, *however,* that kind of freedom is very uncommon.

    _____

    _____

2. For instance, *although* in the United States the boy usually pays for the date, the girl can also pay if she wants to.

    _____

    _____

3. *Unlike* American customs of dating, in Mexico the boy always pays.

    _____

    _____

4. *Even though* in the United States it's okay for girls to ask guys out, this is very unusual in Mexico.

    _____

    _____

Exercise 4 ◆ **Practicing the Use of Contrast Constructions.** Now try using contrast constructions on your own. In each of the following exercises, two ideas are contrasted. Make the contrast more clear by adding a contrast word or phrase. Although many of the sentences could be combined with the same contrast construction, try using a different one each time. Your writing may become boring if you always use the same constructions. The first pair of sentences has been combined using the word *while,* but they also could have been combined using *but, on the other hand,* or *however.*

Example: My favorite sport is baseball. My sister prefers tennis.

My favorite sport is baseball, while my sister prefers tennis.

1. Olivio is very outgoing. Ana is quite shy.

_____

2. This dress is beautiful. It's not my size.

_____

3. School can be demanding. It can also be very rewarding.

_____

4. Raymundo hates dried squid. Yuko likes it.

_____

5. My blue suit must be dry cleaned. My gray pants can be machine washed.

_____

6. Orange juice is refreshing. Hot tea is relaxing.

_____

7. Canada is one of the largest countries in the world. Laos is one of the smallest countries in the world.

_____

8. Big cities often have a lot of violence. Small cities often don't have a lot of violence.

_____

9. Julio learns foreign languages easily. Math is a difficult subject for him.

_____

Unity within a Paragraph

Chapter 1 of this book highlighted the importance of unity within a paragraph. As in other forms of writing, when writing a comparison and contrast essay, it is important to make sure that the essay as a whole is unified. That is, all the details in each paragraph should help explain the controlling idea.

If any of the ideas in the paragraph don't help explain the main idea, the reader may become confused. For example, the controlling idea of the following paragraph is the benefits of a low-fat diet. The third sentence, however, does not help explain the controlling idea, so it doesn't belong in this paragraph.

Recent studies have shown that a low-fat diet can help prevent heart attacks. People who do not eat foods that are high in fat, such as ice cream, beef, and potato chips, generally live longer than those who eat a lot of these foods. Ice cream is delicious. Not only will avoiding high-fat food lead to a longer life, but it will also help the body feel better.

When all the details are related to the controlling idea in a paragraph, that paragraph is *unified,* making it clear and easy to understand. As a reader you can expect that every sentence within a paragraph will in some way expand, explain, or describe the controlling idea of the topic sentence.

Exercise 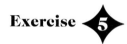 **Unifying Paragraphs.** In each of the following paragraphs, one sentence doesn't belong. First, find the topic sentence (or controlling idea) and underline it. Then, find the sentence that doesn't belong, and cross it out to make a unified paragraph.

1. There are many differences between taking the subway and taking a bus. In the summer, a bus can be hot and stuffy, while the air-conditioned subway is cool and comfortable. The subway also gives a much smoother ride than a bus does. Both have stops in several convenient locations around the city. Perhaps the most important difference is that the subway usually gets its passengers to their stops much more quickly than a bus does.

2. Our family's celebration of Christmas is very similar to our celebration of Thanksgiving. We only get two days of vacation from school for Thanksgiving, whereas we get at least two weeks of vacation for Christmas. On both holidays, we get together for a big dinner. We enjoy a warm fire and soft lights on both days, as we play games and talk. My father stays home from work on Christmas day, as well as on Thanksgiving day, and both days are relaxed and peaceful.

3. The invention of television has helped to change the way people in different countries think about each other. Through the television, we can easily see how other cultures and other races live. We see how others earn a living, how they spend their free time, and how they raise their families. Because we are able to see more about other people through the television, we are better able to understand people who differ from us. The telephone has also been very helpful in expanding our views of others.

4. Though many people think that whales are just like fish, they are actually very different. A whale is a mammal and, like other mammals, it cannot

stay under water all the time. Fish, on the other hand, cannot survive above water for long; they need to stay under water as much as possible. Both fish and whales have similar types of skin that can stand being in water for long periods of time. Fish and whales also differ in the way that their babies are born. A female fish lays her eggs and then waits for them to hatch. A female whale, on the other hand, carries her egg inside, and the baby grows within its mother's body until it is born.

5. My mother's cheesecake is more delicious than any other cheesecake I have ever tasted. Other cheesecakes can be hard on the outside and lumpy on the inside, but my mother's is always smooth and creamy. Her cinnamon rolls are also wonderful. Whereas some cheesecakes are too tart, Mom's is just right—not too sweet but not too sour. Unlike some frozen cheesecakes, my mother's cheesecake doesn't have any artificial ingredients. Real cream cheese and sour cream make my mother's cheesecake the best in the world!

The next essay, "On Friendship," compares and contrasts how four different cultures view the idea of friendship. As you read, try to be aware of some of the things you have learned in this chapter: How is this essay organized? Do the authors make good use of comparison and contrast constructions? Are the paragraphs focused on one controlling idea, and are they unified?

◆ **Prereading Activity**

In the following essay, two anthropologists explore how different cultures view the meaning of friendship. Before you read this essay, discuss the following questions in small groups, and then review the vocabulary words highlighted here.

1. What is your definition of *friendship*?

2. Can a person have several different types of friendships?

3. Have you made friends with someone from another culture who has a different interpretation of friendship? What was your experience?

◆ **VOCABULARY WATCH**

NOUNS	VERBS	ADJECTIVES	ADVERBS	EXPRESSIONS
landmark	constitute	particularized	abroad	surface behavior
temperament	assume	keen	articulately	draws out
compatibility	heighten	compartmentalized	irrevocably	taken into account
wits		enjoined	tentatively	give-and-take
		contrapuntal		

On Friendship

(A)   Few Americans stay put for a lifetime. We move from town to city to suburb, from high school to college in a different state, from a job in one region to a better job elsewhere, from the home where we raise our children to the home where we plan to live in retirement. With each move we are forever making new friends, who become part of our new life at that time.

(B)   For many of us the summer is a special time for forming new friendships. Today millions of Americans vacation **abroad** and they go not only to see new sights but also—in those places where they do not feel too strange—with the hope of meeting new people. No one really expects a vacation trip to produce a close friend. But surely the beginning of a friendship is possible? Surely in every country people value friendship?

(C)   They do. The difficulty when strangers from two countries meet is not a lack of appreciation of friendship, but different expectations about what **constitutes** friendship and how it comes into being. In those European countries that Americans are most likely to visit, friendship is quite sharply distinguished from other, more casual relations, and is differently related to family life. For a Frenchman, a German or an Englishman friendship is usually more **particularized** and carries a heavier burden of commitment.

(D)   But as we use the word, "friend" can be applied to a wide range of relationships—to someone one has known for a few weeks in a new place, to a close business associate, to a childhood playmate, to a man or woman, to a trusted confidant. There are real differences among these relations for Americans—a friendship may be superficial, casual, situational or deep and enduring. But to a European, who sees only our **surface behavior,** the differences are not clear.

(E)   As they see it, people known and accepted temporarily, casually, flow in and out of Americans' homes with little ceremony and often with little personal commitment. They may be parents of the children's friends, house guests of neighbors, members of a committee, business associates from another town or even another country. Coming as a guest into an American home, the European visitor finds no visible **landmarks.** The atmosphere is relaxed. Most people, old and young, are called by first names.

(F)   Who, then, is a friend?

(G)   Even simple translation from one language to another is difficult, "You see," a Frenchman explains, "if I were to say to you in France, 'This is my good friend,' that person would not be as close to me as someone about whom I said only, 'This is my friend.' Anyone about whom I have to say *more* is really less."

(H)   In France, as in many European countries, friends generally are of the same sex, and friendship is seen as basically a relationship between men. Frenchwomen laugh at the idea that "women can't be friends," but they also admit sometimes that for women "It's a different thing." And many French people doubt the possibility of a friendship between a man and a woman. There is also the kind of relationship within a group—men and women who have worked together for a long time, who may be very close, sharing great loyalty and warmth of feeling. They may call one another *copains*—a word that in English becomes "friends" but has more the feeling of "pals" or "buddies." In French eyes this is not friendship, although two members of such a group may well be friends.

(I)   For the French, friendship is a one-to-one relationship that demands a **keen** awareness of the other person's intellect, **temperament** and particular interests. A friend is someone who **draws out** your own best qualities, with whom you sparkle and become more of whatever the friendship draws upon. Your political philosophy **assumes** more depth, appreciation of a play becomes sharper, taste in food or wine is accentuated, enjoyment of a sport is intensified.

(J)   And French friendships are **compartmentalized.** A man may play chess with a friend for thirty years without knowing his political opinions, or he may talk politics with him for as long a time without knowing about his personal life. Different friends fill different niches in each person's life. These friendships are not made part of family life. A friend is not expected to spend evenings being nice to children or courteous to a deaf grandmother. These duties, also serious and **enjoined,** are primarily for relatives. Men who are friends may meet in a café. Intellectual friends may meet in larger groups for evenings of conversation. Working people may meet at the little *bistro* where they drink and talk, far from the family. Marriage does not affect such friendships; wives do not have to be **taken into account.**

(K)   In the past in France, friendships of this kind seldom were open to any but intellectual women. Since most women's lives centered on their homes, their warmest relations with other women often went back to their girlhood. The special relationship of friendship is based on what the French value most—on the mind, on **compatibility** of outlook, on vivid awareness of some chosen area of life.

(L)   Friendship **heightens** the sense of each person's individuality. Other relationships commanding as great loyalty and devotion have a different meaning. In World War II the first resistance groups formed in Paris were built on the foundation of *les copains*. But significantly, as time went on these little groups, whose lives rested in one another's hands, called themselves "families." Where each had a total responsibility for all, it was kinship ties that provided the model. And even today such ties, crossing every line of class and personal interest, remain binding on the survivors of these small, secret bands.

(M)   In Germany, in contrast with France, friendship is much more **articulately** a matter of feeling. Adolescents, boys and girls, form deeply sentimental attachments, walk and talk together—not so much to polish their **wits** as to share their hopes and fears and dreams, to form a common front against the world of school and family and to join in a kind of mutual discovery of each other's and their own inner life. Within the family, the closest relationship over a lifetime is between brothers and sisters. Outside the family, men and women find in their closest friends of the same sex the devotion of a sister, the loyalty of a brother. Appropriately, in Germany friends usually are brought into the family. Children call their father's and their mother's friends "uncle" and "aunt." Between French friends, who have chosen each other for the congeniality of their point of view, lively disagreement and sharpness of argument are the breath of life. But for Germans, whose friendships are based on mutuality of feeling, deep disagreement on any subject that matters to both is regarded as a tragedy. Like ties of kinship, ties of friendship are meant to be **irrevocably** binding. Young Germans who come to the United States have great difficulty in establishing such friendships with Americans. We view friendship more **tentatively,** subject to changes in intensity as people move, change their jobs, marry, or discover new interests.

(N)   English friendships follow still a different pattern. Their basis is shared activity. Activities at different stages of life may be of very different kinds—discovering a common interest in school, serving together in the armed forces, taking part in a foreign mission, staying in the same country house during a crisis. In the midst of the activity, whatever it may be, people fall into step—sometimes two men or two women, sometimes two couples, sometimes three people—and find that they walk or play a game or tell stories or serve on a tiresome and exacting committee with the same easy anticipation of what each will do day by day or in some critical situation. Americans who have made English friends comment that, even years later, "you can take up just where you left off." Meeting after a long interval, friends are like a couple who begin to dance again when the orchestra strikes up after a pause. English friendships are formed outside the family circle, but they are not, as in Germany, **contrapuntal** to the family nor are they, as in France, separated from the family. And a break in an English friendship comes not necessarily as a result of some irreconcilable difference of viewpoint or feeling but instead as a result of misjudgment, where one friend seriously misjudges how the other will think or feel or act, so that suddenly they are out of step.

(0)   What, then, is friendship? Looking at these different styles, including our own, each of which is related to a whole way of life, are there common elements? There is the recognition that friendship, in contrast with kinship, invokes freedom of choice. A friend is someone who chooses and is chosen. Related to this is the sense each friend gives the other of being a special individual, on whatever grounds this recognition is based. And between friends there is inevitably a kind of equality of **give-and-take.** These similarities make the bridge between societies possible, and the American's characteristic openness to different styles of relationship makes it possible for him to find new friends abroad with whom he feels at home.

from *A Way of Seeing*
by Margaret Mead and Rhoda Metraux

✦ About the Reading

1. How is this essay organized?

2. What is the thesis statement?

3. Identify any comparison or contrast constructions.

4. How are American views of friendship different from French views?

5. How are German friendships different from French and American friendships?

6. How do English friendships differ from the others?

7. Are any of the groups' views of friendship similar? If so, how?

8. Which group's views of friendship are most similar to your own views? In what ways?

What Do You Think?

Write about an experience (good or bad) that you have had, which has helped you define the word *friendship.*

Exercise  **Making Your Own Writing Unified.** Now exchange essays with a class-mate, sharing with her or him the writing you have been working on in this chapter. Read each other's essays to see whether the essays are unified. Point out any sentences that do not support the topic sentences of the paragraphs in which they are found.

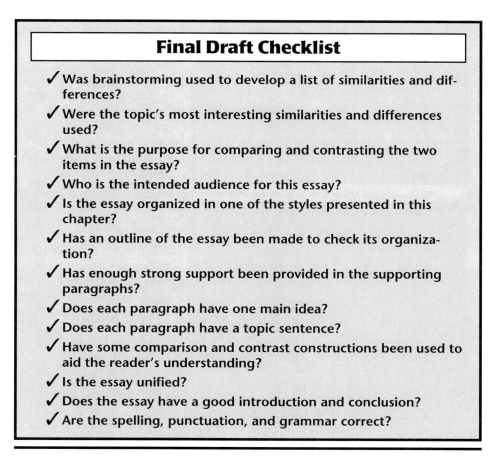

Final Draft

Now you are ready to write the final draft of your comparison and contrast essay. Look at the Final Draft Checklist to help you remember the points that should be included.

Final Draft Checklist

✓ Was brainstorming used to develop a list of similarities and differences?

✓ Were the topic's most interesting similarities and differences used?

✓ What is the purpose for comparing and contrasting the two items in the essay?

✓ Who is the intended audience for this essay?

✓ Is the essay organized in one of the styles presented in this chapter?

✓ Has an outline of the essay been made to check its organization?

✓ Has enough strong support been provided in the supporting paragraphs?

✓ Does each paragraph have one main idea?

✓ Does each paragraph have a topic sentence?

✓ Have some comparison and contrast constructions been used to aid the reader's understanding?

✓ Is the essay unified?

✓ Does the essay have a good introduction and conclusion?

✓ Are the spelling, punctuation, and grammar correct?

Going Further: Idea Generator

Activity ◆**1**   **Commercials.**   Work in teams to select a product (or create one of your own), and design an advertising campaign around that product. Focus on how your product compares with similar products on the market (the competition). If possible, videotape your commercials and present them to your class.

Activity ◆**2**   **What Is Beautiful?**   Bring in magazines from your home country. Cut out pictures of what people in your country consider to be beautiful women and men. Then, cut out pictures from American magazines of what you think Americans view as beautiful men and women. Mount these pictures side-by-side on a large piece of paper. Use them as a basis to compare and contrast the features of these models, both in an oral presentation and in a written essay.

Chapter 7

Cause and Effect

In our everyday lives, it is easy to see how particular actions or events cause other events to happen. For example, when you oversleep in the morning (the cause), you may be late for work or school (the effect). Outside of your personal life, you can see the principles of cause and effect in natural phenomena such as rainfall in the desert or a destructive earthquake. In the global community, you can see the causes and effects of world problems such as war or poverty. Reading and writing about the causes and effects of your own actions, as well as the actions in the world around you, can help you better understand yourself and the world.

217

Part One

Reading and Writing Cause and Effect

In Part One of this chapter, you will concentrate on causes and effects in the real world by identifying causes and effects in written essays. This will help you prepare to write your first draft of a cause and effect essay.

Activity ◆ **Identifying Causes and Effects.** The following activity will help you realize how often cause-and-effect relationships are part of your everyday life. Divide your class into groups. Each group should choose one of the items on the following list, and each person in the group should write as many causes as possible. For example, if your group chooses "catching a cold," you would write as many causes as come to mind (not eating properly, not getting enough sleep, being in the same room with sick people, etc.). Next, discuss your lists with others in your group, and make one master list. Then, together, make a list of effects that follow the causes. (For example, runny nose, high temperature, sneezing, etc., may be outcomes of a cold.) Afterward, share your causes and effects with other groups.

You will notice that some situations are more global, affecting large groups of people and perhaps the whole world, while other situations are more personal, usually affecting a small group or even just an individual. All kinds of situations, large or small, have both causes and effects.

Cause and Effect Items

a good self-esteem	culture shock
freedom	lack of sleep
a strong economy	cheating
too much T.V.	homelessness
illiteracy	falling in love
unemployment	learning a new language
hate	missing a class or a test
good health	catching a cold

Cause and Effect in the Real World

Next, you are going to read two essays that show cause and effect in the real world. The first concerns itself with a more global issue, the second with a more personal one. As you read, see how you can relate the information from both essays to your own life.

Prereading Activity

Often, when people discuss the effects of war, the major focus is on the harmful effects on human beings. The following essay, however, discusses the effects of war on the environment. Before you read, discuss the following questions in small groups, and then review the vocabulary words highlighted here.

1. What are some of the effects war can have on the land?

2. What are some of the effects war can have on animals?

3. What are some particularly devastating effects of war on the environment about which you are already aware?

✦ VOCABULARY WATCH

NOUNS	VERBS	ADJECTIVES	EXPRESSIONS
ecosystem	degrade	barren	gene pool
tactic	contaminate	endangered	domino effect
species	intoxicate	extinct	
habitat	deflate	ecocidal	
defoliation	deforest		
stubble			
poaching			

The Environmental Effects of Armed Conflict

(A)   The effects of armed conflict are devastating to the environments that surround it. Beyond merely killing people, armed conflict can permanently change the face of the land on which it is fought. Physical environments contain many **ecosystems** which suffer and decrease as warriors and technicians prepare for war, fight the war, and attempt to rebuild after their war. Certain war **tactics degrade** the soils which makes the ground fruitless. The consequent death of many plants and animals drains their **gene pool,** thus diminishing the chances of survival for future generations.

(B)   As nations make war preparations, huge amounts of steel, plastic, electronic technology, explosives, and tax dollars are put into the manufacturing of nuclear bombs and other weapons. In the process of researching and developing nuclear warfare, technicians test these bombs and weapons on **"barren"** deserts where the "least" harm can be done. This testing results in tons of pollution which

contaminate soil, animals, plants, and water supplies for years to come. The waste products created by this testing also present another problem: the more that is stored, the less uncontaminated area remains available for many of the desert **species** and their **habitats.**

(C)   Environmental damage from pre-war activities is widespread. The United States and Great Britain have tested some 670 weapons in the Nevada desert, part of which land has been claimed by the Western Shoshone Nation. France's technicians have tested some bombs on the island of Mururoa, destroying a coral reef and promoting single-cell organisms that **intoxicate** several fish, **deflating** the seafood market that is necessary for its islanders' income. Another example of pre-war activities occurred during the Angolan Civil War (1975–91), when soldiers shot rhinos and elephants for their horns and tusks to sell them to buy weapons and uniforms. During preparations for the Persian Gulf War in 1990–91, several camels were reportedly shelled by riflemen in the process of training. Out of 10,000 Kuwaiti camels, only 2,000 survived the war.

(D)   The shooting of too many animals makes them **endangered** or **extinct,** and such extinction can create serious **domino effects** in their ecosystems. If one group of animals disappears, the other levels of its ecosystem either starve and disappear, or multiply uncontrollably and kill off other organisms.

(E)   During a war, certain **ecocidal** tactics are employed to make things difficult for the enemy; however, these tactics destroy more than just the enemy—they destroy the earth. Such tactics include **defoliation** and oil-burning. One heavily spent resource has been poison, made from chemicals, to kill plant life. In the process of the Vietnam conflict, American planes sprayed 19 million gallons of a solution called Agent Orange over trees and crops to kill Vietnam's dense vegetation. At this time, the Americans were trying to destroy the dense jungle vegetation to prevent the Viet Cong from making surprise attacks from behind trees and shrubbery. To make matters worse, 20-ton bulldozers were used to knock trees out of the way in those same areas. By the end of the war, approximately 5.43 million acres of tropical forests were reduced to blackened **stubble.** A more recent example happened in the Persian Gulf War. There, the thick smoke from Kuwait's burning oil fields blocked the sun and killed several thousand birds in flight.

(F)   After the wars are over, as people begin to rebuild their lives and their cities, additional strain is put on forests, wildlife, and other natural resources. For example, approximately forty percent of Vietnam's scrub lands have been **deforested** now because of the post-war lumbering that has taken place. **Poaching** threatened at least four species of monkeys. One man confessed to scientists that he had illegally killed three rare monkeys in Ba Be National Park because he needed meat for his family.

(G)   The effects left by war can be just as bad as or worse than the war itself. The face of the land can be permanently scarred or otherwise changed. Also, the disappearance of one organism affects its natural ecosystem. What used to be Vietnam's battlefields are now covered with some 250 million craters caused by "carpet-bombing," where bombers dropped their cargo over as much land as possible. It is true that several years following a war, nature tends to heal itself to some degree, and new plants and animals replace those that have been destroyed. However, this healing does not justify the extensive damage done to the earth and its living organisms.

(H)   Both the direct and the indirect effects of war result in ecocide. The direct effects of war tactics include the destruction of crops, woodlands, and other valuable resources, and the killing of animals. Even worse are the indirect effects of war, which include huge levels of pollution, defoliation, disease, and the eventual loss of countless animals.

(I)   Usually when people talk about wars, they discuss the people involved and how many died. But they do not always bother to consider what plants, animals, or entire ecosystems were destroyed because of the war. We humans are also organisms in this natural world and depend on the many life forms and other resources that surround us for our survival and well-being. Yes, we might "win" a war, according to political standards, but we lose in the long run, because once the water, soil, and plants go, the animals and micro-organisms go. Once they're gone, we're gone.

by Mark Gillie

✦ About the Reading

1. What are some specific examples of the environmental damage done in prewar activities?

2. What is the thesis of this essay?

3. How is the aftermath of a war sometimes worse than the war itself?

4. Contrast the direct effects with the indirect effects of war.

5. In your opinion, why are many of these effects to the environment seldom mentioned when discussing war?

What Do You Think?

Some people say that war is sometimes necessary. What do you think?

◇ **Prereading Activity**

In this essay, the writer decides that the things he wants require more money than he has. So, he decides to get a job to get the extra money he needs. As you read the essay, pay particular attention to the effects of Jimmy's decision to work while he was going to high school. Before reading the essay, discuss the following questions in small groups, and then review the vocabulary words highlighted here.

1. Look at the essay title, "Needing and Wanting Are Different." What does this title mean to you?

2. As a class, make a list of things you *need*. Then make a list of things that you *want*. Then compare the two lists and discuss the differences.

◇ VOCABULARY WATCH

NOUNS	VERBS	ADJECTIVES	EXPRESSIONS
sneakers	doze	greedy	burning out
priorities	resent	mature	deal with
			screwed up

Needing and Wanting Are Different

"Mom, can I have some money?" Those are the words my mother used to hear all the time. In return, I heard, "Why don't you get a job? Not to make me happy, but so that you have your own money and gain a bit more responsibility." So last year I got a job with Montgomery Ward's photo studio, working about 25 hours a week. For $5 an hour, I was a telephone salesman, trying to persuade people to come in for a free photograph.

All this was during football season and I was on the team as a kicker. To do football and homework and my job at the same time became really hard. I was **burning out,** falling asleep at school, not able to concentrate. My first class was physics and I hated it. I'd just sit there with my hand on my cheek and my elbow

Continued

on the desk, and start **dozing.** One day, the teacher asked my partner what I was doing and she said, "Oh, he's sleeping." The teacher came to the back of the class and stared at me. The whole class looked at me for about two minutes and laughed.

My third-period history teacher was really concerned. She was cool. A lot of times, I'd fall asleep in her class. She'd scream, "Wake up!" and slam her hand on my desk. I'd open my eyes for about two minutes, pay attention and go back to sleep. She asked me if I could handle school, football and work. I said, "Yeah. I'm doing OK so far." She said, "Why? Why all this?"

I told her it was for the things I need, when actually it was for the things I wanted. Needing and wanting are different. Needing something is like your only shoes have holes in them. But when a new pair of **sneakers** came out and I liked them, I'd get them. My parents didn't feel it was right, but they said, "It's your money, you learn to **deal with** it." Within two years I had bought 30 pairs. My parents would laugh. "You got your job, you got your money—but where's your money now?" They didn't realize how much my job was hurting my schoolwork.

My **priorities** were all **screwed up.** On a typical night I did about an hour of homework. A lot of times it was hard for me to make decisions: do I want to be at work or do I want to be at practice? Do I want to worry about what I'll have today or what I'll have in the future? Sometimes I felt there was no right choice. One week in the winter I had to work extra days, so I missed a basketball game and two practices. (I'm on that team, too.) When a substitution oppor-

tunity came at the next game, the coach looked at me and said, "OK, we're running I-5," a new play they had developed during the practices I had missed. I told him I didn't know it, so he told me to sit back down. I felt really bad, because there was my chance to play and I couldn't.

I really did **resent** work. If I hadn't been so **greedy,** I could have been at practice. But I kept working, and the job did help me in some ways. When you have a lot of responsibilities, you have to learn how to balance everything. You just grow up faster. At home, your parents always say, "I pay the bills so while you're here you're under my rules." But now with my money I say, "No, no, no. You didn't pay for that, I did. That's mine."

Slowly, I've come to deal with managing money a lot better. At first, as soon as I had money, it was gone. Now it goes straight into my bank account. This year I decided not to work at all during football season. I have a lot more time to spend with other players after the game and feel more a part of the team. I've only fallen asleep in class once so far. I'm more confident and more involved in the classes. My marks are A's and B's, a full grade better than this time last year. I'm hoping that will help me get into a better college. I don't go shopping as much. I look at all the sneakers in school and think, "I could have those," but I don't need them. Last year I thought that being **mature** meant doing everything. But I'm learning that part of growing up is limiting yourself, knowing how to decide what's important, and what isn't.

by Jimmy Carrasquillo, *Newsweek*, November 16, 1992

✦ About the Reading

1. Where is the thesis statement in this essay?

2. What were some of the ways that Jimmy's job negatively affected his schoolwork?

3. What happened to all the money Jimmy earned at his job?

4. What, according to Jimmy, is the difference between needing and want-ing?

5. How is comparison and contrast used in this essay?

6. What was Jimmy's conflict? What was the turning point, and what was the resolution?

What Do You Think?

Write about a decision you once made that was not a wise one, and ex-plain why you made it. Why was it unwise?

Inferring from the Text.   The answers to the following questions are not ex-plicitly stated by Jimmy. However, you can infer these answers from other in-formation in the text. In the blanks below, write short answers to the ques-tions, and note the clues in the text that helped you to infer the answer. The first one is done as an example.

1. How did Jimmy's parents feel about his working?

   They felt good. They wanted him to have his own money and gain responsibility.

2. Why did Jimmy start working?

   _____

3. What was the history teacher's attitude about Jimmy?

   _____

4. What did the basketball game teach Jimmy?

   _____

5. How does Jimmy feel about working now?

   _____

Inferring Vocabulary.   Use the words listed from "Needing and Wanting Are Different" to fill in the blanks in the following sentences.

substitution	mature	responsibility	burned out
dozing	greedy	deal with	concentrate

1. When it is noisy Kyung can't _____ on his homework.

2. After putting it off for weeks, I decided that the time had come to _____ the noisy neighbor in the next apartment.

3. When Marco was a child, it was his _____ to milk the cows.

4. Elsa acts older than she really is. She is _____ for her age.

5. The child was so _____ that she would not share her toys with anyone.

6. The cat was stretched out on the floor _____ in the sunlight that shone through the window.

7. If you don't have sugar, honey can be a wonderful _____ in a cup of tea.

8. Raphael studied all night. In the morning, he felt _____ .

Identifying Causes and Effects

In this section, you will read two cause-and-effect essays. As a reader, it will be your job to identify all of the causes and effects each author wrote about. As you read, you will notice that sometimes the authors chose to focus more on the causes, sometimes more on the effects. You may also think of some additional causes and effects the writers didn't discuss.

 **Prereading Activity**

Sometimes, something as routine as a daily exercise program can be a good example of cause and effect. The following essay, "Why I Run," tells about what caused the author to begin a running program and about the effects of that running program. Before you read this essay, discuss the following questions with your classmates in small groups, and then review the following vocabulary words.

1. Do you like to exercise? Why or why not?

2. What kinds of exercise do you enjoy doing the most? (If you aren't a fan of exercise, what kind do you *dislike* the *least*?)

3. What are some of the benefits (the effects) of a good exercise program?

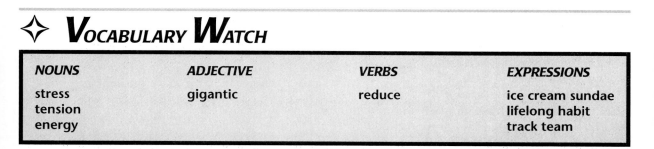

✦ VOCABULARY WATCH

NOUNS	ADJECTIVE	VERBS	EXPRESSIONS
stress tension energy	gigantic	reduce	ice cream sundae lifelong habit track team

Why I Run

(A)   It is often said that you should exercise for your health. Daily exercise will help your heart and lungs become stronger, and as a result, you will live longer. I believe that, but the reason I began a routine of daily exercise had more to do with ice cream than with a healthy heart.

(B)   I started to exercise when I was eleven years old. My brother was a runner, and he wanted me to start running, too, but running seemed like a lot of work to me. However, my brother understood me well. He told me that if I would run a ten kilometer race with him at the end of the summer, he would buy me the biggest **ice cream sundae** that the ice cream shop made. I thought of the **gigantic** 27 scoop ice cream sundae the shop was famous for, and decided that I was ready to try running.

(C)   I ran almost every day for the rest of the summer. By the end of the summer I was able to run ten kilometers. I ran the race in about an hour. Later that week, I ate the biggest ice cream sundae that I had ever seen. I ate until I was sick to my stomach. I felt so sick that I wished I had never run the race. However, beyond giving me a stomachache, that mountain of ice cream helped me to develop a **lifelong habit** I have continued for many reasons.

(D)   Fifteen years later, I am still running. Now it is not for ice cream or for my heart and lungs. Rather, I run because it makes me a happier person. My daily exercise helps to **reduce** the **stress** I feel from school and work. The pounding of my feet against the road helps me to release the **tension** that has built up in my body during the day. Running also gives me time to think about the things that I want to think about instead of the things that somebody else is telling me to think about.

(E)   Another reason that I run is that it makes me feel better about myself. When I exercise, I am doing something for myself. Running gives me more **energy.** It also helps me to look better. For a year and a half, I wasn't able to run. At the end of that time, I weighed 162 pounds. After I began running again, my weight dropped to 133 pounds. Now I

Read to Write

feel much better in my clothes and, as a result, I am happier and even nicer to the people around me.

(F)   Running has also helped me to meet many interesting people and make many friends. In junior high and high school, I was on the **track team,** and my teammates became my best friends. Later in college, I got to know my husband when we began to run together. Recently, I have become better friends with a neighbor because I have started to run with her.

(G)   Although I started running for an ice cream sundae, I continue to run for my happiness and for my health. Running has made my life more fun and enjoyable. It is a habit I hope I never give up.

Exercise 3 **Identifying Causes and Effects.**   Go back and scan the essay, "Why I Run." On a separate sheet of paper, list all the causes and effects that you can find in the essay. Remember, sometimes an author focuses on either the causes or the effects, so you may find more causes than effects or more effects than causes. After you have listed all of the author's causes and effects, think of at least one more cause and one more effect that could have been used in the essay. Share your list with the rest of your class.

Prereading Activity   In the final essay in this section, the author writes about a more global problem: prejudice. Sometimes it is difficult to realize that you have prejudicial attitudes about someone or something. Before you read "The Ill Effects of Prejudice," ask yourself these questions:

1. How do you usually react when you meet someone whose skin color, culture, religion, or way of life is not like yours?
2. Have you been the victim of prejudice?

The Ill Effects of Prejudice

(A)   Why do we form opinions or attitudes about someone or something without really knowing much about them? Just hearing something good or bad about a person, a group of people, a place, or thing can influence our opinions for good and for bad. But letting the opinions of another person determine what our opinions will be is dangerous. Forming opinions about someone or something, before really knowing them well, is called *prejudice*—"pre" means *before* and "judice" refers to *judgment.* Hence, prejudice means to judge before having adequate knowledge.

(B)   We can be prejudiced *toward* or *against* someone or something. To be prejudiced toward something means that we can only see the good in it, while to be prejudiced against something means that we can only see the bad. In either case, we are only allowing ourselves to see half of the picture. Very few people or things in this world are all good or all bad.

(C)   Prejudiced attitudes are usually based on myths, half-truths, or incorrect information, and they are dangerous because they can keep us from learning the truth about someone or something. People form prejudices against others for many reasons—differences in their race, language, religion, gender, age, geographic location, or occupation.

(D)   Prejudices keep people apart. They keep us from really knowing and understanding each other. We should feel proud of who we are and the group of people we represent. If feelings of pride begin to turn to feelings of superiority when we think that our group, our language, or our beliefs are better than those around us, however, then we begin to develop prejudiced attitudes that can be harmful. For example, the prejudiced attitudes of one group may keep another group from attending certain schools, from living in any neighborhood they want, or from getting a job or a promotion. Extreme feelings of prejudice have even caused the deaths of innocent people.

(E)   We are responsible for our own thoughts and opinions. When we let someone else tell us what to think about someone or something, we are giving up some control of our own lives. Before you form an attitude or opinion, find out for yourself about the person, the place, or the thing in question.

(F)   Sometimes we don't realize that we hold prejudicial attitudes toward or against someone or something. We need to carefully examine our lives and our fears, and to ask ourselves whether our attitudes and our opinions come from our personal knowledge and experience or from rumors and fear of the unknown. The good news about prejudice is that we are not born with it. Prejudicial attitudes and opinions develop over time, but with education and knowledge, we can replace our prejudices with cooperation and understanding.

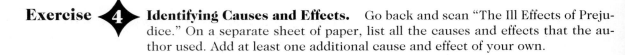

Exercise 4 ▶ Identifying Causes and Effects.   Go back and scan "The Ill Effects of Prejudice." On a separate sheet of paper, list all the causes and effects that the author used. Add at least one additional cause and effect of your own.

                                                         Read to Write

Getting Started: Brainstorming Causes and Effects

As you have found in previous chapters, taking time to brainstorm before you begin writing can help you produce material you can use later in your essay. Begin by selecting a topic. You may choose either something from the list of "Cause and Effect Items" on page 218 or another topic of your own.

Exercise 5 **Listing Causes and Effects.** On a separate sheet of paper, list as many causes and effects associated with your topic as you can think of. For now, write everything that you can; don't worry about what you will actually use in your essay. Later, you can carefully select only the most important or interesting causes and effects. This brainstorming may also help you determine whether your essay should focus on either causes or effects for your topic.

Essay Writing: First Draft

Now that you have done some brainstorming for ideas to use in your essay, it is time to write the first draft of your essay. Remember that in this first draft, the most important thing is to develop your ideas for the essay. Think about which is most important—the causes or the effects. Perhaps both are equally important, and you will want to give them equal consideration in your essay. Look at the list you wrote when you were brainstorming for ideas, and choose the most important and interesting causes and effects to include in your first draft.

Before you write your first draft, read over the First Draft Checklist to help guide you in your writing. Then, after you have written your draft, use the checklist to evaluate what you have written. Make any changes that will improve your writing.

First Draft Checklist

✓ Have you had experience with this topic?
✓ Did you brainstorm for ideas before writing the essay?
✓ Were several of the topic's most interesting causes and/or effects selected for the essay?
✓ Does each paragraph have one main idea?

Part Two

Developing Cause and Effect

In Part One, you learned how to identify causes and effects. In this section of the chapter, you will concentrate on the organization of cause-and-effect writing. You will focus on various styles of organization, two new ways to write an introduction, and the use of good transitions. You will also learn how cause-and-effect essays make use of narration, description, and comparison and contrast, and how they are sometimes used to explain the process of something or to offer a solution to a problem.

Organizational Style in Cause-and-Effect Writing

Cause-and-effect essays can be written in several ways, depending on the author's purpose. You can focus on all of the causes of a problem or situation, or you can write about all of the effects of the same problem or situation. You may also choose to write about both the causes and the effects, or finally, you may write a chain-reaction essay, where something causes an effect, which in turn causes another effect, which in turn causes another and another, and so on.

As a reader, when you understand the style of a cause-and-effect essay, you can more readily determine the author's purpose. The author may have chosen to explain only the effects, in order to alert you to the far-reaching consequences of a specific action. On the other hand, the author may write about only the causes, to analyze a process or to explain the origin of a certain issue or phenomenon.

Diagram 1. When you concentrate on the causes of a situation, your essay might look like this:

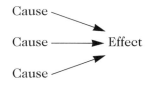

Diagram 2. On the other hand, when you focus on the effects of a situation, your essay might look like this:

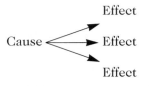

Diagram 3. An essay written about both the causes and the effects of a phenomenon could look like this:

Cause ←——→ Effect

Cause ←——→ Effect

Cause ←——→ Effect

Diagram 4. Finally, an essay that uses the chain-reaction method could look like this:

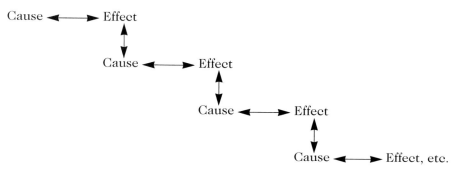

Cause ←——→ Effect
↕
Cause ←——→ Effect
↕
Cause ←——→ Effect
↕
Cause ←——→ Effect, etc.

Exercise  **Diagramming Organizational Styles.** In small groups, decide the organizational styles for the essays you read earlier in this chapter. On a separate sheet of paper, diagram the style for each of the essays identified here: "The Environmental Effects of Armed Conflict," "Needing and Wanting Are Different," "Why I Run," and "The Ill Effects of Prejudice."

Compare the organizational styles used in the preceding essays with the style used in the following essay, "Stress."

✧ Prereading Activity

Nowadays, stress is a common condition for many people. Although some stress is good, in that it may help urge people to get things done, too much stress can have negative effects, as the following essay points out. Before you read the essay, discuss the following questions in small groups, and then review the vocabulary words highlighted here.

1. What are some causes of stress?
2. What are some negative effects of stress?
3. What helps get rid of stress?

✦ VOCABULARY WATCH

NOUNS	VERBS	ADJECTIVES	EXPRESSIONS
demand	procrastinate	depressed	keeps you on your toes
prevention	meditate	vulnerable	putting things off
commitment		hectic	look on the bright side
talent			

Stress

(A)   All people have some stress in their lives. A little stress makes life interesting, and it **keeps you on your toes.** However, too much stress can be unhealthy. You may find your life becoming stressful whenever there are changes in your environment, in your relationships, or in the **demands** you put on yourself. Stress can be caused by having too many problems in your life, such as trouble with money, school, job, or family. Stress can also be caused by good things in your life, such as getting a new job, moving to a new place, or getting married.

(B)   How can you tell when your life is getting too "stressful"? You will probably find yourself always feeling rushed, as though you must hurry everywhere you go. There is never enough time to do everything that you need to do. You may find yourself walking, talking, and eating more quickly than usual. If you find that you eat more or less than usual, or that you don't sleep very well, it may be that you are under a lot of stress. Too much stress can also make you feel **depressed** or bored; it can rob you of your excitement for life.

(C)   Besides causing emotional problems, stress can also cause real physical problems. If you have too much stress in your life, you may suffer from stomach problems, headaches, or neck and shoulder pain. Too much stress can make you more **vulnerable** to illness and can even make you more likely to have accidents! Doctors estimate that 50 to 80% of all disease is directly related to stress. The cost of treating both stress and illness caused by stress is said to be in the billions of dollars each year.

(D)   **Prevention** is the best way to deal with stress. There are many things that you can do to keep stress under control so that it will help you, not hurt you. First of all, be organized—there is nothing so stressful as a disorganized life. Put your life and your surroundings (your home, apartment, or desk at work or school) in order. Don't **procrastinate.** Stop **putting things off.** Do what needs to be done today. On the other hand, if there are things that you can put off for another day, do. Don't always feel that you have to do everything right now. Learn to say "no" to activities and **commitments** that will only add more stress to your life. Remember that you are only human, and that you can only do one thing at a time.

(E)   Learn to relax. Slow down. Take a break or a walk when you feel yourself getting stressed. Find a quiet place where you can go and **meditate,** breathe deeply, and bring back the balance in your life. Find a hobby that you enjoy. Reading, listening to music, or creating something with your hands are all great ways to bring some peace to a **hec-**

tic life. Learn to laugh at yourself and your life. Try to **look on the bright side** of life. Even when things seem pretty dark and stressful, there is usually a place for some humor and a smile. Perhaps that is the most important time to find something to laugh about.

(F)   Finally, one of the best ways to deal with stress is to take care of yourself physically and mentally. You will be able to handle the stress in your life much better if you eat a healthy diet, get plenty of rest each day, and find time for some exercise such as a brisk walk several times a week. Keep mentally healthy by reminding yourself of your **talents** and abilities (everybody has them!) and by appreciating the good things in your life each day.

✦ About the Reading

1. What organizational style does this essay follow?

2. What is the purpose of the essay?

3. How does the author use comparison and contrast in this essay?

4. What are some of the bad things that can cause stress?

5. What are some good things that can cause stress?

6. What are some of the signs of stress?

7. What are some things you can do to reduce or eliminate stress?

What Do You Think?

What are some things that cause you to have stress? How do you deal with stress in your life?

Analyzing Organizational Styles

Now that we have briefly discussed organizational styles, let's analyze how they work. Following is the first paragraph of "Stress." Reread it.

All people have some stress in their lives. A little stress makes life interesting, and it keeps you on your toes. However, too much stress can be unhealthy. You may find your life becoming stressful whenever there are changes in your environment, in your relationships, or in the demands you put on yourself. Stress can be caused by having too many problems in your life, such as trouble with money, school, job, or family. Stress can also be caused by good things in your life, such as getting a new job, moving to a new place, or getting married.

If you were to diagram this paragraph, it would look like this:

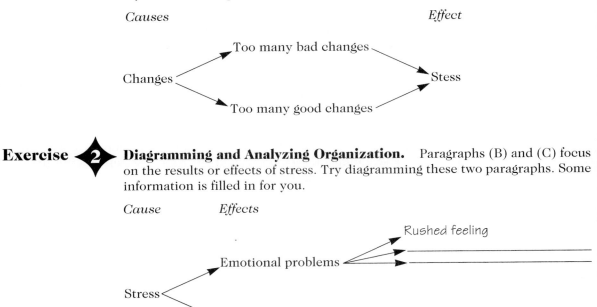

Causes   *Effect*

Too many bad changes

Changes

Too many good changes

Stess

Exercise 2 ◆ Diagramming and Analyzing Organization. Paragraphs (B) and (C) focus on the results or effects of stress. Try diagramming these two paragraphs. Some information is filled in for you.

Cause   *Effects*

Rushed feeling

Emotional problems

Stress

Stomach problems

The remaining paragraphs discussed solutions to the problem of stress. Providing solutions to the problem is not necessary for cause-and-effect essays. However, if you have some good solutions to the problem you have chosen, you might want to include them.

Exercise 3 ◆ Reviewing Outlines. In Chapter 6, you learned how to make an outline. Practice your outlining skills by filling in the blanks with the missing information in the following outline for "Stress."

Stress

   I. Introduction of stress
      A. Changes in environment
         1. _____
         2. good changes

  II. Signs of stress
      A. Time problems
      B. _____
      C. Sleeping problems
      D. _____

                          Read to Write

III. _____
   A. _____
   B. Vulnerability to sickness or accidents
   C. _____

IV. General prevention of stress
   A. _____
   B. Prioritizing activities
   C. Saying "no"

V. Prevention of stress through relaxation
   A. Slowing down
   B. Meditating
   C. Getting interested in hobbies
   D. _____
   E. _____

VI. _____
   A. _____
   B. Getting enough rest
   C. _____
   D. Keeping a positive attitude

✦ Prereading Activity

Gangs are becoming an increasing problem in the United States. Many citizens are asking the government to step in and find some solutions. The author of the following essay, however, looks to other solutions as he explains what he feels are the underlying causes of gangs. As you read the following student essay on gangs, notice how the author organizes the cause-and-effect information. Before you read the essay, discuss the following questions with your classmates, and then review the highlighted vocabulary words.

1. Why do you think people form gangs?
2. What kinds of damage are caused by gangs?
3. Do you have gangs in your native country?

NOUNS	VERBS	ADJECTIVES
stability	collide	recreational
arcade	cooperate	criminal
hostility		fake
		dedicated
		antisocial
		self-destructive

Why Gangs?

(A) America has a problem. The number of gang-related crimes is rapidly increasing. So far, we have not found a way to stop this problem, which has become out of control. If we don't find a way soon, we may find the problem is too large to stop. Understanding the causes of this problem is the first step in ending it. If we can understand why youths become gang members, perhaps we can find a way to lead them in a different direction.

(B) It is a well-known fact that the environment in which we are raised strongly affects us as we grow up and develop our social and personal skills. If this environment lacks important qualities, such as love, **stability,** and safety, a child will seek these comforts elsewhere—maybe in a peer group of kids looking for what their families did not give them. Members of such a group share feelings of unity, protection, and belonging. As these feelings grow stronger over time, group members grow closer to one another and become a gang.

(C) Gangs often form in areas where there are few after-school or other **recreational** activities. If gang members can't find meaningful or interesting activities to do, they may go looking for places where "things happen." Often, these places are shopping malls, since there are a lot of people and many things to do at malls. If the gang does not have much money, they may just hang out—often in an **arcade,** where they can find cheap entertainment such as video games. Suppose that a gang member also finds this kind of activity boring and suggests to the gang that they do something dangerous or **criminal.** Because it is important to feel part of a group and there is no other peer group but the gang to associate with, the chances are good that the rest of the gang members will join in such a dangerous or crime-related activity.

(D)   Besides stealing, spray-painting on walls, and other activities that give gang members a rush of excitement, various gangs often collide with each other. Gang members show their loyalty to their group by standing up for their friends. Proving this loyalty often results in their fighting with members of other gangs. Fighting and other gang activities scare most people. As a result, instead of trying to help these kids deal with their hostility, we distance ourselves by creating a wall between "them" and "us." Thus, gang members feel even more like outsiders, living in a society that fears and hates them. Only when they are in a gang do members feel that they share an identity with people like themselves.

(E)   This sharing of identity attracts kids to gangs, even those from strong families, because most teenagers are afraid of being alone. When they join a gang, kids instantly become members of a strong group. This group membership often makes them feel energized. It also gives them a feeling of power, that they can fight back at the society that has ignored or rejected them. For its part, society fears and hates the gang, so the cycle of fear and mistrust continues. As the gang grows stronger, it is more likely to cause problems in the community. Then, when problems start, society puts its foot down and wants gang activity stopped. At this point, however, it may be too late. The gang sees any attempt to destroy or control it—for example, through police action or help from a government or private agency—as a threat or challenge from its "enemies," and it will usually refuse to **cooperate.**

(F)   The way I see it, the only way to solve the problem of gang-related crime is to stop the process at an early stage. The most effective solution is making families aware of how important it is to give their children a strong foundation of love. If children feel this love, they will not need to seek it elsewhere. They will also be able to see through the **fake** image of unity that a gang provides. If more people try to help their kids through the hard process of growing up, we will be able to avoid a great deal of the problems associated with gangs in our cities. Society must become **dedicated** to preventing gangs if we do not want to keep losing a valuable part of our younger generation to the **self-destructive** and **anti-social** world of gangs.

by Rene

✦ **About the Reading**

1. What is the author's thesis statement?

2. Does each paragraph support the thesis statement? How?

3. In which organizational style was this essay written?

4. List some of the reasons that kids join gangs, according to this essay.

5. According to the author, what are the things lacking in the environment, which cause a person to seek comfort in gangs?

6. According to the author, how important is it to a gang member to be part of a group?

7. What does the author mean in paragraph (E) when he says, "At this point, however, it may be too late"?

8. What are some of the effects of joining gangs?

9. What additional information or topics would you have liked to see included in this essay. Why?

What Do You Think?

What are your ideas for a possible solution to the gang problem?

Understanding Idiomatic Expressions.   Use your scanning skills to locate the idiomatic expressions in "Why Gangs?" listed next. Read the sentences in the essay where these expressions occur, and try to understand their meaning from the context. Then read the following sentences 1–5. Each sentence has an expression missing. Use the context of these sentences—and those from the sentences in the essay—to fill in the blanks with the correct expressions. When you finish, discuss your answers with one or more fellow students.

hang out   put (his) foot down
stand up for   to see through
creating a wall between

1. When John got a low grade in math, his father _____ . He told John that he couldn't play football again until he got a better grade in math.

2. Mary isn't communicating with her parents. She is _____ her parents and herself. She needs to start talking to them more about how she feels.

3. After class, many students like to _____ in the cafeteria, where they eat snacks and talk about their experiences.

4. Martin Luther King, Jr., was an important civil rights leader who helped people _____ their rights.

5. Advertisers are always trying to get people to buy their products. Sometimes, they write advertisements to make people *think* they need a product in order to get them to buy it. It is important for people _____ this kind of advertising and to buy only the things that they really need.

Making Your Introduction Inviting

When you write, you want to make your whole essay inviting for others to read. You can begin by making your introduction inviting. As you learned in Chapter 5 on exposition, there are different ways to write an introduction. You already learned about the funnel approach. In this chapter, you will learn two other ways of introducing your essay: the surprise and the dramatic introduction.

The Surprise Introduction

The *surprise introduction* begins by presenting a viewpoint that is *not* the view that will actually be discussed in the essay. The writer begins as if he or she is going to discuss a specific viewpoint, then, suddenly, at the end of the introductory paragraph, the author changes directions and states the opposite point of view. The effect is to surprise the reader.

One reason authors may use this surprise technique is their anticipation that their readers may not agree with their viewpoint. By starting with what they believe to be their readers' point of view, writers try to interest their readers enough to continue reading the paragraph to discover the writer's perspective. Read the following paragraph for an example of this surprise approach.

Television is at its worst. An abundance of violence, sex, and other inappropriate material fills the screen every day and night. Last year, a new TV show began, which contained such highly questionable scenes that a "parental discretion" notice is placed on the screen every time the program is shown. Recently, a child advocacy group made a formal complaint to the Federal Communications Commission, stating that commercial television does not air enough wholesome children's shows. The group has demanded that something be done about the situation. With seemingly so little to offer, many feel that abandoning television altogether might be our best and only solution. However, although television offers numerous programs of little or no value, it need not be seen in a completely negative light. Television offers many opportunities to learn and grow—opportunities that should not be missed.

This paragraph begins as if the author supported the opinion that television has no positive use; then, at the end of the paragraph, the author turns around and supports the opposite view. The next example comes from the essay, "A Tale of Two Schools," on page 196 in Chapter 6. Because this essay is much longer, the introduction takes four or five paragraphs to get to the point. See how it uses the surprise technique.

Two schools—one public and the other parochial—stand just four blocks apart in the crime-ridden St. Louis neighborhood of Walnut Park. Both boast dedicated, no-nonsense principals and integrated faculties. Both student bodies are 100 percent black.

At Northwest High, the public school, I found no litter or graffiti, heard no hollering in the halls. The youngsters rushing up and down the long corridors seemed intent only on pursuing their studies.

At Cardinal Ritter College Prep, crucifixes and religious portraits adorned the walls, and all the students wore uniforms. In other respects, its atmosphere was exactly the same as Northwest's: no distractions, a low noise level and a seriousness of purpose evident on the kids' faces.

Yet when it comes to results, the two schools are quite different. . . .

This introduction begins by showing the similarities between the two schools, so it originally seems as though the schools might be quite similar. However, in the beginning of the fourth paragraph the author suddenly turns about, and it is apparent that he will discuss the differences for the remainder of the essay.

Exercise 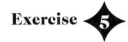 **Writing a Surprise Introduction.** Look back at the essay, "Why I Run," on page 226 and rewrite the introduction, using the surprise technique.

Exercise 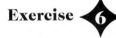 **Writing a Surprise Introduction to Your Essay.** Rewrite the introduction to the essay you have been working on for this chapter, using a surprise introduction. Later, you can choose which introduction you will actually use for your final draft; for now, however, practice writing a surprise introduction.

The Dramatic Introduction

A *dramatic introduction* begins with some scenario—a narrative—that shows, more than explains, a reason to be discussing the topic. The essay "The Ill Effects of Prejudice," on page 227 began with a funnel approach. However, it could have begun with a dramatic introduction. It might have looked like this:

Late last Friday night, on my way home from a friend's party, I stopped at a convenience store to buy some orange juice for the next morning. Instead of being part of a simple transaction, I was witness to a terrible drama, which is repeated in some form hundreds of times a day.

When I brought my juice to the counter, there were two very drunk guys hassling the sales clerk, who happened to be Pakistani. In fact, the clerk was in my biology lab, and although we weren't close friends, I knew he was American-born: His parents had immigrated more than 20 years ago. Nevertheless, these two drunk guys, who didn't have enough money to pay for their six-pack, were making fun of his accent and screaming things at him such as "Why don't you go back to where you came from?" "I bet you don't even wear shoes!" and "Where's your elephant?" They were laughing and giving each other high-fives, but I could see that the clerk was getting more and more angry, as well as more and more sad. Just as I was about to step in between them and say something, one of the drunk guys' friends came in, gave them the extra two dollars, and they all left.

"I'm so sorry that happened," I said to the clerk.

"Thanks," he said sadly, "but it happens almost every night."

Why do we form opinions or attitudes about people or things without really knowing much about them? . . .

The new introduction provides drama, and gets the reader immediately involved, both intellectually and emotionally. This introduction compels the reader's interest before even presenting the thesis statement. Next, reread the dramatic introduction to the essay, "Needing and Wanting Are Different," on page 222. How does the dramatic approach enhance this introduction?

Exercise 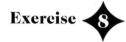 **7**   **Writing a Dramatic Introduction.**   Go back to the essay, "Stress," and rewrite the introduction as a dramatic introduction.

Exercise **8**   **Writing a Dramatic Introduction to Your Essay.**   Rewrite the introduction to the essay you have been working on for this chapter, making it a dramatic introduction. Later, you can choose which introduction you will actually use for your final draft.

◆ Prereading Activity

Procrastination (delay in doing things) is a common problem that all of us have faced at some time in our lives. Like stress, procrastination can lead to other problems. The following essay, "Put it Off," begins with a dramatic introduction. Before you read it, discuss the following questions in small groups, and then review the vocabulary words highlighted here.

1. Are you a procrastinator?

2. Why do you think people procrastinate?

3. What are some of the effects of procrastination?

◆ Vocabulary Watch

NOUNS	VERBS	ADJECTIVES	ADVERBS	EXPRESSIONS
pit	wander	irrational	diligently	to put off
escalator	doom			runs out
spurt				summed up
desperation				being on top of

Put It Off

(A)   It is late Thursday night. My eyelids droop as I think about the English assignment before me: Write an introductory paragraph to an essay on one of the five selected topics. I give some thought to the topics, but soon I find my eyes as well as my mind **wandering** to the mosquito bites on my leg. "They sure are big." Next I notice a stain on the shirt I am wearing. "How did that get there?" Next my eyes wander to the clock. Suddenly I am jerked back into reality as I realize that in a matter of hours I will be sitting in English class, and I still don't have a paragraph written.

(B)   This is a classic situation for me. I have managed **to put off** writing this paragraph all afternoon, just like I manage to put off nearly all my assignments for hours, days, and even weeks. And when time **runs out,** I am in trouble. Henry David Thoreau once said, "The mass of men lead lives of quiet desperation." Because of my procrastination, I belong to that same mass. As a result, I waste a great amount of valuable time, and I find myself always one step behind in life.

(C)   The results of my procrastination can be **summed up** in Edward Young's statement, "Procrastination is the thief of time." I spend more time thinking up weak excuses for why I can't do an assignment now than I ever spend on the actual assignment. And the ways I avoid an assignment definitely leave something to be desired, such as calling my friend for the eleventh time today, or watching a television show meant for a four-year-old. Procrastination also causes me to waste time when I finally get down to the task I've been avoiding. The simplest task takes on extreme proportions in my mind because of the panic I feel for having put it off for so long. I become an **irrational,** unclear thinker when I am rushed, and this causes me to be much slower at any task. However, the clock ticks on; it does not stop for procrastinators like me.

(D)   Furthermore, procrastination keeps me one step behind in life and school as I try to catch up on what should already be done. While most students **diligently** do homework for tonight, I diligently do the homework from last night, or even last week. Because I can never seem to do a task when it is assigned, I never get that satisfied feeling that comes with getting things done, with **being on top of** everything. Rather, I always end up feeling as if I am at the bottom of a **pit,** trying to climb out—one late assignment at a time. But since I am always behind, catching up on my work is like trying to walk up the down **escalator**—very difficult and nearly impossible. Because of procrastination, I am never free to live in the present; instead, I always find myself trapped by unfinished business from the past.

(E)   Thus, procrastination continues to rob me of time. My life is continually interrupted by **spurts** of anxiety and **desperation** as one due date or another flies by. I have yet to grasp the concepts of organization and promptness. I hope that I will grasp them soon; otherwise, I will be **doomed** to a life in the procrastinator's prison that I have built for myself.

Melia James

✦ About the Reading

1. Find the topic sentence in each paragraph, and underline it.
2. What kind of effect did the introductory paragraph have on you?
3. What are the two main effects of procrastination on the author?
4. How hopeful does the author seem about being cured of procrastination?
5. How does the author use quoted speech in this essay?
6. What are some other effects of procrastination?

What Do You Think?

The author quotes Henry David Thoreau, who wrote, "The mass of men lead lives of quiet desperation." Write a response to this quote.

Making the Connections between Ideas

As you know, an essay is made up of many paragraphs, all centered around the same topic and its controlling idea. Each paragraph discusses a different aspect of the controlling idea. How do these paragraphs connect to one another, though? In most of the chapters of this book, you have discussed and practiced using cohesive devices or transition words that help to connect your ideas. Just as transitions in sentences and paragraphs are necessary to help a reader understand how small ideas are related, transitions between paragraphs are necessary to help a reader see how the controlling ideas of paragraphs fit together to create one controlling idea for the whole essay.

Often, the first sentence of a paragraph, whether it is the topic sentence or not, refers back to the ideas in the paragraph that precedes it. Sentences such as these link the ideas from two paragraphs. To see how this works, read the following excerpts from two cause-and-effect essays. The first sentence of the second paragraph has been underlined. The portion of the first underlined sentence that refers to an idea from the previous paragraph has been circled, and arrows have been drawn to those ideas in the previous paragraph.

1. One of the negative effects of smoking is that it can cause <u>serious health</u> ◄ <u>problems.</u> Smoking can increase the chance of getting lung cancer, as well as cancer of the mouth, throat, bladder, pancreas, and kidneys. Heart disease and ulcers are also related to smoking. Further, pregnant women who smoke are more likely to have premature babies than women who do not smoke.

   Beyond (causing bad health,) smoking can begin to control a person's life. Many people who smoke feel like they *have* to smoke because they feel good when they puff on a cigarette. Most people start by just smoking a few cigarettes a day. However, they often begin to smoke more and more until they feel impatient or unable to relax when they can't smoke.

2. How can you tell when your life is getting too "stressful"? You will probably find yourself always feeling rushed, as though you must hurry everywhere you go. There is never enough time to do everything that you need to do. You may find yourself walking, talking, and eating more quickly than usual. If you find that you eat more or less than usual, or that you don't sleep very well, it may be that you are under a lot of stress. Too much stress can also make you feel <u>depressed or bored.</u>; it can <u>rob you of your</u> <u>excitement for life</u>.

   Besides causing (emotional problems,) stress can also cause real physical problems. If you have too much stress in your life, you may suffer from stomach problems, headaches or neck and shoulder pain. Too much stress can make you more vulnerable to illness and can even make you more likely to have accidents! Doctors estimate that 50 to 80% of all disease is directly related to stress. The cost of treating both stress and illness caused by stress is said to be in the billions of dollars each year.

◆ Prereading Activity

Learning a foreign language can be a very exciting experience. You can meet new people, learn new ways of thinking, and discover new cultures. Nonetheless, learning a new language requires lots of hard work. It can sometimes be frustrating and even embarrassing as you struggle to make yourself understood. The following essay was written by a student who learned Spanish as a second language. As you read, see how many of her experiences you can relate to.

As you read "Learning a Foreign Language," pay special attention to the transitions between paragraphs. Before you read, discuss the following questions in small groups, and then review the highlighted vocabulary words.

1. What have been the best things about learning English?

2. What have been the worst things?

3. What helps you the most to learn a new language?

Read to Write

NOUNS	ADJECTIVES	EXPRESSIONS
praise	challenging	off and on
insight	rewarding	reap the benefits
determination	intimidated	bridge the gap
persistence	intensive	

Learning a Foreign Language

(A)   Learning a foreign language was one of the most **challenging** yet most **rewarding** experiences in my life. Although at times, learning a language was very frustrating, it was well worth the effort. Now that I can speak a second language, I appreciate another culture, and best of all, I can communicate with many wonderful people I would never have known had I not learned their language.

(B)   My first experience with a foreign language was in junior high school, when I took my first Spanish class in seventh grade. I was very excited to learn a language. I had a wonderful, patient, and kind teacher who gave plenty of **praise** to all the students. Because of this positive environment, I eagerly answered all the questions I could, never worrying much about making mistakes. I was at the top of my class for two years.

(C)   When I went to high school, I was naturally eager to continue studying Spanish; however, my experience studying Spanish in high school was very different from that of junior high school. While my former teacher had shown patience to all the students, my new teacher was quick to punish students who gave incorrect answers. Whenever we answered questions incorrectly, she took a long pointed stick, and, while pointing it at us and shaking it up and down, would shout, "No! No! No!" Well, with this new fear, it didn't take me long to lose my eagerness to answer questions. Not only did I lose my excitement for answering questions, I totally lost my desire to say anything at all in Spanish. Because I didn't participate much in class, I lost most of the Spanish I had learned in junior high school. In fact, I just about decided I would never again take a foreign language, least of all, Spanish.

(D)   However, that decision didn't last long. When I went to college, I learned that in order to fulfill some general education requirements, all students were required to take a certain number of courses in either mathematics or foreign languages. Because I was an even worse math student than a foreign language student, I decided to try again with Spanish. I enrolled in a couple of Spanish classes and, to my delight, had wonderful teachers. Unlike my high school teacher, they were patient and kind, and none of them carried sticks! However, the situation was far from ideal. As our classes were very large, I was only able to answer a couple of questions in each class period. Also, after a few weeks of classes, I noticed that there were many students who had lived in Spanish-speaking countries. Because of this, they were able to speak much better than I was. I began to feel **intimidated.** So, once again, although for different reasons, I was afraid to speak. It seemed my Spanish was just going to stay at the same level forever.

(E)   That was the case until a couple of years later, when I was offered an opportunity to study in a Spanish-speaking country in South America. Here was one last chance, I thought! If I couldn't learn Spanish after this experience, I would just have to give up forever. So I decided to take the opportunity. I went to an **intensive** Spanish program, where I "relearned" a lot of what I had been trying to learn, **off and on,** in previous years.

(F)   Finally, it was time to go to South America. I'll never forget the day I got off the plane and realized that this was going to be a lot harder than I had expected. Everywhere I heard this new language that I "thought" I had learned. Everything anybody said to me sounded like one big word stuck together. These people didn't sound at all like my American Spanish teachers. I wondered whether I had really learned the right language. Because I talked very slowly and my communication was poor, people looked at me and talked to me as if I were stupid. I felt so frustrated sometimes, I just wanted to scream. But there was no use in doing that. I realized that the best thing to do was to try, try, and try again.

(G)   So practice I did. I carried a little dictionary with me everywhere I went, as well as a notebook in which I listed any new words I heard. I woke up an hour early every morning to study. I tried new vocabulary and grammatical structures every day. I made many mistakes, and sometimes they were embarrassing mistakes. Once, while trying to tell my friend that her hair was fluffy, I mixed up two similar words and told her it was scary. Another time, while trying to say that I was hungry, I got confused again and told my friend that I had a lover! Needless to say, I had to learn to have a sense of humor and laugh at myself a little. Once in a while I cried with frustration, and occasionally I felt like giving up. But I kept trying, and little by little I let go of my fear. And then, one day I realized that I could understand just about everything that anybody said to me, and most important, I could "say" anything I wanted to in Spanish. Although I still made many mistakes and was continually learning, I had finally **reaped the benefits** of all that hard work.

(H)   Not only did learning another language teach me the value of hard work, but it also gave me **insights** into another culture, and my mind was opened to new ways of seeing things. Although we had many differences, because I was able to speak with these people in their own language, I realized that we were often much more similar than different.

(I)   Finally, the most wonderful aspect of having learned a second language was that I could communicate with many more people than before. Talking with people is one of my favorite activities, so being able to speak a new language lets me meet new people, participate in conversations, and form new, unforgettable friendships. Now that I speak a foreign language, instead of staring into space while Spanish is being spoken, I can participate, and I can make friends. Because I have learned a second language, I am able to reach out to others and **bridge the gap** between my language and culture and theirs.

(J)   Learning a second language has been a most challenging experience for me, but one that I wouldn't trade for anything. The character traits that I have gained are invaluable. I have learned **determination** and **persistence.** My mind has opened up to new ways of thinking and of seeing the world. Most important, learning a second language has brought me new and lasting friendships.

✦ About the Reading

1. What made the author's experience with Spanish in junior high positive (the causes)?

2. What made the author's experience with Spanish in high school negative (the causes)?

3. How was the author's experience in college different from her experience in high school (the effect)? What caused the situation to be somewhat negative?

4. Once the author was in South America, what were some of the strategies that she used in order to learn the language?

5. How does the writer use comparison and contrast in this essay? Give several examples.

6. How is narration used in this essay? For what purpose?

7. What are some of the strategies (causes) you use to learn a new language?

8. What were some of the benefits (effects) the author gained from learning a new language?

What Do You Think?

What are some of the benefits you feel you have gained from learning a new language? What has been the most frustrating aspect of learning a second language?

Exercise 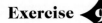 **9** **Finding Connections between Ideas.** Go back to "Learning a Foreign Language." Underline the first sentence of each paragraph. Then find the idea in each of these sentences, which refers to an idea mentioned in the previous paragraph. Circle that idea, and then draw arrows to that same idea mentioned in the preceding paragraph.

Exercise **10** **Making Transitions in Your Essay.** Now that you have seen how ideas can be connected between paragraphs, work on connecting the ideas in your own writing. Return to your essay, and see whether you have made effective transitions between your paragraphs. Rewrite any transitions that need to be more clear. You may want to get some feedback about your transitions from another reader.

 ## Now Revise: Second Draft

Use the organizing skills you have practiced in this part of the chapter to organize your essay for the most effective presentation of your ideas. Don't forget to write good topic sentences with clear controlling ideas to let your reader know what information each paragraph will contain. Also, make sure that each paragraph is connected to the paragraph before it, through the use of transitions. Use the Second Draft Checklist to evaluate and make changes to your essay.

When you have finished your second draft, exchange papers with a classmate. Read and discuss each other's essays. Make suggestions for additional changes that will improve the writing.

Second Draft Checklist

✓ Have you had experience with this topic?

✓ Did you brainstorm for ideas before writing the essay?

✓ Did you select several of the topic's most interesting causes and/or effects for the essay?

✓ Are the connections between the topic's causes and effects logical and fully developed so that the reader will easily see the connections?

✓ Does each paragraph have one main idea?

✓ Has one of the organizational styles for cause and effect been used?

✓ Is the introduction inviting to the reader?

✓ Are transitions between paragraphs used to connect the main points?

Part Three

Refining and Reviewing

In this chapter, you have learned some of the uses for cause-and-effect writing as well as several ways to organize such essays. In this section, you will learn cohesive devices that help readers to understand relationships in cause-and-effect writing. In addition, you will review the importance of having a good thesis statement.

Cohesive Devices: Logical Connectors

The transition words that help to make cause-and-effect relationships clear are *logical connectors*. When you are reading, these logical connectors will help you understand how events relate to one another. When you are writing, these connectors will help you give your readers a clear understanding of the cause-and-effect relationships in your essay. Logical connectors can be divided into two groups, those that indicate a *cause* and those that indicate an *effect*. The following chart lists some of these words and how they are used.

Cohesive Devices: Logical Connectors		
Uses	**Cohesive Devices**	**Examples**
To show effect	*therefore*	I have been a competitive swimmer since my youth; *therefore,* I have very strong muscles.
Can follow a semicolon (;) or a period (.)	*consequently,*	I really studied hard for the exam last night; *consequently,* I received a perfect score.
Are followed by a comma (,) and a complete sentence	*for this reason,*	I eat a very healthy diet; *for this reason,* I have plenty of energy.
	as a result,	
Follows neither a semicolon nor a period Is not followed by a comma	*so*	I got up late this morning, *so* I missed the exam.
To show cause	*because . . . ,*	*Because* my sister had a swimming accident when she was young, she is afraid to swim. (My sister is afraid to swim *because* she had a swimming accident when she was young.)
Are followed by a noun and a verb	*as . . . ,*	*As* Jake had not attended the meeting, he did not know the new rules. (Jake did not know the rules, *as* he had not attended the meeting.)

Uses	Cohesive Devices	Examples
To show cause Are followed by a noun phrase	*because of . . . ,* *due to . . . ,* *owing to . . . ,*	*Because of* the storm last night, the electricity has gone out. (The electricity has gone out because of the storm last night.) *Due to* the fire, the house is going to be torn down. (The house is going to be torn down *due to* fire.) *Owing to* her ability to work well with people, the mayor asked her to take the job as Public Relations Manager. (The mayor asked her to take the job of Public Relations Manager, *owing to* her ability to work well with people.)

Exercise 1

Creating Sentences Using Logical Connectors. Practice creating sentences that use the logical connectors from the previous chart. Complete the sentences by writing in the cause or the effect in the blank. You will know whether you should use a cause or an effect, based on the logical connector that is used.

Example: Crime has continued to rise, even though more police officers have been hired; therefore, <u>it is necessary to look at some other ways to deal with this problem.</u>

1. The President had lost popularity with the voters; consequently,

   _____.

2. _____ ;

   for this reason, I cannot drive at nighttime.

3. Yener's parents were not happy with his new girlfriend. As a result,

   _____.

4. _____

   so I wasn't able to go to the movie tonight.

5. Because pollution has such bad effects on our health, _____.

   _____

6. As I could not understand the explanation given by my teacher, _____

   _____.

7. Because of _____ ,

   everyone had to leave the party earlier than expected.

8. Due to the recent political problems, _____

   _____

9. Owing to _____

   Yukie could not pay her rent.

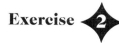

Exercise **2** **Using Logical Connectors.** Use logical connectors to revise five of the sentences in your cause-and-effect essay. On a separate sheet of paper, write the original sentences, then the revised ones.

Thesis Statements

As discussed in previous chapters, a thesis statement contains the controlling idea of the entire essay and usually comes at the end of an introductory paragraph. Each paragraph in the rest of the essay should be connected to and support the thesis statement. As you read the next essay, look for the thesis statement, and note the ways in which other paragraphs support it.

Can you think of some possible thesis statements that might be made about volcanoes? When reading the following essay, note the student's thesis statement, and observe how well he supports it.

◆ **Prereading Activity**

The following report is about the effects of a frightening natural phenomenon. Before you begin to read it, discuss the following questions in small groups, and then review the vocabulary highlighted here.

1. What natural phenomenon (such as fire, floods, etc.) are you most afraid of? Why?

2. Have you ever experienced the effects of a volcano? If so, share your experience with the class. If no one in the class has had such an experience, share what you know about volcanoes.

◆ V*OCABULARY* W*ATCH*

NOUNS	ADJECTIVES	EXPRESSIONS
lava	dormant	tipping the balance
eruption	agricultural	
phenomenon	essential	

Volcanoes

(A)   Throughout history, volcanoes have been feared by many people, and for good reasons. Even though a **dormant** volcano seems to be just a hill or a mountain, inside it, a great amount of heat, in the form of **lava,** ash, and steam is waiting to get out. In the past 10,000 years, at least 500 volcanoes have produced more than 600 volcanic **eruptions.** These eruptions have had a great effect on the world, changing the climate, damaging agriculture, and causing disasters that have killed countless people.

(B)   The climate around the world has changed dramatically due to volcanic eruptions. When an eruption occurs, a volcano blows small particles of volcanic dust into the atmosphere. This dust causes the temperature to drop several degrees for up to two years. The temperature drops because the volcanic dust dims the sunlight in the tropical Pacific area, and, as a result, the warm tropical winds are weakened, thus **tipping the** delicate climatic **balance.** This situation occurred when "El Chiconal" erupted in Mexico. At that time, winds near the equator became weaker, causing the water in the western Pacific Ocean to cool and wash eastward. This change in the climate is a **phenomenon,** which has been named "El Niño."

(C)   The change in the weather due to volcanic eruptions can also damage **agricultural** resources. For instance, in 1815 "Mount Tambora" in Indonesia erupted. The climatic change caused by this eruption resulted in crop failure the following summer. As a result, a food shortage occurred. At the same time, many people in the United States found their fields white with ice on the Fourth of July, probably a result of the eruption of "Mount Tambora."

(D)   Another way in which volcanic eruptions can hurt agricultural resources is in damage to the land itself. When fields are covered with lava, the land cannot be used for many years to come. For example, after the eruption of "Mount Etna," the lava-covered land was not able to support agriculture for 300 years. The farmers in this area were no longer able to use this land to grow their **essential** crops.

(E)   Finally, volcanic eruptions and mud flows have caused many deaths. In this century alone, there have been thousands of deaths directly related to volcanic eruptions. An example of the deadly power of volcanoes occurred in 1985, when "El Nevada del Ruiz" erupted in Colombia. The mud flow that followed this eruption killed more than 25,000 people. Earlier, in 1883, another volcanic eruption that took many lives occurred when the volcano "Krakatoa" erupted near Java. This eruption caused mud flows that were as high as 130 feet, killing 36,000 people. Since 1600, more than 168,000 deaths have been recorded as a result of volcanic eruptions.

(F)   In summary, volcanoes can cause serious, worldwide damage. This damage includes changes in climate, damage to agriculture, and widespread death. Although volcanoes have not taken as many lives as many other natural phenomena, they continue to be among the most frightening disasters to humankind.

by Norberto

◆ About the Reading

1. Underline the essay's thesis statement. What are the controlling ideas in the thesis statement?

2. In what organizational style is the essay written?

Read to Write

3. What do you think the author's intended audience and purpose are?

4. What are three destructive effects of volcanoes? Which of these three effects do you think is most devastating? Why?

5. Circle all the logical connectors in this essay. How are they used?

6. What other expository techniques does the author use? Explain.

What Do You Think?

Have you ever been involved in a natural disaster? Write about it. If you have not, write about someone you know who has.

Exercise 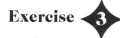 **Identifying Controlling Ideas.** "Volcanoes" has a clear thesis statement. Furthermore, each paragraph that follows the introduction has a controlling idea that supports the thesis. In the blanks below, write the thesis statement from "Volcanoes," then write the controlling ideas in each paragraph, which support the thesis.

Thesis Statement: _____

Controlling Idea from Paragraph (B):

_____

Controlling Idea from Paragraph (C):

_____

Controlling Idea from Paragraph (D):

_____

Controlling Idea from Paragraph (E):

_____

Thesis Focus

Several qualities define a thesis statement:

- It must be a *complete sentence,* with *one* clear focus.
- It must *limit* the topic and control the entire essay by stating an *opinion or attitude* about the subject. (The topic must be sufficiently narrowed.)
- It usually mentions the *major controlling ideas,* which will appear in the following paragraphs. Almost always, these controlling ideas are presented in the order in which they will appear in the essay (from least important to most important, from smallest to largest, from most familiar to least familiar, etc.).

There are several characteristics to avoid in writing a thesis statement:

- *Do not state an obvious fact* without some limiting opinion or attitude about your subject. (For example, "Paris is a city" is not a thesis statement because there is no attitude or opinion. "Paris is a romantic city" can be a thesis statement because the word "romantic" limits the topic.)
- *Do not write a title instead of a full sentence.* (For example, "Sports I like" is not a thesis statement; "My favorite sports are soccer, kayaking, and marathon running" is a thesis statement.)
- *Do not tell the reader what you are going to write about.* (For example, "I am going to tell you about my plans for the next five years." Instead, try "Over the next five years, I intend to learn to speak English fluently, enter college, and start my career.")

Exercise  **Identifying Good Thesis Statements.** Explain why the following sentences are *not* good thesis statements. Next, rewrite each sentence, so that each one is effective.

1. I am going to explain why I decided to become a doctor.

   Reason not a good thesis: _____

   _____

   Rewritten thesis: _____

   _____

2. The reasons that earthquakes happen.

   Reason not a good thesis: _____

   _____

   Rewritten thesis: _____

   _____

3. There are many similarities and differences between cats and dogs.

   Reason not a good thesis: _____

   _____

   Rewritten thesis: _____

   _____

4. Bees make honey.

   Reason not a good thesis: _____

   _____

Read to Write

Rewritten thesis: _____

_____

5. Living in Minneapolis can be challenging and there are many cultural experiences to be had in this city.

   Reason not a good thesis: _____

_____

   Rewritten thesis: _____

Final Draft

It is time to use the ideas and skills that you have practiced in this chapter to put the finishing touches on your essay. In this final draft, concentrate on making sure that you have a clear and strong thesis statement with paragraphs to support it. You should also make sure you have logical connectors in your essay, which make the cause-and-effect relationships more clear to your readers. Read over the Final Draft Checklist to help you remember all the points that should be included.

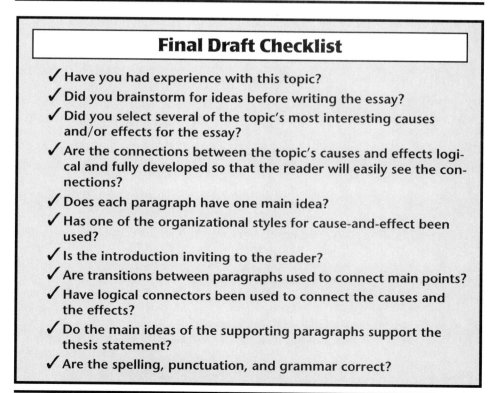

Final Draft Checklist

✔ Have you had experience with this topic?

✔ Did you brainstorm for ideas before writing the essay?

✔ Did you select several of the topic's most interesting causes and/or effects for the essay?

✔ Are the connections between the topic's causes and effects logical and fully developed so that the reader will easily see the connections?

✔ Does each paragraph have one main idea?

✔ Has one of the organizational styles for cause-and-effect been used?

✔ Is the introduction inviting to the reader?

✔ Are transitions between paragraphs used to connect main points?

✔ Have logical connectors been used to connect the causes and the effects?

✔ Do the main ideas of the supporting paragraphs support the thesis statement?

✔ Are the spelling, punctuation, and grammar correct?

Going Further: Idea Generator

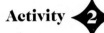

Activity 1   **World Events.**   Cut out pictures from newspapers and magazines of major world events, such as earthquakes, political riots, wars, elections, etc., and bring them to class. Post these pictures around the room. First, identify the event with your classmates, then talk about what the causes of this event might be. Finally, lead a class discussion about the possible effects of this event.

Activity 2   **Chain Reactions.**   Often, the effects of one action cause a new situation, which in turn causes a new set of causes and effects. This is called a *chain reaction.* In groups of four or five, work together to tell a story in which the effect that one person tells causes a reaction in the next person's story, and so on. For example, you may want to start by saying "Li Mei woke up three hours late, so she missed the bus for work." The next student might add, "As a result, she was very late for an important meeting at work." And so on. Continue the story until each person in the group has added ten sentences. One person in the group should record everyone's responses, and afterwards, you can write this as a group story to share with the rest of your class.

Chapter 8

Persuasion

Persuasion is a familiar concept. We have all tried to persuade someone to do or to believe something, and we have all been persuaded
by others. We try to persuade friends to go to one movie instead of
another or to think that one sports team is better than another.
Every day, advertisers attempt to persuade consumers to buy certain
products, and politicians try to make us believe that their program is
best. In this chapter, you will read persuasive essays and learn how to
write persuasively. All the techniques you have learned so far will apply here. A good persuasion essay can make use of description, narration, exposition, comparison and contrast, and cause and effect.

Part One

Reading and Writing Persuasion

When you write a persuasive essay (sometimes called an "argument"), you do more than simply see a problem, present a solution, and have everyone agree with your position. As a persuasive writer, you must know your audience and anticipate what some of your audience's opposing arguments might be. You must also offer sufficient support to make your own argument strong. In this section, you will learn that you must know all sides of the issue about which you are writing. You will also become familiar with different kinds of support that make a persuasive essay.

Activity ◆ **Debating Both Sides of an Issue.** A debate is a common activity in which persuasion is used. As a class, choose a controversial topic, such as one from the following list. Then, divide your class into two groups. One group will be *pro* (for), the other group will be *con* (against). In your groups, write down ideas that support your position. Even though you may find yourself on a side with which you don't particularly agree, you must still try to find strong support for your team's position. Your teacher will decide which side has supported its position with the strongest arguments.

Ideas for Debate

1. Capital punishment
2. Divorce
3. Technology: Is it beneficial to society?
4. Gun Control
5. Children in competitive sports
6. Choosing the gender of your child (e.g., through technological means)
7. Requiring students to learn a foreign language while in elementary and secondary school
8. Public assistance for the needy: Is it necessary?
9. Intercultural marriages
10. Censorship

Persuasion in the Real World

Persuasive writing is one of the most common essay forms. One of the main reasons you write is to influence others. Alternatively, because you read to become informed on different issues, you often become influenced by various writers' opinions. Whether you are reading a newspaper editorial, a movie review, or an advertisement, the writer may sway you to consider his or her viewpoint.

The first two essays are about the legalization of marijuana, sometimes referred to as "pot," in the United States. Although both essays discuss the same subject, the authors represent opposing viewpoints. After you read, choose the essay that you found most persuasive, and state why. Then discuss your opinions with the class.

Prereading Activity

Cannabis sativa, or hemp, a plant grown in many countries in the world, has many useful functions. For example, it can be used to make rope and to alleviate pain. However, some products of the *cannabis sativa* plant, if used improperly, can have harmful effects. Because of these sometimes destructive effects, the use of marijuana, which comes from the cannabis plant, was made illegal in the United States about the time of World War II. Before you read these two essays, discuss the following questions in small groups, then review the vocabulary words highlighted before each essay.

1. What positive uses can be served by marijuana or other substances made from plants?
2. What negative uses can they have?

✦ VOCABULARY WATCH

NOUNS	VERBS	ADJECTIVES
fiber	perpetuate	durable
varnish		versatile
sedative		respective
nausea		addicting
euphoria		
deterioration		
outlawing		

Hemp Can Help Heal

(A)   Imagine a plant that produces long, tough **fibers,** which not only can produce solid, **durable** rope and twine, but also can make a sturdy cloth that is stronger yet softer than cotton. Imagine these same plant fibers being used to produce all kinds of paper and building materials, freeing a society from its dependence on products made from trees. In addition, the oil from the plant's seeds provides food protein and can be made into products ranging from **varnish** to cooking oil. Along with the fibers and seeds, imagine that this same plant has leaves, which naturally contain a chemical found to be useful as a **sedative** and in relieving pain and **nausea.** Imagine that this incredible plant can be grown almost anywhere in the world, and it can be successfully grown without the use of chemical fertilizers and toxic insecticides. Can a plant like this really exist, or is it too good to be true? Fortunately, this plant really does exist and it can produce all of the wonderful benefits described above and more. Unfortunately, this miraculous plant, known as hemp (*cannabis sativa*), is not being used as widely as it should be; in fact, growing hemp is against the law in the United States.

(B)   Why would such a beneficial plant be outlawed in the United States? Before 1937, hemp was not illegal in the U.S. In fact, it was widely used in the early Colonial settlements and by the pioneers who settled the western United States. For many years, farming families in the U.S. would set aside at least one section of land specifically for growing hemp, which was long recognized as one of the most **versatile** and valuable plants grown in the U.S. Even the Constitution of the United States was originally written on paper produced from hemp! Although it was already illegal during World War II, farmers and 4-H Clubs* were encouraged by the government to grow hemp as part of the U.S. war effort. Hemp crops yielded oil used to lubricate plane engines, parachute webbing, ropes, and canvas.

(C)   It is no longer legal to grow hemp in the United States for two main reasons: 1) misinformation about the effect of the chemical tetrahydrocannabinol (THC) found in the leaves and flowers of the hemp plant which began to appear in newspaper articles in the mid-1930s, and 2) the efforts of powerful petroleum and timber producers who fought to eliminate hemp as a competitor for their markets. Today, oil and timber producers still maintain almost total control of their **respective** markets, and the U.S. government's war on drugs continues to **perpetuate** misinformation about hemp and THC.

(D)   THC, like other drugs including tobacco, caffeine, and alcohol, can be harmful if abused. Marijuana and hashish are produced from hemp leaves and flowers, and marijuana is classified as a *narcotic*, a chemical which produces drowsiness. Someone who uses marijuana will usually feel relaxed and may also have "an increase in heartbeat, heightening of the senses, feelings of **euphoria**," according to *The Cambridge Factfinder*. Like any narcotic, marijuana will also temporarily reduce a person's powers of concentration, reaction, and coordination.

(E)   But this chemical, unlike other drugs such as tobacco, caffeine, and alcohol, is not physically **addicting**. A person who uses marijuana or hashish *cannot* become addicted. In fact, in two separate studies, scientists argue that there is no evidence suggesting that marijuana is a "gateway drug." The use of marijuana will not automatically lead to the use of hard drugs such as heroin. In addition, many other studies mentioned in the book, *Hemp & the Marijuana Conspiracy: The Emperor Wears No Clothes*, indicate that there is no evidence of cannabis use

---

* Organizations sponsored by the U.S. Government to teach young people about modern farming methods; the 4 "Hs" stand for: head, heart, hands, and health.

harming the human brain or intelligence; there is no link between cannabis use and criminal behavior; there is no evidence of any kind of permanent physical **deterioration** associated with cannabis use.

(F)   In fact, hemp has been found to have great value in improving health. It has been shown to ease pain and relieve stress. Illnesses such as glaucoma, migraine headaches, and insomnia can be treated and even prevented with hemp. Patients suffering from AIDS, cancer, tuberculosis, and eating disorders have found that hemp products help them relax and even stimulate their appetites. When these patients are able to eat, they gain or maintain their weight, and their strength improves. The hemp flower also contains a natural antibiotic that has been used to treat burns and bacterial infections of the eyes, ears, mouth, and throat.

(G)   The U.S. Government's continuing policy to prohibit marijuana use appears to be an overreaction to a growing hard drug (heroin, cocaine, etc.) problem. It seems as though the baby has been thrown out with the bath water. With the **outlawing** of marijuana, all of the beneficial effects have also been outlawed. For example, recently in the state of Utah there was a young man who suffered from a rare autoimmune disease which caused him to have violent attacks of nausea. Even after the nausea episodes passed, the young man was very weak and still felt unable to eat. Marijuana was the only thing that he found that helped him keep his nausea attacks under control. Synthesized, or manmade, versions of THC were expensive and not as effective for him as marijuana, so the young man went to court to get permission to legally use marijuana as part of his therapy. Unfortunately, the court denied his request, and this young man continues to suffer without relief.

(H)   What should the U.S. do about hemp and controversial hemp products such as marijuana? The country of Holland may provide the best route for the U.S. government to follow. Since the government of Holland made the sale and use of cannabis legal, marijuana and hashish are no longer sold by hard drug dealers. According to a 1989 *L.A. Times* article, since its legalization, cannabis use among teenagers in Holland has gone down considerably.

(I)   Hemp has been grown for thousands of years as a source of food, fiber, fuel, and medicine. It may, in part, be the answer to many of our country's concerns as we look for new sources of renewable fuel, as well as food and fibers that can be grown and produced with fewer chemicals. Furthermore, manmade drugs are usually more expensive and not always as effective as natural chemicals. For the health of the planet and its people, we must look to natural "miracle" plants such as hemp.

by S. Scott

◆ VOCABULARY WATCH

NOUNS	VERBS	EXPRESSIONS
prohibition	endorse	side effects
decriminalization	entice	
deterrent	differentiate	
perks	surpass	
proponent		

Pot Promotes Further Drug Use Problems

Preston was a glaucoma sufferer during the time it was legal to carry marijuana for medical use.

But he refused to do so. "It sends the wrong message," he said, adding that he didn't want to add to the "national high."

In the late '70s, the Nixon administration **endorsed** "partial **prohibition**" or "**decriminalization.**"

The belief was some young people may be labeled drug abusers for life if they were prosecuted for possession of small amounts of pot. The definition of "small" varied from state to state. It was a time of drug law experimentation.

Later the Bush administration reversed a federal policy that allowed the Food and Drug Administration to permit people with certain illnesses to use pot.

Decriminalization had proven not to be a **deterrent** of drug abuse. Possession of small amounts began again.

Legal efforts to legalize the medical use of marijuana have failed, and for good reason.

Marijuana is a gateway drug: It leads to the use of harder drugs. Legalization would give young minds, and burned-out minds, a green flag to use or continue to use. It would give the OK that would **entice** and lead others down the high road of drug abuse.

Recently released by Columbia University, a study termed "Gateway Drugs" (tobacco, alcohol and marijuana) found that children 12 through 17 years old who use marijuana are 85 percent more likely to use cocaine than children who have not used marijuana.

And Salt Lake City is no exception.

Rick, a native of Salt Lake City, began smoking marijuana around age 15. Despite the **perks** of a middle-income family, good family ties and a strong religious base, he and every friend he can recall smoked pot.

There were none of these friends, to his recollection, who didn't move on to harder drugs. "We tried them all," Rick claims. "Many even used heroin."

About half of Rick's friends are still abusing drugs and alcohol, he said.

It would be unfair to say marijuana is the wild card that brings about drug addiction.

It is fair, however, to say that there is more evidence that marijuana leads to drug abuse than there is evidence that cigarettes are related to lung cancer, emphysema and heart disease.

Legalization of marijuana would increase the availability of the drug and its by-products.

Intervention programs competing with advertisements for marijuana harvests would send mixed messages to children.

The drug companies would be claiming marijuana's ability to end nausea, pain and increase ap-

Continued

Pot Promotes Further Drug Use Problems Continued

petite, while schools, parents and role models would continue to advocate "just say no."

Children and some adults don't always have the ability to **differentiate** between the good and the bad.

Proponents of legalization feel the medicinal use of marijuana is reason enough for legalization.

But THC, the primary active ingredient in marijuana, has been synthesized and used routinely as dronabinol capsules.

The National Institutes of Health (NIH) has found no scientific justification that smoking marijuana is effective in treatment of glaucoma or multiple sclerosis.

AIDS patients are being studied now, and no evidence has been obtained proving natural THC works better than synthesized THC.

In fact, the NIH maintains that manufactured drugs like serotonin and dronabinol are more effective, less dangerous and the dose is more accurate.

Marijuana, when smoked, combusts into more than 2,000 chemicals, which include carcinogens and toxins.

Bill Grigg, spokesman for US Public Health Service, said, "The only reason we're having the medical debate is because 'advocates' want it legalized for recreational use."

Rick saw damage done to the lives of friends and families. He knows first-hand the power of pot: a gateway to nowhere.

Even removing the threat of long-term marijuana abuse and further drug involvement, loss of memory and the inability to concentrate are considerable **side effects.** They are side effects that can occur with medical and personal use.

There is no logical reason to legalize pot.

Medically we have **surpassed** whatever benefit it provided.

by Kathy Barnett, *Salt Lake Tribune,*
February 7, 1995

✦ About the Reading

1. Briefly describe the purpose of each article.

2. According to the articles, how can marijuana be helpful? How can it be harmful?

3. Identify the thesis statement in each article.

4. After identifying the thesis of each article, make a list of at least five items that each writer used to persuade the reader.

5. What is a "gateway drug"? What is each author's attitude toward marijuana as a gateway drug?

6. For each article, identify where and how each author used outside experts.

7. According to Kathy Barnett, how would the legalization of marijuana and intervention programs send a mixed message to children?

8. According to S. Scott, what other substances, besides marijuana, can be harmful?

9. In what ways does each author use cause and effect to develop persuasive arguments? How did either author use comparison and contrast?

10. Which article do you find more persuasive? Explain why.

Exercise  **Recognizing Specialized Vocabulary.** Both of these articles mention various diseases and physical or mental ailments. Scan both articles, underline all such references, and be prepared to discuss them with your class.

✧ **Prereading**
✧ **Activity**

Having access to clean water is a daily problem in many parts of the world. In some parts of the world, however, people may never give clean water any thought. The author of the following essay thought that this subject is important for us to think about. Before you read the essay, discuss the following questions with your classmates in small groups, and then review the vocabulary words highlighted here.

1. In your country, do most people have easy access to clean water—water they can drink or cook with—in their homes?

2. Do you worry about having clean water today, tomorrow, or a year from now?

✧ VOCABULARY WATCH

NOUNS	VERBS	ADJECTIVES	EXPRESSIONS
manufacturing	dump	turbulent	seep down
creature	guarantee	downstream	
shore		precious	
privilege			
litter			
waste			

Clean Water:
Our Most Valuable Resource

(A)   Oceans, rivers, streams, and lakes cover about three fourths of the earth's surface. Looking at a world map there seems to be water everywhere, but only about 2.5% of all the water on the earth's surface is fresh water—water that can be used for drinking, cooking, farming and **manufacturing**. Luckily for the living things that depend on fresh water, there is also water found beneath the surface of the earth. In fact, 90% of the water that is used by plants, animals and humans comes from below the ground.

(B) Every living thing needs water. Humans can live without food longer than they can live without water. Nevertheless, all over the world, we have made the water in our oceans, rivers, streams, and lakes polluted and dirty. Although water is the most valuable resource we have, we are not doing a very good job of keeping it clean and usable.

(C) According to the Earth Works Group, publisher of such books as *50 Simple Things You Can Do To Save The Earth*, 14 billion pounds of garbage and poisonous chemicals are **dumped** into the world's oceans every year. The plastic bags, garbage, and chemicals that are dumped or spilled into the ocean kill as many as one million sea **creatures** every year. Like the ocean, our rivers and lakes are also used as places to dump both garbage and chemicals. Thirty years ago, there was a river in Ohio that was so polluted with chemicals that it caught fire. Today in parts of Eastern Europe there are still rivers that can catch fire due to the large amount of chemicals in them. Even the water that runs below the ground is not safe from pollution. These underground sources of clean water are polluted by chemicals that are dumped on the surface of the earth and then **seep down** into the water beneath the ground. According to the Earth Works Group, a gallon of gasoline spilled on the ground can seep into the water below and pollute 250,000 gallons of drinking water.

(D) Fortunately, many bodies of water are able to cleanse themselves over time. Oceans that are **turbulent** and rivers that flow quickly can rid themselves of some of the pollution. But the oceans that are quiet, such as the Baltic Sea, and rivers that flow slowly may take as many as 80 years to cleanse themselves of the pollution that has been poured into them by unthinking humans. And the underground pools of water that don't move at all may never be able to rid themselves of the pollution that seeps down from the surface above.

(E)　　We have to stop thinking that what we dump into the ocean or in a river or on the ground will just flow away and not cause a problem for anyone else. The trash you throw into the ocean today will wash up on someone's (maybe even your own!) **shore** tomorrow. The chemicals that you pour into the river flowing by your home will flow by someone else's home, too. The chemicals you let spill on the ground may end up in the water you drink. Someone once said, "We all live **downstream.**" We are all affected by the pollution that is ruining our **precious** sources of water.

(F)　　Some of us are fortunate to have access to clean water in our homes, and may not even be aware of the lack of clean, fresh water in other parts of the world. Because of the polluting of our fresh water sources, many people must buy the water they use for drinking and cooking, or they may have to travel far from their homes to find a source of clean water. In some parts of the world, people have no access to clean water; the water they are forced to use actually makes them sick. By one estimate, there are over 25,000 deaths each day from dirty water. However, even if we have access to clean water today, this doesn't **guarantee** that we will *always* have access to clean water.

(G)　　In the past few years, some countries such as England, the United States, and Japan have realized the importance of clean water and have made greater efforts to take better care of their water supplies. Yet even though most bodies of water in the United States are cleaner today than they were several decades ago, there is still a problem with polluted water in the U.S. According to a survey done by the U.S. Environmental Protection Agency, almost half of all rivers, lakes, and streams in the U.S. are damaged or threatened by pollution. Obviously, there is still much more work to be done.

(H)　　Clean water should be a worldwide human right for everyone, not just a **privilege** for a select group of people. To make clean water available for more people, there are some important steps we can all take. You may think that there is nothing that you can do as one person to control what your government or the local factory does to your source of water, but remember that every little bit helps. One person *can* make a difference. Some things that you can do personally are the following:
　1)　Don't throw any kind of **litter** on a beach or in any water. Next time you visit your favorite beach, river, or lake, take along a bag and pick up the litter you find. Take the bottles or aluminum cans you find to a recycling center if possible. If you fish, don't ever

leave plastic fishing line behind; birds and sea creatures can get tangled in it and die.

2) Don't pour chemicals such as paint, gasoline, or motor oil on the ground, in any water, or even in the garbage where it may be dumped onto the ground later. Even the chemicals you spray on plants and trees eventually are washed into the ground and can seep down to the groundwater. Use these chemicals sparingly.

3) Don't leave any kind of **waste** near a stream. Human and animal waste pollute water.

4) Report any kind of chemical or other polluting leaks to a local authority.

(I)   Some of us have been lucky to have lived most of our lives in a place where we can drink and cook with clean water. But there are those of us who have also lived where clean water was scarce, and every drop was valuable. Anyone who has had to go without clean water for even a day can appreciate how valuable clean water is to human life. If you want to help, organize with other people who also care about clean water and the future of our planet. Write to the local newspapers, and meet with the local authorities about cleaning up the water where you live. In the words of Al Gore, Vice President of the United States, "The lakes and rivers sustain us; they flow through the veins of the earth and into our own. But we must take care to let them flow back out as pure as they came, not poison and waste them without thought for the future."

✧ **About the Reading**

1. What kinds of information does this author use to persuade the reader? Is it effective? Why or why not?

2. How does the author use authorities in this essay? Are they used effectively? Why or why not?

3. What is the thesis statement of this essay?

4. Evaluate the introduction to this essay. How many paragraphs does it cover?

5. What is the meaning of the sentence, "We all live downstream" in paragraph (E)? Does it matter that the author doesn't mention exactly who said it?

6. How does the author use cause and effect in this essay? How does the author use comparison and contrast?

7. What specific recommendations does the author make to the reader?

What Do You Think?

Write about an issue that you think people need to think about that will make the world a better place today and in the future.

Identifying Persuasive Support

The support that writers use for persuasive essays is critical to the effectiveness of the writing. An author will either convince you or not, depending on the quality and quantity of the support he or she uses. When you write your own persuasive essays, you will more likely get your readers to agree with you if your support is clear and strong.

The major types of support used for persuasion are *examples* (e.g., facts and personal experiences), *personal opinion,* and *citations of expert authorities.* Examples are usually the most effective type of support.

Examples. Examples are the heart of your support. Examples can be general or specific, but usually the more specific, the better they are. The following are two possible types of examples.

1) **Facts.** Facts are actual statistics or documented events. Facts are often given in the form of numbers, such as statistics. "Clean Water" is loaded with important and convincing statistics, such as "14 billion pounds of garbage and poisonous chemicals are dumped into the world's oceans every year" and "only about 2.5% of all the water on the earth's surface is fresh water."

2) **Personal Experience.** Although personal experience is often not considered to be as strong as hard facts, no one can dispute true experiences, either your own, or those of someone you know or have heard about. Experience adds reality to facts that can often seem far removed from true life experience. Both articles on marijuana make use of personal experience. In "Hemp Can Help Heal," S. Scott relates the positive experiences with marijuana of a young man in Utah suffering from an autoimmune disease, while in "Pot Promotes Further Drug Use Problems," Kathy Barnett tells about the negative experiences of another young man in Utah.

Personal Opinion. Personal opinion is often expressed in a thesis statement or a topic sentence. The examples used in the essay are chosen to support the stated opinion as strongly as possible. The author of "Clean Water" states emphatically, "We have to stop thinking that what we dump into the ocean or in a river or on the ground will just flow away and not cause a problem for anyone else." Also, the closing sentences of both articles on marijuana make the respective authors' personal opinions very clear: "There is no logical reason to legalize pot," and "For the health of the planet and its people, we must look to natural 'miracle' plants such as hemp."

Personal opinion is not the strongest form of support because it relies on the point of view of the writer, and people can always disagree with an opinion. However, there are ways to make your personal opinion more convincing. For instance, avoid using the personal pronoun *I* or phrases that begin with *I:* "I think that . . . , I believe . . . ," etc. Notice that the author of "Clean Water" does not write *"I feel that* we have to stop thinking what we dump into the ocean . . . will just flow away," but rather, "We have to stop thinking that what we dump into the ocean . . . " [paragraph E], and the author of "Hemp Can Help Heal" writes "In fact, hemp has been found to have great value in improving health" [paragraph F], rather than "I think that hemp has great value in improving health."

Citations of Expert Authorities. One of the best ways to persuade your reader is to cite (e.g., quote) convincing authorities on your topic. However, such authorities must be chosen and used very carefully. For example, if you wanted to convince your reader about the benefits of antismoking legislation, you probably would not use the president of a tobacco company, except to show an opposing viewpoint. In the antimarijuana article by Kathy Barnett, she effectively used such reputable authorities as Columbia University and the National Institutes of Health.

Exercise 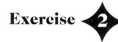 **Identifying Persuasive Support.** For each of the following categories of support, there is one example from the essay "Clean Water: Our Most Valuable Resource." List at least two more examples from the same essay for each category of persuasive support.

Examples

Facts Only about 2.5% of all the water on the earth is fresh water.

_____

_____

_____

Personal Experience Some of us have been lucky to have lived most of our lives in a place where we can drink and cook with clean water.

_____

_____

_____

Personal Opinion We have to stop thinking that what we dump into the ocean or in a river or on the ground will just flow away and not cause a problem for anyone else.

_____

_____

_____

Citation of According to the Earth Works Group, a gallon of gasoline spilled
Authorities on the ground can seep into the water below and pollute 250,000
gallons of drinking water.

_____

_____

_____

Getting Started: Brainstorming Types of Support

It is always a good idea to take some time to think about what you want to write before you even begin writing. Before you write a persuasive essay, you will first want to have a clear goal in mind regarding what you want to convince your reader to do or to believe. Then you will want to spend some time brainstorming for the various types of support you can use to reach your goal.

The writer's brainstorming for "Clean Water: Our Most Valuable Resource" may have looked like this:

Goal: To convince the reader that clean water is valuable, and each person

has a responsibility to work for clean water in his or her community.

Types of Support

Examples

Facts

1. Water covers 3/4 of the earth's surface, but only 2.5% is fresh

2. 90% of fresh water is underground

3. Every living organism needs water to survive

4. 14 billion pounds of garbage and chemicals are dumped into the oceans

5. 1 gallon of gasoline can pollute 250,000 gallons of fresh water

6. 25,000 people die each day from the effects of dirty water

7. Some rivers in the United States and eastern Europe are so polluted
   that they catch fire

8. Baltic Sea cannot cleanse itself very quickly

Personal experience

1. Some people have been without clean water

Personal opinion

1. <u>Whenever any one of us pollutes our water, all of us are affected by the pollution</u>

2. <u>People should clean up their own water sources—don't litter, don't dump chemicals, etc.</u>

Citation of authorities

1. <u>Earth Works Group</u>

2. <u>U.S. Environmental Protection Agency</u>

3. <u>Vice President Al Gore</u>

Exercise  **Brainstorming for Your Persuasive Essay.** Now it is time for you to decide what your goal is and to brainstorm for ideas you can use in your own persuasive essay. If you need ideas for a topic, look at the list at the beginning of this chapter (page 258), use the topic your class debated, or choose a completely different topic.

To give a structure to your goal and your possible support, use the following outline. Copy the outline onto a separate sheet of paper, and fill in the details for your topic.

Goal:

Types of Support:

   Examples:

    Facts:

    Personal experiences:

   Personal opinions:

   Citation of authorities:

Essay Writing: First Draft

After you have spent time brainstorming about possible types of persuasive support for your essay, and you have recorded all of your ideas for possible types of support, you can select your best ideas and begin writing. Try to use at least two different kinds of support in your essay.

Before you write your first draft, read over the First Draft Checklist to guide your writing. Then, after you have written your draft, use the checklist to evaluate what you have written. Make any changes that will improve your writing.

Part Two

Developing Persuasive Writing

In persuasive writing, as in all other types of writing, organization is extremely important. A well-organized persuasive essay has the power to convince its readers of its argument. This section explains how to organize a persuasive essay, including a review of strong thesis statements and an introduction to *coherence* (the tendency for ideas to hold together logically).

Organizational Style in Persuasive Writing

A writer's purpose in persuasive writing is to convince readers that the author's viewpoint is the correct one. This often involves trying to get readers to change their opinion about a subject. Because of this, authors need to be especially aware of their audiences when writing persuasive pieces. It is important to think about why a reader might hold an opposing viewpoint and then to explain why the reader's opinion is incorrect or inadequate. In such essays, after refuting the opposing arguments, writers go on to present additional arguments in support of what should be a clear and direct thesis statement. The following essay exemplifies this pattern of organization in persuasive writing.

 **Prereading Activity**

The following essay was written by a student who thought at first that a dishwasher would be a wonderful appliance to have. However, after using one, her opinion changed. Before you begin reading, discuss the following questions with your classmates in small groups.

1. Are dishwashers a common appliance in your country?

2. What do you like and dislike about using a dishwasher?

272

Against Dishwashers

(A)   Dishwashers are one of the most common American household appliances. When I first came to America, I knew that dishwashers were viewed as a necessity by most Americans. Because dishwashers are not common in my country, Japan, I really looked forward to having a chance to use this wonderful appliance. However, after having used a dishwasher, my first impressions have changed. I now feel that dishwashers are not necessary. In fact, rather than being a helpful tool, dishwashers are an inconvenience.

(B)   Most Americans believe that a dishwasher is a great tool because it saves time. However, a dishwasher actually "takes" time. For example, because a dishwasher takes a lot of water to run, most people like to make sure that it is completely full before they run it. As a result, when there are only a few dishes to be washed, the dishes are not cleaned immediately. While these dishes sit in the dishwasher, the leftover food dries, and this dried-on food takes more time to clean off the dishes. On the other hand, when there are many dishes to wash, not all of the dishes can fit in the washer at the same time. Consequently, some dishes must be left unwashed until the first set of dishes is cleaned. Waiting for those dishes takes time. So, how can people say that dishwashers save time?

(C)   Americans also believe that dishwashers are helpful appliances because these appliances can wash and dry dishes completely, without human work. On the contrary, a dishwasher takes a lot of human work to fully clean the dishes. If dishes aren't rinsed before they are put into the dishwasher, the heat of the washer bakes food onto the plates. This dried-on food is very difficult to get off the dishes. Actually, a dishwasher only washes dishes cleaner after people have already washed the majority of the food off of them. Further, even if the dishes are rinsed before they are washed, there are usually detergent spots left on the dishes. These spots must then be washed off of the dishes before they can be used. For these reasons, dishwashers actually make a lot more work than they save.

(D)   In conclusion, if we want to wash our dishes completely and quickly, washing them by hand is the answer. In the time that it takes to get the dishes ready to be washed by the dishwasher, we can wash them ourselves. When we wash dishes by hand, we also can be sure that the dishes are clean, and we can finish the job all at once. Certainly, washing dishes by hand is the smarter decision.

by Ryoko

✦ About the Reading

1. Why does the author think that dishwashers are not helpful?

2. How does she attempt to persuade her readers?

3. Find the thesis statement. Is it a strong statement of her opinion?

4. Which of the author's arguments do you agree with? Are there arguments that you disagree with?

5. How has the writer used comparison and contrast?

What Do You Think?

Is there some tool or appliance in your country that you think helps in daily life? Write about the purpose of the tool and why it makes life more convenient.

If you look closely at "Against Dishwashers," you can see that Ryoko organized her essay in a very straightforward way. In her opening paragraph, she explained the issue, which is whether dishwashers are helpful. She also strongly stated her opinion when she wrote, "dishwashers are an inconvenience." Next, Ryoko explained why the opposing viewpoint is wrong. She understood that people who like dishwashers think that they save time and wash dishes more cleanly than hand washing. However, to refute these ideas, she explained to her reader why she believes these opinions are incorrect. Finally, she added a conclusion in which she restated her opinion.

The following box summarizes key points to remember when organizing a persuasive essay.

An Effective Way to Organize Your Persuasive Essay

1. Introduction
   - Explain the problem or argument: Briefly explain what each side believes.
   - Use a strong thesis statement to explain or state your opinion.
2. Refute the opposing arguments: Explain why the other side is wrong.
3. Explain additional reasons and give supporting arguments.
4. Conclusion
   - Briefly restate the reasons argued previously.
   - Restate your opinion.

Arguing a Case

In order to effectively argue against the other side, a writer must first understand why the reader might hold the opposing opinion. Only then can the writer argue effectively. For example, if a writer were trying to persuade us that putting older people in rest homes is wrong, some of his or her arguments might be these:

- People get lonely in rest homes.

- Rest homes are expensive.

- Rest homes can't provide the kind of care for a person that a family member can.

The opposition will probably agree with some but not all of these reasons. For example, the opposition might easily agree with the first two points yet not with the third. Thus, the writer would focus on explaining why this point is valid and important.

As an informed reader, it is important not to believe everything you read. In other words, you should read critically. Don't just accept the reasons the author gives as being strong enough to convince you of his or her arguments. As you read, think of other points that may support an opposing view. Keeping opposing arguments in mind while reading is called being a "devil's advocate." By being a devil's advocate, you will get more out of your reading, as you can add your own judgment and criticism.

Exercise 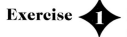 **Being a Devil's Advocate.** Look at the following topics, and think of all of the reasons that you or another reader might give to show that the writer's point of view is wrong. Use the following example as a guide in writing your own responses on the lines.

Example.   A woman should stay at home and take care of her children.

          Women need to work to be independent.

          Women are needed in the work force to support their families.

          Women should be able to have the same opportunities as men to

          work.

1. Mothers should be encouraged to work outside their homes.

    _____

    _____

    _____

2. People who commit murder should be killed.

    _____

    _____

    _____

3. Divorce is always a wrong decision.

    _____

    _____

    _____

4. Teachers should not be allowed to discipline students physically.

_____

_____

_____

5. No country should trade with countries that abuse human rights.

_____

_____

_____

 **Prereading Activity**

Divorce is very common in the United States. Traditionally, in the majority of the cases, the children live with the mother after the divorce. The author of the following essay challenges this tradition. Before you read the essay, discuss the following questions with your classmates in small groups, and then review the vocabulary words highlighted here.

1. Should one parent be more responsible for parenting than the other?

2. Who do you think should decide what happens to the children in a divorce? How should it be determined?

✧ VOCABULARY WATCH

NOUNS	VERBS	ADJECTIVES	ADVERBS
spouse	enact	uncontradicted	unanimously
assets		contested	
custody		unfit	
hearing			
advent			

I, Too, Am a Good Parent: Dads Should Not Be Discriminated Against

Divorce is a fact of modern life. A great number of people simply decide that they do not wish to stay married to their **spouse**. A divorce is not a tremendously difficult situation unless there are minor children born to the couple. If there are no minor children you simply divide the **assets** and debts. But you cannot divide a child. The child needs to be placed with the appropriate parent.

Continued

I, Too, Am a Good Parent: Dads Should Not Be Discriminated Against Continued

In my own case, my former wife chose not to remain married to me. That is her right and I do not fault her decision. My problem is that I do not believe it is her right to deny me the privilege of raising our children. Some fathers want to go to the parent/teacher conferences, school plays, carnivals and to help their kids with homework. I have always looked forward to participating on a daily basis in my children's lives. I can no longer enjoy that privilege—the children live with their mother, who has moved to a northern Midwest state.

I tried so hard to gain **custody** of my children. I believe the evidence is **uncontradicted** as to what an excellent father (and more important, parent) I am. My ex-wife is a fairly good mother, but unbiased opinions **unanimously** agreed I was the better parent. Testimonials were videotaped from witnesses who could not attend the out-of-state custody **hearing.** I choose to be a father. When I was 3 years old, my own father left my family. While I've loved my father for many years, I did and still do reject his parental pattern.

A couple of centuries ago, a father and mother might have shared equally in the care and raising of children above the age of infancy. But with the coming of the Industrial Revolution the father went to work during the day, leaving the full-time care of the young to the mother, who stayed at home. It was easier to decide who should get child custody under those circumstances. That would be true today even if the mother were put into the position of working outside the home after the divorce.

Now, a majority of married mothers are in the workplace—often because the family needs the second income to survive. With the **advent** of the working mother, we have also seen a change in child care. Not only have we seen an increase in third-party caregivers; there is a decided difference in how fathers interact with their children. Fathers are even starting to help raise their children. I admit that in a great many families there is an uneven distribution of childcare responsibilities. But there are fathers who do as much to raise the children as the mother, and there are many examples where men are full-time parents.

But, because we have this past history of the mother being the principal child caregiver, the mother has almost always been favored in any **contested** child-custody case. The law of every state is replete with decisions showing that the mother is the favored custodial parent. The changes in our lifestyles are now being reflected in our laws. In most, if not all, states, the **legislature** has recognized the change in child-care responsibilities and **enacted** legislation that is gender blind. The statutes that deal with child custody now say that the children should be placed with the parent whose care and control of the child will be in the child's best interest.

This legislation is enlightened and correct. Society has changed. We no longer bring up our children as we did years ago. But it is still necessary to have someone make the choice in the child's best interest if the parents are divorcing and cannot agree on who takes care of the kids. So we have judges to make that enormous decision.

The state legislature can pass laws that say neither parent is favored because of their gender. But it is judges who make the ultimate choice. And those judges are usually *older males* who practiced law during the time when mothers were the favored guardians under the law. These same judges mostly come from a background where mothers stayed home and were

Continued

I, Too, Am a Good Parent: Dads Should Not Be Discriminated Against   Continued

the primary caregivers. By training and by personal experiences they have a strong natural bias in favor of the mother in a child-custody case. That belief is regressive and fails to acknowledge the changed realities of our present way of life. Someone must be appointed to render a decision when parents cannot agree. I would ask that those judges who make these critical decisions re-examine their attitudes and prejudices against placing children with fathers.

After the videotaped testimony was completed, one of my lawyers said he had "never seen a father put together a better custody case." "But," he asked me, "can you prove she is **unfit?**" A father should not be placed in the position of having to prove the mother is unfit in order to gain custody. He should not have to prove that she has two heads, participates in child sacrifice or eats live snakes. The father should only have to prove that he is the more suitable parent.

Fathers should not be discriminated against as I was. It took me three years to get a trial on the merits in the Minnesota court. And Minnesota has a law directing its courts to give a high priority to child-custody cases. What was even worse was that the judge seemed to ignore the overwhelming weight of the evidence and granted custody to my ex-wife. At the trial, her argument was, "I am their mother." Other than that statement she hardly put on a case. Being the mother of the children was apparently deemed enough to outweigh evidence that all the witnesses who knew us both felt I was the better parent; that those witnesses who knew only me said what an excellent parent I was; that our children's behavior always improved dramatically after spending time with me; that my daughter wished to live with me, and that I had a better child-custody evaluation than my wife.

So I say to the trial judges who decide these cases: "Become part of the solution to this dilemma of child custody. Don't remain part of the problem." It is too late for me. If this backward way of thinking is changed, then perhaps it won't be too late for other fathers who should have custody of their children.

by Dorsett Bennett, *Newsweek*, July 4, 1994

◆ About the Reading

1. What kinds of information did the author use to persuade the reader? Where does the writer use personal experience and facts as examples?

2. What did the author do to try to gain custody of his children?

3. What explanations does the author give for the fact that most judges give custody of the children to the mother?

4. What does the author suggest that the state legislature do to make the child-custody laws more fair?

5. What was the main argument of the author's wife at the custody trial?

6. What might be some possible arguments against this author's viewpoint?

Read to Write

What Do You Think?

What solutions would you propose to the problem of child-custody cases?

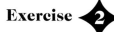 **Use Rebuttal Writing.**   A *rebuttal* gives the opposing viewpoint to a persuasive essay. Write a short rebuttal, from the wife's point of view, to "I, Too, Am a Good Parent." Be as imaginative as you like.

Reviewing Rhetorical Forms

Among the tools available to help the author write a convincing persuasive essay are all the rhetorical forms or styles that you have learned throughout this book. For example, if a writer were to argue that one type of car was better than another, the writer would want to use the techniques of *comparison and contrast* writing. On the other hand, if an author were to argue that people should not smoke because it is harmful to their health, he or she would want to use *cause–effect* writing tools. The following exercise will help you to determine which kinds of writing may best strengthen your persuasive essays.

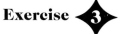 **Deciding on a Style.**   Indicate the writing style(s) that you feel would be most effective in explaining each of the following statements. (*Note:* The writing styles are biography, description, narration, exposition, comparison and contrast, and cause and effect.) Be prepared to explain your choice.

Example.   Television programming should be regulated because many topics contained in programs can be harmful to children.

 Cause and Effect _____

1. Taxes should be raised so that schools can afford the best equipment and supplies for students.

   _____

2. Nighttime is the best time to come up with new ideas.

   _____

3. It is important for the government to regulate information on the Internet.

   _____

4. Pollution is the responsibility of big industries, not individuals.

   _____

5. The most calming place I have ever been is my backyard.

   _____

6. Einstein was the smartest man who ever lived.

   _____

7. Diet programs are useless because they only cause people to become fatter than they were before they began.

_____

Making Your Position Clear: Thesis Statements

Part Three of Chapter 7 reviewed the qualities of an effective thesis statement, which contains the controlling idea of the essay (see the Thesis Focus box on page 253). In persuasive writing, the thesis statement contains an especially strong statement of the author's opinion. The author strongly and clearly takes a side and explains what he or she thinks that the reader should do or think.

Exercise  **4** **Recognizing Strong Opinions as Thesis Statements.** Following are several thesis statements. Some of them state an opinion or present a side of an issue strongly enough to be used in persuasive writing. Others do not. Read the following statements, and put a checkmark next to the thesis statements that would be suitable for a persuasive essay. Be ready to discuss your choices.

1. _____ When I came to the United States, I experienced culture shock.

2. _____ A woman should never consider the idea of having an abortion.

3. _____ Smoking is one of the worst problems in our society today.

4. _____ English should be the official language in the United States.

5. _____ Iranian body language is quite different from Chinese body language.

6. _____ Being a mother is the best profession for every woman.

7. _____ Learning to speak another language can be stressful.

8. _____ Parents should not find out the sex of their babies before they are born.

9. _____ Telling a lie often results in telling another lie.

10. _____ All university students should be required to study in a foreign country before they graduate.

 **Prereading Activity**

This persuasive essay was written by a student who experienced the importance of learning from other cultures when he studied in the United States. As you read, pay special attention to how he develops his thesis statement. Before you read, discuss the following questions in small groups.

1. How are foreigners treated in your home country?

2. What do you think you can learn from living in another culture?

Accept or Reject Foreigners?

(A)   Should people from a minority culture forget their original traditions and customs and try to adapt to the dominant culture's way of life when they immigrate to a new country? Or, should the people of the dominant culture try to learn something from the immigrant subcultures? These two viewpoints have been discussed widely in the media and wherever people meet. The question "What is best for our society?" concerns everyone. In the United States, it seems that many people feel that foreigners are dumb, lazy, and an economic burden to the society. However, this opinion is ignorant, narrow-minded, and wrong. The "new  blood" which comes from immigrants and refugees can actually benefit the dominant culture. Americans should be willing to learn from the minorities and immigrants in their culture.

(B)   Some people believe that cultural differences make it impossible for different groups to live together. One of the better examples of how cultural pluralism is good for a society is Switzerland. In Switzerland, three cultures live side by side: French, German, and Italian. These cultures have worked together for many years. The result of their mutual acceptance and cooperation is a broadly represented government which has had many innovative ideas. The lesson we can learn from Switzerland is that people can live together successfully despite cultural differences.

(C)   Cooperation is the solution to dealing with cultural differences within a nation. Instead of fighting the minority cultures that are in the United States, Americans should ask themselves, "What can we learn from these groups?" It is a matter of learning tolerance and, over time, forming a broader definition of American culture—a culture formed by taking the best from the many American subcultures and adding these qualities to the existing American culture. I have learned how important this is since I have lived in the United States. I come from Europe, and I am not used to living "side by side" with people who are not from western cultures. By getting to know people from Asia, I have learned that we can learn a lot from other people's ideas and perspectives. We all can learn more about ourselves when we allow ourselves to learn more about other people.

(D)   Some Americans feel that immigrants and refugees only come to the United States to receive welfare. It is true that some foreigners come to the United

States and become welfare recipients. However, we should not believe this false stereotype. Think about how many Americans receive welfare. It would be unfair to say that because a few Americans receive help from the government, all Americans are lazy and on welfare. Furthermore, statistics show that many highly educated people from the rest of the world choose to come to the United States for education and work because of the opportunities in this land. Over the years, the immigrant work force has greatly contributed to making the United States what it is today. It is important to bear in mind that most immigrants to the United States have been able to immigrate because of their brainpower and determination. This is an extremely valuable asset that has helped America in the past and will continue to help the United States in the future.

(E)   In the end, we must ask ourselves whether the United States can afford the narrow-mindedness that makes some Americans believe that immigrants and other minority groups should totally adapt to the American culture. Conversely, Americans can gain cultural, political and economical enrichment from the many different people who enter their society.

by R. Thornfeld

 **About the Reading**

1. What is the thesis statement in the essay? What is the author's opinion in this statement?

2. Why does the author use a series of questions in the first paragraph? What is the effect?

3. What is the meaning of "new blood" in the first paragraph?

4. What is your opinion of the author's use of facts? Are there places where more facts or statistics would have been helpful? Explain.

5. Find the topic sentence for each paragraph, and underline it. How does each relate to the thesis?

6. Why do some people dislike foreigners in their country?

7. What methods did the author use to convince you that his opinion is the correct one?

8. Do you agree or disagree with this author? Explain your answer.

What Do You Think?

What have you learned from another culture's way of doing something?

Guessing Meaning from Context. Use one of the following words from the essay to fill in the blanks in the following sentences 1–8. If you do not know the meaning of the word, look back at the essay and try to determine the meaning from the sentence (the context). After you fill in each sentence, write your own sentence using the word or expression.

media	despite	narrow-minded
burden	perspective	side by side
mutual	minority	

1. African-Americans are one of many _____ groups in the United States.

   Your sentence: _____

2. When Marty became a student again after being a teacher, he gained a different _____ on teaching.

   Your sentence: _____

3. _____ her busy schedule, Melanie still finds time to help her grandmother.

   Your sentence: _____

4. Both Ivan and Adriana know Anya; she is their _____ friend.

   Your sentence: _____

5. People who have never traveled outside of their hometown can be very _____ .

   Your sentence: _____

6. Working _____ with people of another culture can be a great learning experience.

   Your sentence: _____

7. Members of the _____ are always sure to report on tragedies in the lives of celebrities.

   Your sentence: _____

8. Even though taking care of his mother in her old age was a financial _____ , Kyochi felt it was his responsibility.

   Your sentence: _____

Exercise **6** **Writing a Good Thesis Statement for Your Essay.** Look at your own essay. Do you have a strong, persuasive thesis statement? Revise it, as needed.

Coherence

In addition to being organized in a form that will convince the reader, persuasive essays, like all essays, must be coherent. *Coherence* means that all the sentences in a paragraph or essay are presented in a logical order. The order that is most logical often depends on the type of writing you are doing. For persuasive writing, you are likely to argue about your opponent's point first, and then to present your other arguments. You want to be concerned not only about the order of your argument, but also about the content. For example, sometimes, it is tempting to add some new ideas at the end of the paragraph where they don't belong. Doing this, however, may make your writing less coherent. Each sentence in a coherent paragraph should logically connect to the sentences that precede and follow it. As you read the next essay, notice how each sentence in each paragraph flows naturally from the thought in the sentence that precedes it.

Prereading Activity

The student who wrote the following essay discusses a current issue, but with a surprising twist. Before you read it, discuss the following questions with your classmates.

1. What does recycling mean to you?

2. What recycling efforts are made in your country?

3. How do you personally try to save or recycle?

Defend the Forests

(A)   Most people want their descendants to have a comfortable life. However, we have already consumed many of our natural resources in order to provide a comfortable life for ourselves without often thinking of the consequences for the future. Only very recently have we begun to understand the environmental destruction that we have caused and to fear the effect that this destruction will have on our descendants. Americans seem to be especially concerned about their environment. They recycle their newspapers and aluminum soda pop cans, and many now bike to work instead of driving because they think that these measures will solve environmental problems. On the contrary, despite these measures, Americans remain very wasteful. There are many things that Americans could do to help solve one of the major environmental problems—saving the forests. Rather than recycle, Americans need to change their attitudes toward using paper.

(B)   Americans might be surprised to learn that their attitude toward paper use is quite wasteful. For instance, many people take a lot of paper napkins at fast food restaurants or cafeterias, and they rarely use as many as they take. Additionally, they use too many paper towels in public bathrooms. They also waste paper when they write. It seems that they like to write memos for messages that

---

are unimportant or could be communicated in other ways, often using big pieces of paper for short messages. Further, there is a lot of "junk mail" delivered daily that is never read but only thrown away.

(C)   Some Americans feel that they are really trying to help save the forests by recycling the paper that they use. However, recycling is not the real answer to the problem. A report from the Forest Resources Project explains that, "Recycling vast amounts of paper could do more harm than good to the environment." One obvious detriment of recycling is the increased air pollution it causes. Further, it is very expensive to recycle. Most people are unaware that it takes seventeen mature trees to make one ton of paper. However, when this amount is recycled, only one tenth of the original paper is produced. Therefore, recycling is actually not very efficient for the amount of money spent on it.

(D)   Rather than recycling the forests, Americans could help to save the forests by conserving the amount of paper they use in the first place. First, they should only take as many paper napkins as they need, or they should use cloth napkins. In addition, they could bring handkerchiefs to the public bathrooms, as is the custom in other countries. This could save great amounts of paper. Further, they could tell their messages to people directly or send them by electronic mail instead of writing memos. Moreover, if they don't read their junk mail, they can have their names removed from junk mail listings. These measures will save more trees from becoming paper. If we really think about defending the forests, we realize that changing our attitude about paper usage is the only way to really save the trees.

by Masae

◆ About the Reading

1. What is the thesis statement of this essay? What is the controlling idea of the essay?

2. Which kind of introduction does this essay have?

3. Did this essay seem coherent? Why or why not? How was each sentence connected to the one preceding it?

4. List four ways that Americans waste paper, according to the author.

5. Where does the author cite authorities? How effective is her use of authorities? Why?

6. What suggestions does the author give for conserving paper?

What Do You Think?

Give suggestions of your own for conserving paper, as well as other natural resources.

Exercise ◆**7**▶ **Making Coherent Paragraphs.** Each of the following paragraphs contains one sentence that is misplaced. Read the paragraphs, circle the misplaced sentences, and indicate with an arrow where the sentences should properly go. The first one has been done as an example to guide you.

Having too much money can make us lazy. When I was in my own country, I used to go to an English conversation school. Once, one of our teachers asked us to imagine what we would do if we were rich. Most of the class said they would want a huge house with a swimming pool, a tennis court, and a big garden. I was shocked and asked my classmates, "If you had a huge house such as this, who would clean it?" and they answered that they would have servants. But this would be harmful because, if they had servants to do everything for them, they would end up doing nothing. Of course, if you become lazy, you might enjoy it for a while, but you would probably not develop many positive personal characteristics. (Not doing anything leads to laziness.)

It is important to become independent at a young age. It gives people confidence in new situations, such as going to school for the first time, getting a job, or finding a place to live. Being independent also helps you to accomplish things on your own, without the help of your parents or relatives. Realizing your own goals can help you feel a sense of pride. Gaining independence helps you lose fear of unfamiliar situations. Although some people feel it is better to remain dependent on their parents for awhile, becoming independent will lead to more confidence and success in the future.

Many people would say that watching television is a complete waste of time; however, there are many benefits from watching television. We can see news throughout the world, documentaries, and other programs that teach us more about life. The television can be an excellent educational tool. It can also be a wonderful pastime. Imagine watching a good movie with your family, snacking on peanuts and popcorn. Imagine watching a good program on a cold rainy night, cuddled up in your favorite blanket. Watching television is definitely not a waste of time; it can be a wonderful way to spend free time.

Now Revise: Second Draft

Now you are ready to organize your own essay. Review your essay again. Use the questions in the Second Draft Checklist to make sure that you have implemented the ideas that were discussed in this section.

When you have finished your second draft, exchange papers with a classmate. Read and discuss each other's essays. Make suggestions for additional changes that will improve your writing.

Read to Write

Part Three

Refining and Reviewing

In this section, you will review three concepts to which you have already been introduced. First, you will review the different kinds of *cohesive devices* that you have studied in previous chapters. Second, you will review the importance of writing *effective transitions* between paragraphs. Third, you will review how to provide *adequate support* for the ideas that are presented in the topic sentence of each paragraph. Finally, you will have the opportunity to apply these concepts to your own writing.

Review of Cohesive Devices.

In previous chapters, you have learned how to use cohesive devices. *Cohesive devices* are those words and phrases that help to tie together an essay's ideas or events. Readers depend on these cohesive devices to help them see relationships between ideas or understand a sequence of events. Various cohesive devices may have different names, such as *chronological, comparison, contrast,* or *logical constructions,* but their purposes are the same—to help build connections and relationships between the ideas or events of an essay.

In persuasive writing, you may want to describe something, compare or contrast things, explain a cause-and-effect relationship, or narrate a brief personal experience to persuade your reader to see your point of view. No matter which rhetorical style you choose to use in your essay, be sure to use those cohesive devices that will make your writing clearer and more convincing to your reader.

The following is a brief review of some of the many cohesive devices you have discussed in earlier chapters. (For more complete lists, go back to the specific chapter where the device is first presented.)

Chronological Connectors	
Uses	**Cohesive Devices**
To make a sequence of events more clear	*first, second, third . . . , next, finally, last*
To show a specific time	*today, tomorrow, yesterday, at noon, in 1966, on March 6th*
To help establish a time relation-ship between events	*before, after, later that day, while, during, since, as soon as, immediately*

Comparison and Contrast Constructions	
Uses	**Cohesive Devices**
To show that two things are similar	*both, is the same as, is similar to, like, as, similarly*
To show that two things are different	*is different from, however, contrary to, on the other hand, in contrast*

Logical Connectors	
Uses	**Cohesive Devices**
To show a cause	*because, as, because of, due to, owing to*
To show an effect	*therefore, consequently, for this reason, so, as a result*

Exercise  **Using Cohesive Devices in Your Own Essay.** Look at the persuasive essay that you are writing now. Where are you using description, narration, comparison and contrast, or cause and effect in your essay? Try to include those cohesive devices that will make the relationships among your ideas and the sequence of the events more clear for your reader.

Review of Transitions between Paragraphs

Earlier, you learned how important transitions between paragraphs are for linking one paragraph to the next. A good transition will remind your reader what was written in the previous paragraph and will also prepare the reader for what will be presented in the following paragraph. Transition sentences between paragraphs also help a reader understand how separate events are related.

Read the following paragraphs from the essay "Culture Shock" on page 18 in Chapter 1. Notice how the first sentence of the second paragraph acts as the transition that links the ideas presented in the first paragraph to the ideas presented in the second paragraph.

> Studying in a different country is something that sounds very exciting to most people. Many young people who leave their home to go study in another country think that they are going to have a lot of fun. Certainly, it is a new experience which brings us the opportunity of discovering new things and a feeling of freedom. In spite of these advantages, however, there are some difficulties we will face. Because of the different beliefs, norms, values, and traditions that exist among different countries, we may have difficulty adjusting to a new culture and to all of the parts of the culture that are not familiar to us. This is culture shock. There are at least four essential stages of culture-shock adjustment.
>
> The first stage is called "the honeymoon." In this stage, we are excited about living in a different place, and everything seems to be marvelous. We like everything, and everybody seems to be so nice to us. Also, the amusement of life in a new culture seems as though it will never end.

The thesis statement at the end of the first paragraph introduces the idea that there are four stages to culture shock. Then, the first sentence of the following paragraph begins by referring back to the thesis statement by introducing the first of those four stages.

✦ Prereading Activity

The world of style and fashion is very influential, often affecting our looks, our comfort, and our finances. The following essay was written to show how ridiculous the products of the fashion industry can sometimes be. See how well you are persuaded to adopt this position. Before you read this essay, discuss the following questions in small groups, and then review the vocabulary words highlighted here.

1. How does the fashion industry persuade people to buy their products?
2. How do you feel about fashion trends? Are you aware of them? Do you try to follow them?
3. From the title of the essay, what can you tell about the author's position?

✦ VOCABULARY WATCH

NOUNS	VERBS	ADJECTIVES	EXPRESSIONS
deception	aerate	detrimental	standing on tiptoe
downfall	endanger	deformed	rise to the call
podiatrist			
ostrich			
stilts			

There Are No Heels in Heaven

(A)   In department stores and closets all over the world, they are waiting. Their outward appearance seems rather appealing because they come in a variety of styles, textures, and colors. But they are ultimately the biggest **deception** that exists in the fashion industry today. What are they? They are high heels—a woman's worst enemy (whether she knows it or not). High heel shoes are the **downfall** of modern society. Fashion myths have led women to believe that they are more beautiful or sophisticated for wearing heels, but in reality, heels succeed in posing short as well as long term hardships. Women should fight the high heel industry by refusing to use or purchase them in order to save the world from unnecessary physical and psychological suffering.

(B)   For the sake of fairness, it must be noted that there is a positive side to high heels. First, heels are excellent for **aerating** lawns. Anyone who has ever worn heels on grass knows what I am talking about. A simple trip around the yard in a pair of those babies eliminates all need to call for a lawn care specialist, and provides the perfect sized holes to give any lawn oxygen without all those messy chunks of dirt lying around. Second, heels are quite functional for defense against oncoming enemies, who can easily be scared away by threatening them with a pair of these sharp, deadly fashion accessories. And finally, anytime a hammer can't be found, a high heel shoe makes the perfect substitute tool for pushing in a nail.

(C)   Regardless of such practical uses for heels, the fact remains that wearing high heels is **detrimental** to one's physical health. Talk to any **podiatrist,** and you will hear that the majority of their business comes from high-heel-wearing women. High heels are known to cause problems such as **deformed** feet and torn toenails. The risk of severe back problems and twisted or broken ankles is three times higher for a high heel wearer than for a flat shoe wearer. Wearing heels also creates the threat of getting a heel caught in a sidewalk crack or a sewer grate and being thrown to the ground—possibly breaking a nose, back, or neck. And of course, after wearing heels for a day, any woman knows she can look forward to a night of pain as she tries to comfort her swollen, throbbing feet.

(D)   Besides the obvious physical damage heels can cause, they are also responsible for a large amount of psychological damage. A woman with a closet full of heels may **endanger** her own social well-being as well as that of any man who chooses to date her. A night on the town in a pair of shoes that makes a woman feel as if she is a towering **ostrich** on **stilts** is not something to look forward to. In addition, an evening with a woman twice his height may make an insecure man slightly less than comfortable. Instead of enjoying the date, he may be feeling uncomfortable about his own height as he attempts to equal her height by stretching his back, holding up his chin, and **standing on tiptoe.** Ultimately, the man will lose interest in the heel-wearer as he realizes that no woman is worth the price of his diminishing self-esteem. In short, a woman who feels like a walking skyscraper and a man who feels like an ant are not likely to feel high self-esteem.

(E) Are high heels really worth it? It is clear that in spite of their clever uses, high heels can cause severe physical and psychological problems. No amount of surface beauty is worth such terrible inconvenience and potential danger. Women of conscience must **rise to the call** and fight the low-minded mentality of the high heel industry.

by Melia James

◆ About the Reading

1. What is the thesis statement? Do the paragraphs that follow it support the thesis?

2. What rhetorical form(s) is/are used to help persuade?

3. How does the author feel about high heels? How do you know?

4. What are some of the positive benefits of wearing high heels, according to the author? What are the negative effects of wearing high heels, according to the author?

5. How would you characterize the author's overall attitude in this essay? Why?

6. What is the meaning of the expression "those babies" in paragraph B?

7. Why does the author use parentheses in paragraph A?

8. How does the author use humor in this essay? What is her purpose for doing so?

What Do You Think?

The fashion industry often controls our comfort, as well as our pocketbook. Why do you think people often follow the styles of the world and ignore their own comfort and common sense?

Exercise ◆**2** **Making Transitions between Paragraphs.** Practice connecting the idea that was presented in the previous paragraph with the one in the following paragraph. Following are the first sentences of several of the paragraphs in

"There Are No Heels in Heaven." For each topic sentence, write the ideas from the *previous* paragraphs that are mentioned in the topic sentence.

Paragraph B: For the sake of fairness, it must be noted that there is a positive side to high heels.

_____

_____

Paragraph C: Regardless of such practical uses for heels, the fact remains that wearing high heels is detrimental to one's physical health.

_____

_____

Paragraph D: Besides the obvious physical damage heels can cause, they are also responsible for a large amount of psychological damage.

_____

_____

Using Transitions to Find the Central Points

The author of the next essay very effectively uses transitions between paragraphs. If a writer uses transitions well, the reader can often get the central idea of the entire essay by just reading the first sentence or two of each paragraph. Skimming, as you have learned, will help you glean the main idea of an essay to help you know whether you want to continue reading. Skimming can also help you review a text you have already read.

Exercise 3 · Skimming. Before you read the following essay or do the Prereading Activity, skim the essay, by reading the first sentence or two of each paragraph, and list three central points you glean from it.

Central Point 1: _____

Central Point 2: _____

Central Point 3: _____

Prereading Activity

We seldom recognize thinking as an art. The author of the following essay does so, and she gives many reasons for why we don't think as much as we should, and why thinking more will be beneficial to us as individuals and as a society. Before you read the essay, discuss the following questions in small groups, and then review the highlighted vocabulary words.

Read to Write

1. Do you consider yourself more of a thinker or a doer?

2. Which does your culture value more—thinking or doing?

✦ Vocabulary Watch

NOUNS	ADJECTIVES	ADVERBS
villain	spineless	suspiciously
loafing	humane	spontaneously
seclusion	guilty	
sociability	insurmountable	
	sacrilegious	

Thinking: A Neglected Art

It is generally agreed that the American educational system is in deep trouble. Everyone is aware of the horrible facts: school systems are running out of money, teachers can't spell. Most of us know, or think we know, who is to blame: liberal courts, **spineless** school boards, government regulations. It is easy to select a **villain.**

But possibly the problem lies not so much in our institutions as in our attitudes. It is sad that although most of us profess to believe in education, we place no value on intellectual activity.

We Americans are a charitable and **humane** people: we have institutions devoted to every good cause from rescuing homeless cats to preventing World War III. But what have we done to promote the art of thinking? Certainly we make no room for thought in our daily lives. Suppose a man were to say to his friends, "I'm not going to PTA tonight (or choir practice or the baseball game) because I need some time to myself, some time to think"? Such a man would be shunned by his neighbors; his family would be ashamed of him. What if a teen-ager were to say, "I'm not going to the dance tonight because I need some time to think"? His parents would immediately start looking in the Yellow Pages for a psychiatrist. We are all too much like Julius Caesar: we fear and distrust people who think too much. We believe that almost anything is more important than thinking.

Continued

Thinking: A Neglected Art Continued

Guilty: Several years ago a college administrator told me that if he wanted to do any serious thinking, he had to get up at 5:30 in the morning—I suppose because that was the only time when no one would interrupt him. More recently I heard a professor remark that when his friends catch him in the act of reading a book, they say, "My, it must be nice to have so much free time." And even though I am an English teacher—a person who should know better—I find myself feeling vaguely guilty whenever I sneak off to the library to read. It is a common belief that if a man is thinking or reading, he is doing nothing. Through our words and our actions, we express this attitude every day of our lives. Then we wonder why our children refuse to take their studies seriously and why they say to their teachers, "This stuff won't do me any good because I'll never need to use it."

It is easy to understand the causes of this prejudice against thinking. One problem is that to most of us, thinking looks **suspiciously** like **loafing.** *Homo sapiens* in deep thought is an uninspiring sight. He leans back in his chair, props up his feet, puffs on his pipe and stares into space. He gives every appearance of wasting time; he reminds us more of Dagwood and Beetle Bailey than of Shakespeare and Einstein. We wish he would get up and *do* something; mow the lawn, maybe, or wash the car. Our resentment is natural.

But thinking is far different from laziness. Thinking is one of the most productive activities a human being can undertake. Every beautiful and useful thing we have created—including democratic government and freedom of religion—exists because somebody took the time and effort to think of it.

And thinking does require time and effort. It is a common misconception that if a person is "gifted" or "bright" or "talented," wonderful ideas will flash **spontaneously** into his mind.

Unfortunately, the intellect does not work in this way. Even Einstein had to study and think for months before he could formulate his theory of relativity. Those of us who are less intelligent find it a struggle to conceive even a moderately good idea, let alone a brilliant one.

Seclusion: Another reason why we distrust thinking is that it seems unnatural. Human beings are a social species, but thinking is an activity that requires solitude. Consequently, we worry about people who like to think. It disturbs us to meet a person who deliberately chooses to sit alone and think instead of going to a party or a rodeo or a soccer match. We suspect that such a person needs counseling.

Our concern is misplaced. Intelligence is just as much a part of human nature as **sociability.** It would certainly be unnatural for a person to retreat into total seclusion. It would be equally unnatural for a person to allow his mind to die of neglect.

If Americans ever became convinced of the importance of thought, we would probably find ways to solve the problems of our schools, problems that now seem **insurmountable.** But how can we revive interest in the art of thinking? The best place to start would be in the homes and churches of our land. Ministers should admonish their congregations to do some purposeful procrastination every day, to put off one chore in order to have a few minutes to think. Family members should practice saying such things as, "I'll wash the dishes tonight because I know you want to catch up on your thinking."

This may sound un-American, possibly **sacrilegious.** But if we are to survive as a free people, we will have to take some such course of action as soon as possible, because regardless of what some advertisers have led us to believe, this country does not run on oil. It runs on ideas.

by Carolyn Kane, *Newsweek,* December 14, 1981

About the Reading

1. What is the thesis statement of this essay?

2. According to the author, why would people react negatively to others who decline social invitations to stay home and think?

3. Why does the author, as well as some of her colleagues, feel guilty about spending time to think or read?

4. How does the author explain the cause of America's prejudice against thinking?

5. How does thinking differ from laziness?

6. How does the author explain that thinking seems unnatural?

7. What suggestions does the author give for reviving people's interest in the art of thinking?

8. The author uses several allusions in the sixth paragraph. (An *allusion* is a historical, social, or literary reference to something or someone outside the main idea of the writing.) See whether you can identify each of the following: Dagwood, Beetle Bailey, Shakespeare, Einstein.

9. Explain how the author uses each of the following expository styles in this essay as support for her thesis: narration; exposition; comparison and contrast; cause and effect. Which style did you find most convincing?

What Do You Think?

What do you think about thinking?

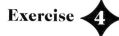 **Exercise** **4** **Making Paragraph Transitions in Your Own Writing.** Now return to the persuasive essay that you are writing, and read the first sentence of each paragraph. If your sentences are not acting as good transitions, which link the ideas from one paragraph to the next, rewrite your first sentences for each paragraph to make them more effective. If you need to, look back at the essay you just read and note how the author made transitions between her paragraphs. Have a classmate read your essay to give you feedback on which transition sentences were effective and which need more work.

Final Draft

As you write the final draft of your persuasive essay, remember to watch for opportunities to use cohesive devices, and make sure that your paragraphs begin with effective transition sentences. Read over the Final Draft Checklist to help you remember all the points that should be included.

Final Draft Checklist

✓ Did you brainstorm to discover the types of support that would be used in the essay?

✓ Did you use at least two different types of support in the essay?

✓ Is the essay convincing? Why or why not?

✓ Is your opinion stated strongly and clearly in the thesis?

✓ Have opposing arguments been refused?

✓ Have additional reasons been added?

✓ Has the topic been matched with a rhetorical form, and have the techniques appropriate to that form been used?

✓ Is the essay coherent?

✓ Have you included some cohesive devices that tie together ideas within a sentence or paragraph?

✓ Does each paragraph begin with a sentence that acts as a transition, linking the ideas presented in one paragraph to the ideas presented in the next?

✓ Are the controlling ideas for each paragraph supported by the use of facts, personal opinions and experiences, and authorities?

✓ Are the spelling, punctuation, and grammar correct?

Going Further: Idea Generator

Activity 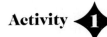 **1** ▶ **Persuasion in the World of Advertising.** Bring to class either a videotape of a television commercial or a print advertisement from a magazine. Write a short analysis of what the advertiser does to try to persuade the consumer to buy the product (for example, comparing one product to another, making consumers look glamorous or sophisticated if they use the product, or using famous people to sell the product). Then, present your analysis orally to your class.

Activity **2** ▶ **Editorials.** Whether they appear in newspapers, magazines, or on television, editorials are good examples of people trying to convince others of their viewpoints on issues. Read several editorials in a variety of sources. Then, choose a local issue about which you feel strongly, and write your own editorial to the local newspaper. Mail it! See how many from your class get published.

Index

Notes

<u>Notes</u>

<u>Notes</u>

Notes

<u>**Notes**</u>

<u>Notes</u>

<u>Notes</u>

<u>Notes</u>